The
BACKSTORY:
Scenes and Stories from My Unscripted Life
COREY MAHER

The Backstory : Scenes and Stories from My Unscripted Life

Library of Congress Control Number: 2026902438

Note on the Text: This book is an autobiography. It reflects the author's present recollections of experiences over time. Some names and identifying characteristics have been changed to protect the privacy of those involved. Certain events, dialogue, and details have been reconstructed from the author's best memory.

ISBN: 979-8-9947055-0-6 (Ebook) ; 979-8-9947055-1-3 (Paperback 5.5x8.5) ; 979-8-9947055-2-0 (Hardback 6x9) ; 979-8-9947055-3-7 (Audiobook)

Edited by: Alwin Baum

Cover Photography by: Anitra Photography www.anitraphotography.com

Audiobook recorded at Greenlight Studios – Charlotte, NC

Cover Graphic Design by: Brandon Padgett @BigDogsStudio

Published by 1301 Press LLC

https://www.coreymaher.net

Printed in the United States of America

THE BACKSTORY

To my family and friends:

Thank you for these moments

Contents

Introduction

Admit it, you picked up this book and opened it because the pictures on the front and back covers caught your eye and you thought to yourself, *"Hello Daddy. What's your story?"*

To be honest, I'm flattered that most women and a few men have reportedly swooned over me whenever I walk into a room. It actually cracks me up because I wasn't always considered a handsome fella. When I graduated college in 1997, I weighed almost 300 pounds and wore glasses. Nobody bothered to take a second glance at me when I walked into a room back then.

Now you're thinking:

"OK, this must be another "self-empowering" book, filled with superficial statements of the obvious and other bullshit, written by an egocentric, narcissistic prick. Another story of some fat boy who worked out, got in shape and is now full of himself and seeking external validation. Just like that

guy who played the fat kid in Stand By Me. What was his name? Uggh, why did I drink a whole bottle of wine last night? My head is killing me. I need to slow down. Where the hell is my husband? We need to go soon. We have to stop by the grocery store on the way home. What kind of cheese did Susan say went well with Pinot Noir?"

Before you put this book down to look up cheese pairings on your phone or to go find your spouse (try the front of the store, they're probably waiting for you there), let me clarify a few things first.

This is not a self-help book filled with platitudes about the obvious. At least, I don't think it is. I can't say whether you'll find me to be an egocentric, narcissistic prick. I don't think I am and have never been accused as such. But nobody is without a critic in this world. I'm sure somebody thought Mother Teresa was full of herself.

So, what's this book about?

Well, to state the rather obvious, this book is my *Backstory*.

The term "backstory" is typically used in reference to a process that an actor uses when developing a character's mannerisms and motives. I'm a part-time actor and have worked on several major motion pictures and television shows over the last decade as well as produced my own award-winning, independent films.

Now, before you say *"Nope"* and put this book down, hear me out.

When developing a character's backstory, an actor creates a history of moments and life experiences that have shaped the character's principles, values and outlook on life. Basically, everything that has happened in that character's life that has made him or her into the person they are today. The actor then creates a headspace in their mind and dives into those experiences, trying to find the truth within the character so it can be properly played. Just watch any movie featuring Daniel Day Lewis or Meryl Streep and you'll know what I'm talking about.

Recently I reached a low point and had to come to grips with the fact that my life is half over. I'm closer to the grave than the crib now. In accepting that fact, I decided I wanted to play the second act of my life properly. And to do that, I need to understand my backstory. Who wouldn't benefit from a better understanding of themselves?

Plus, "backstory" sounds cooler than memoir or autobiography. Saying this book is my memoir makes me sound ancient and uptight. Saying it's my autobiography makes it sound dull and boring. So, Fuck That! I think I've had an interesting life so far. It's time I put it under a microscope and took notes.

This book is a collection of stories, moments, people and experiences in my life that have shaped the core of who I am today at 50. I'm not a recovering addict or here to sell you an ideology of any particular variety. Politics, in general, bore me, and I don't like people who preach or proselytize. I wish I could say that I have the recipe for a fulfilling life, but I don't. I do think I can share a few ingredients with you that have made my life more palatable though. Because, in my experience, life can be pretty bland at times and downright inedible occasionally.

I wrote this book to analyze my life's story up to this point in the hope that I can better appreciate it and understand all that I have to be grateful for. I know that most self-published books sell very few copies and that the odds of anyone other than my wife and my mother reading my book are slim. But I decided to write it anyway. At the very least, I'll have it for some added perspective when my life takes a wrong turn down shit creek again.

I'm not a war hero or a billionaire tech mogul, and I'm certainly not a famous actor by any stretch. This book isn't a retelling of all my experiences on a film set meant to wow you with stories about working with celebrities. There's some talk about that, but it's minimal.

I think you would be interested in my story. I've experienced quite a few triumphs and dismal failures in just about every facet of my life over the last 50 years. Plus, it's my nature to be a wise ass. Finding the humor in everything is my *modus operandi*.

As you have already noticed, I do use some curse words, but I don't pepper my language with them as much as my wife peppers her salads with cayenne and garlic. *Seriously sweetheart, that's enough!* I use profanity to accentuate and highlight feelings that I feel deserve a little more attention, or to get a laugh. That kinda shit.

Living in the 21st Century, with all its technological marvels and constant bombardment of information, our civilization has evolved to have a very limited attention span. If you have something that you'd like to share with the world, you have about 30 seconds to grab someone's attention before they get bored and decide to scroll down to find something else to form an opinion about. I understand and accept that.

That said, I encourage you to dive into this book. My primary goals when writing it were to keep it interesting and filled with humor. After all, I am my own worst critic, and if I enjoyed writing it and reading it, I'm confident you will too.

So, that's it. That's my pitch. I'm not trying to sell you a ten-step program or get you to download an app. I just want to share with you my backstory. Maybe it'll encourage you to write and share yours someday.

I hope you enjoy it.

Corey

~ My phone says that 'soft, bloomy rind cheeses, like Brie and Camembert, are best to pair with a Pinot Noir. But it is a versatile wine and goes well with 'semi-hard, nutty cheeses as well'.

Semi-hard.

That sounds like how I felt when watching Baywatch as a kid.

The Towering Inferno

L et's get one thing straight from the beginning: I had a fantastic childhood.

My father coached little league baseball in the spring and summers and then basketball in the fall and winters. Mom would bake cupcakes for my class when it was my birthday and would taxi my brother, sister and I to and from various after school activities and the like.

We took regular family vacations together and, for the most part, all got along. There were occasional fights among siblings, of course, but never any serious confrontations. Although my sister, Cami, once drew blood and left a scar on my arm after I shot her with a super soaker squirt gun. She also slugged my brother, Carey, pretty hard once after we ignored her when she came outside to tell us it was time to come in for dinner. I promptly headed inside for dinner to avoid her wrath. I learned at an early age not to fuck with my baby sister.

My family has its origins in Indiana. My mother, Wanda Kay Cheek, was one of seven children who grew up in a small town called Circleville, while my father, Steven Lynn Maher, was the second of four children and grew up on a farm outside of Kokomo, Indiana. Neither of my parents came from money, but they were both raised in loving and supportive households, which thankfully set the tone for how they raised Carey, Cami and me.

Being a farm boy, Dad spent his childhood getting up at the crack of dawn to collect eggs from the hen house, milk the cows and feed the hogs before having breakfast and going to school. He certainly had it tougher growing up than we did, but Dad was never one to throw that in our faces. He was always full of optimism and cheer in the mornings, almost *ad nauseam*. I remember him singing *"Zip-a-Dee-Doo-Dah"* to us every morning before school, trying to get us to think positive and have a productive day.

At the age of fourteen, my father and his younger brother, Patrick, left the family farm to attend seminary school, where they were both put on the path to become Catholic priests. That usually doesn't surprise people after meeting my father. He's always been a kind and generous man, with a hearty laugh and a genuine interest in people.

Neither my father nor his brother pursued priesthood after finishing high school at the seminary. In 1964, the Second Vatican Council declared that priests could perform mass in English rather than explicitly in Latin. The change was made to make Catholic services more palatable to Americans and hopefully to boost church congregation numbers in the United States. But Dad, who was 17 in 1964, says that the change from Latin to English made him seriously question his faith and the authoritative power of the Church. To be honest, I think Dad just didn't find the life of a priest very appealing. He wanted to get married and start a family. Obviously, I'm thankful for that.

My parents met in 1970 at a Savings and Loan bank where my mother was a teller and Dad worked in the evenings doing audit work, balancing the books. They were poor and barely scraping by, but happy together. So, in August of 1972, they got married and have been happily wed ever since. This summer they will celebrate their 53rd wedding anniversary, which just boggles my mind. *Where the hell did the time go?*

It was on a cold Sunday night in February of 1975 when I began to make my way into this world. Mom and Dad had gone out to dinner with Dad's boss and his wife. Dad was 27 years old at the time and a rising star at the Kaiser Aluminum Corporation, where he was considered a natural born salesman, breaking all kinds of records within the company.

After dinner that night, my mother told my father that she wanted to go see a movie. Why Mom wanted to sit in an uncomfortable movie theater at nine months pregnant is beyond my comprehension. Nonetheless, my parents went to see the 1975 film *The Towering Inferno*, which featured Paul Newman, Fred Astaire and Steve McQueen battling for their lives at the top of a high rise building engulfed in an uncontrollable fire.

I'm pretty sure the nightmares I had as a child stemmed from me hearing the screams from that movie while still inside my mother's womb. I imagine I was banging on Mom's uterus screaming *"What the hell's going on out there?! Let me outta here!"*

After the movie ended, I promptly sent my mom into labor, and at approximately 9 a.m. on the morning of February 10, 1975, I entered this world and was given the name Corey Paul Maher. My middle name, Paul, is my grandfather's name on Dad's side.

Every year on my birthday, my father likes to remind me that after I was born, he was so proud he went out and bought cigars, real and bubblegum, to hand out to everyone at his company. My mother likes to tell me that, while holding me for the first time, she remembers hearing the song "Morning Has Broken" by Cat Stevens being played somewhere in the hospital.

I, on the other hand, distinctly recall hearing the opening riff to Black Sabbath's "Children of the Grave" being played in the distance that morning.

Two years later, in January of 1977, my brother, Carey Lynn Maher, was born, and three years after that, my sister, Cami Lee Maher, was born in April of 1980.

Growing up, it was always a bit confusing that my parents named me and my brother within one letter of each other. Whenever we'd visit with friends or extended family, my brother and I would always have to correct people on what our names were. *"No, I'm Corey, and he's Carey."* I suppose my brother had it rougher than I did because everyone thought Carey was a girl's name, but actually, he was named after the popular silver screen icon, Carey Grant.

My brother and I had a typical relationship growing up. We played together as kids and occasionally fought. Being the oldest, I always got seniority to be the more powerful superhero or good guy in our adventures together. I would be Superman and make Carey be Batman. Or, if I wanted to be Batman, I would make Carey be Robin.

Like most siblings, my relationship with Carey took many twists and turns through the years. We had periods of close friendship and communication along with a few periods where we wouldn't speak to one another for one stupid reason or another. This has been the case with me and my brother throughout our adult lives.

My relationship with my sister, Cami, was fairly nonexistent as a child because she's five years younger than I am, and that age gap was just too wide for me and her to have anything in common. However, as we reached adulthood, Cami and I would become very close and end up supporting one another through difficult times.

I love my brother and sister dearly and would do just about anything for them.

Because I was the first born, I was the trend setter with our parents and had to push boundaries for me and my siblings to gain independence from childhood. Mom and Dad were fairly liberal with us though and, thankfully, neither I nor my brother or sister ever did anything too stupid, like getting arrested or addicted to drugs. I'm very grateful for that and think that it's a testament to how well our parents raised us.

We lived in Indiana until I was 5 years old before moving to North Carolina in 1980. Dad continued to do well at Kaiser Aluminum and was eventually promoted to regional sales of the rapidly growing southeast market. He sold aluminum culvert pipe and bridge systems to developers and municipalities in the region. We settled in the township of Pineville, N.C. – a suburb just south of Charlotte, close to the South Carolina state line. My parents still live in the house they bought in 1980, and it's where I will always consider home to be.

Obviously, I don't remember much about life before 1980. However, one strong memory I have in Indiana is of crying non-stop for hours because I lost my Star Wars C3P0 action figure in the sandbox of our backyard. I was devastated that C3P0 was dead and that I was the reason R2D2 lost his best friend.

Like most of Generation X, I was raised on blockbuster movies from the 70s, 80s and 90s. My parents would take me and my brother to the drive-in movie theater at night to watch the original *Star Wars* under the stars. Carey and I would lie on the warm hood of Mom's Ford Pinto, wrapped in blankets, and be captivated by the visual spectacle that George Lucas had created for the world. When The *Empire Strikes Back* came out in 1980, Dad took me and Carey to see it on opening weekend, and I was hooked for life.

After moving to North Carolina in 1980, we would routinely take trips back to Indiana to visit with my grandparents and cousins. Mom and Dad would pile all of us kids into a 1970s cargo van that Dad had bought used. The van was your stereotypical 'shaggin' wagon', with a large bed in the back and dirty brown shag carpeting throughout the entire interior to muffle noise. Every summer and holiday season our family would pile into that van to make the long 12-hour trip up north.

I have a lot of great memories of the 'shaggin' wagon'. Because it was built in the 70s, it only had an eight-track cassette player and the only cassettes we owned were the few that came with the van when Dad bought it. That meant that during our many roundtrip drives to Indiana, we usually only had a handful of albums to listen to. The two albums we listened to the most were *The Best of the Monkees* and the soundtrack to *Saturday Night Fever*. To this day, whenever I hear the song "Stayin' Alive" by the Bee Gees, my hips start gyrating and I sing along in falsetto with Barry Gibb. And everyone in my family can still sing along with The Monkees. My first concert ever was when Mom and Dad took all of us kids to see The Monkees live.

Driving to Indiana was grueling for me at times though because I would get motion sickness easily as a child and it gave me horrible headaches.

But I loved visiting my family in Indiana, especially my father's family because I got to play on the farm. I liked running through the corn fields, chasing field mice. They were everywhere because they ate the leftover corn after harvest. Every now and then though my brother and I would find a black snake in the fields and run inside, scared to death.

Dad's family farm also backed up to an active railroad. You could hear the train coming from miles away while inside my grandparents' house and my brother and I would race out into the fields to wait for the train to pass so that we could try and get the conductor to blow his horn.

As I got a little older and braver, I would often sneak into the two-story barn to inspect all the old tractors and farming equipment that my grandpa and my dad used to operate decades before I was born. I used to get into trouble for going into the barn though because Mom thought it was unsafe. But I loved it and sneaked in anyway. To this day, whenever I smell hay, I'm always transported back to that barn and all the fond memories I had playing in it.

Going to see my mom's family in Indiana was not as much fun as visiting the farm that my father grew up on. My grandmother, Daisy Cheek, lived in an old, run-down, two-story home in the town of Frankfort, Indiana. It wasn't exactly a cosmopolitan town because it was filled primarily with homes either abandoned or in disrepair. Unlike my father's family farm, Frankfort wasn't someplace where Carey and I could run around and explore without an adult present. It was a blue-collar, postwar community, overlooked by time.

But Grandma Cheek was always very kind to us and would cook all sorts of delicious sugary treats when we visited her, like chocolate sheet cake and butterscotch balls. Mom was very close with her mother and the two of them would talk nonstop for days whenever we visited, usually leaving me bored to tears with nothing to do and nowhere to explore. I never got along very well with my cousins on my mom's side of the family, and I don't remember much about my mom's father, Charlie Cheek, because he died when I was 4 years old.

Like my father's family farm, Frankfort had an active railroad running through it too. But hearing the trains go by at Grandma Cheek's house scared me as a child because the trains would barrel through in the middle of the night, blasting their horns. The train tracks were so close to my grandmother's house that we would often wake up with our beds shaking uncontrollably, as if possessed. While the train at my dad's family farm delighted me, the train at Grandma Cheek's terrified me.

When I was about 6 or 7 years old, my parents once left us with Grandma Cheek for the day, and a tornado touched down in Frankfort. I remember grandma scooping Cami up into her arms and grabbing Carey by the hand while yelling at me to follow her outside to the underground cellar to take shelter. As soon as we stepped outside the back door, I remember a shovel flew by me, barely missing my head. If I had stepped out just a second sooner, I'm sure that shovel would have killed me.

But being as young as I was, I did not fully comprehend the level of danger we were in. I remember thinking it was all incredibly exciting. Thankfully, though, nobody got hurt and we made it safely to grandma's cellar. Carey, Cami and I huddled in the darkness with Grandma Cheek while the fierce winds outside roared, causing destruction and mayhem. Miraculously, when we emerged from the cellar, we found Grandma's house to be seemingly untouched by the chaotic twister.

I have only a few memories of my dad's mom, Hilda Maher, because she died in 1984 from lung cancer, when I was just 9 years old. I do remember her having a loud, cackling laugh though. According to mom, Grandma Maher had a strange sense of humor. When the first zombie movie, *Night of the Living Dead* aired in 1968, Mom says that Grandma Maher laughed throughout the entire movie while everyone else was horrified. Based on that information, I'm guessing that my sense of humor comes from my dad's mom.

My dad's father, Paul Maher, had the strongest impact on me while I was growing up. He was a small man, lean and sinewy from a long life of farming, but he also had a heart of gold and was a devout Catholic.

One of the strongest memories I have of Grandpa and Grandma Maher was when they took me to see the movie *Superman 2* when I was 7 years old, with Christopher Reeve portraying the iconic Man of Steel. I became a huge fan of Kal El after watching that movie and, to this day, I still wear t-shirts and hats with the Superman insignia on them.

The Shadow Man

I've always had a vivid imagination. Creativity and play just come naturally to me. Throughout my entire life I've been in constant search for a creative outlet to occupy my busy little mind. I consider it both a blessing and a curse because I can get bored easily if I'm not entertained with whatever I'm doing. Naturally, I disliked school while growing up because I found it tedious and uninteresting.

Once, when I was in the first grade, I was so bored that I told my teacher that my mom died so that I could go home. I played it rather convincingly too, bringing on the water works and crying. I had an elaborate story about it being a car accident or some nonsense. It fooled both my teacher and the principal at first, but the ruse fell apart when they called my house and my mom answered the phone. I'm not exactly sure how I expected that to work out, but what can I say, I was only 6.

I faked being sick quite often so that I could skip school, usually on days when I had a test that I didn't study for or when some project that I hadn't even started was due. I developed some pretty good acting chops in my youth trying to fool my mother. But Mama Bear knew me too well and almost always saw through me. She did let me stay home quite a bit, but I knew I was pushing it too far whenever she would threaten to take me to the doctor's office. That's when I'd give up the act. I made some miraculous recoveries back from the brink of death throughout my childhood.

In high school, when I had a car, I would sometimes skip school to drive out into the country, park somewhere inconspicuous and read fantasy books all day. I found that immensely more enjoyable than calculus, biology or reading *The Scarlet Letter* for English Literature. In my opinion, Nathanial Hawthorne sucks compared to Stephen King or Anne Rice.

As I got older, I eventually found some discipline and patience to help focus on the tedious necessities of life. But as a child, my imagination ran wild and, as a result, I would often have vivid nightmares.

The nightmares started when I was five or six years old, after my family moved to North Carolina. Sometimes they gave me insomnia because I was just too frightened to go to sleep. I was quite the lucid dreamer in my youth and would often sleepwalk through the house in the middle of the night while in one of my nightmares.

Lucid dreaming is when you are semi-conscious and self-aware that you are dreaming. It occurs while in R.E.M. (rapid eye movement) sleep—the borderline between the waking world of reality and the sleeping world of the subconscious. They say about 50% of people experience lucid dreaming at least once in their lives.

As I got older, my lucid dreams became less frequent, but the ones I have had as an adult have been powerful and, for the most part, positive. One experience I had at the age of 33 altered my life completely, but the lucid dreams I experienced as a child terrified me because I didn't understand them. I felt helpless, like I was trapped inside my dream and couldn't get out.

I don't think the nightmares I experienced as a child were the result of any repressed abuse or trauma. Maybe I have repressed something, but I seriously doubt it. I think I just had a hyperactive mind and needed to learn how to control it.

One nightmare I frequently had as a child was of falling through empty space. It was a terrifying feeling, being stuck in a void of emptiness. It was just pure anxiety, kind of like when you lean back in a chair too far and, for a brief second, feel like you're going to fall backwards onto the floor. That fear of toppling over and spinning out of control was perpetual whenever I would have lucid dreams as a child. I couldn't scream for help because there was nothing for my voice to even resonate against. It was very much like staring into the abyss.

While I was in one of these nightmares I would sleepwalk and wander around our house, semi conscious and quietly sobbing. I never woke anyone up while I was sleepwalking. In fact, I don't think I've ever told anyone about the dreams. Most of the time I would wake up on my own, usually when standing in front of the large mirror in the front foyer of our house. Staring at myself in the mirror seemed to always pull me out of my dream state and bring me back to reality.

The moment right before I woke up was always the most terrifying because I would see myself in the reflection of the mirror as if detached from my existence, falling helplessly through empty space with nothing grounding me in reality. Eventually, my semi-conscious mind would recognize my eyes in the reflection of the mirror, and I would slowly slide back into full consciousness and wake up.

They say dreams of falling are most often associated with subconscious feelings of instability or a lack of control. So, I guess at 6 years old I was carrying around a lot of insecurity, about what, I have no idea. Perhaps I was processing the trauma of moving so far away from our family in Indiana. Or maybe it was the initial anxiety of starting grade school and not liking it. Or it very well could have been listening to the "Towering Inferno" inside Mom's belly hours before I was born.

A similar nightmare I frequently had involved being stalked by the *Shadow Man*. Or, at least, that's what I call him. For me, the *Shadow Man* was the personification of nothingness or *non-being*. Whenever he appeared in my dreams, it made my heart race. Feeling his presence would cause me to become semi-conscious within my dream, and I would become overwhelmed with the urge to escape his gaze.

For several years, my brother and I shared a bedroom on the second floor of our Cape Cod home in North Carolina. Our bedroom had a dormer that overlooked the street outside with my bed on one side of the dormer and my brother's on the other. Whenever I dreamed about the *Shadow Man*, I would slowly climb out of bed and be compelled to look out our dormer window.

Outside, I would see the *Shadow Man* standing motionless in the street, silhouetted by the dull white light emanating from our neighbor's sodium lamp on their garage. Ironically, the *Shadow Man* didn't cast a shadow, he seemed to simply absorb the light around him. I never saw him physically move, and I could never make out any of his features. He always appeared like a shroud of darkness, his presence always more felt than seen. But he definitely seemed real to me, with substance and form. Whenever I looked at the *Shadow Man*, it made me feel like I was staring into the void, and I could sense that it was staring back at me.

After seeing the *Shadow Man* in the street, I would hastily leave our bedroom and try to make my way downstairs to mom and dad's room, being careful not to make too much noise. I was terrified that the *Shadow Man* would hear me on the move and would come to get me.

When I would reach the bottom of the stairs, I would peek out of the small window that was centered in the foyer landing of our house to see if the *Shadow Man* was still there. Almost always he'd be standing motionless in the driveway, somehow getting closer to me.

As my anxiety grew stronger, my pace would quicken, and I would finish climbing down the last few steps into our foyer. In those few seconds, the *Shadow Man* would move from the driveway to standing right on our front porch, staring into my soul through the front glass door.

I don't know how long I would stand in the foyer staring at the *Shadow Man*. Hours maybe? It certainly felt like eternity. Sometimes I would begin to fall through empty space again and go deeper into the dream. At other times I could break free of his gaze and turn to face the mirror on the wall so that I could wake up. When I was able to pull myself out of the dream and back into reality, the *Shadow Man* would disappear.

I eventually stopped having the nightmares, but even now, I can still feel the *Shadow Man* watching me in the darkness. He doesn't frighten me anymore though. My perception of him simply changed. Because when I was 11 years old, I experienced something very real that would help me re-define what the *Shadow Man* represented, and it became permanently engrained in my psyche.

The Worm Farmer

My grandfather, Paul Maher, was nearly deaf without his hearing aid. He also drank more coffee than I thought was humanly possible, which is probably why I remember his hands trembling constantly. I also remember being delighted to see his dirty overalls and muddy boots sitting in the utility room of his house every time we visited. But Grandpa cleaned up well too and wore a tweed sport coat with a snappy fedora to mass every Sunday.

Whenever we visited Grandpa, my brother and I would sleep in the living room, on either the floor or one of the couches. There was no air conditioning, of course, so during the summers, we'd sleep with all the windows in the house open to create airflow.

Because the living room was in the front of the house, closest to the road, my brother and I would hear cars, trucks and motorcycles race by sporadically in the night. Sometimes you could hear them coming from miles away, and whenever they passed the house, their headlights would flood the living room with white light for a brief second, then bathe the room in crimson red from their taillights as they sped by.

Despite the rumbling noise and vehicle lights flooding the room every now and then, I slept very well in Grandpa's house. I always felt safe and at home there, and I sleep better with white noise anyway. It's in dead silence that I have trouble sleeping.

Grandpa would wake up at sunrise every morning to start drinking coffee, and the smell of freshly brewed coffee would wake up my father, which is why my brother and I would almost always be awakened to the sound of raucous laughter coming from the kitchen.

Dad and Grandpa were both boisterous and, most mornings, we would find the two of them smoking cigarettes and drinking pot after pot of coffee while laughing themselves to tears, reminiscing about the past. It got especially loud when Grandpa's hearing aid went dead because you would have to shout for him to hear you.

In the summer of 1985, I spent a lot of time with Grandpa Maher. My brother and sister stayed with Mom at Grandma Cheek's house while I got to stay with Dad and Grandpa on the farm for a week. Grandpa had long since retired by this time, but like my father and me, he couldn't sit still for too long and had to have something to do. So, to make a little extra money every month, Grandpa raised worms in his basement to sell to the local bait shop.

As a 10-year-old boy, I thought Grandpa's worm farm was astronomically cool. He had several large wooden beds filled with black soil and compost which he used to breed fat, wiggly night-crawlers, the kind local fisherman used almost exclusively as bait at the nearby reservoir.

During that week in the summer of '85, I spent most of my time glued to Grandpa's hip, wanting to help him with his worm farm. Grandpa would let me go down into the basement with him to help feed the worms and then let me help package them up in Styrofoam containers to sell. To me it was a lot of fun collecting 20 wiggly worms to put into pint size containers.

After we collected our worm harvest, Grandpa and I would hop into his old flatbed Chevy and deliver our worms to the bait shop. I never enjoyed the stench of the bait shop, but overall, the entire experience delighted me. For a short time, I remember wanting to be a worm farmer when I grew up.

When we finished up at the bait shop, Grandpa would take me out to lunch at a fast-food joint called "Scotty's", where he would buy me a cheeseburger, fries and a coke. Most of the time Grandpa would just drink coffee, but sometimes he would have a hamburger.

You may be thinking, *"How the hell do you grow worms?"* And the answer to that lies in the coffee.

Used coffee grounds are rich in nitrogen, which is a perfect food source for worms. Every time somebody made a pot of coffee in Grandpa's house, it was a well-known imperative that you saved the used coffee grounds. I thought it was genius of my grandfather to raise worms because they fed on the by-product of something he consumed everyday. It felt very efficient and smart to me at 10 years old. And it still does.

Going down into Grandpa's basement was always a little scary to me because, according to Grandpa, worms thrive in darkness, so we couldn't have any bright lights on. When Grandpa would remove the old brown paper bags covering the worm beds, he would jiggle the beds slightly, which would cause the worms to rise to the surface. We would then spread out the fresh coffee grounds on top of the composted soil while the worms blissfully rolled around in the nutrient rich food.

In the evenings, after our long day of worm farming, Grandpa and I would sit in the living room and watch TV together. We would watch reruns of all the classic '70s shows, like *Starsky and Hutch*, *CHiPs*, *Hawaii 5-0*, *Kojak*, *Rockford Files* and *Hogan's Heroes*. If we were really lucky, *Smoky and the Bandit* or *Cannonball Run* would be on, and we'd laugh hysterically at the antics of Burt Reynolds, Sally Field, Jackie Gleason and Dom DeLuise.

Because Grandpa was hard of hearing, he would sit in an old reclining chair about 4 feet from the television. But as the evening grew late, he would always take off his hearing aid and slide out of his recliner to sit on the floor, about 2 feet from the TV, so that he could hear. The night usually ended with us watching *The Tonight Show* together, hosted by the king of late night, Johnny Carson.

I developed a very special bond with my grandfather during the summer of 1985. It is a bond that I still hold sacred today.

One Second

The following summer, in 1986, my family returned to Indiana over the July 4th holiday for a couple of weeks. Dad was in a temperamental mood on that trip because he had quit smoking a few months earlier at the behest of my mother. I, too, was in a foul mood during the first week of that trip because my family stayed in a rented RV at a local campground called Jellystone National Park. My mom's sister, Jo, worked at the campground and a lot of my cousins were staying there for Carey, Cami and I to play with.

But I hated that campground. It was hot, uncomfortable and full of mosquitoes. Plus, as I mentioned earlier, I never really got along well with my cousins on my mother's side of the family. So, I complained incessantly about wanting to leave Jellystone to go see Grandpa at the farm.

After a few days at the campground, I caught a lucky break when my mom came down with terrible flu while my dad had to fly away on a short business trip. Because Mom was sick, Grandpa drove down to take Dad to the airport. When I saw Grandpa at the campground, I begged my mom to let me go back to the farm with him for the remainder of the vacation, and she happily agreed. She was too sick to put up with me any longer and wanted me out of her hair.

When Grandpa and I dropped Dad off at the airport I remember Dad kissing me on the cheek and putting his hand on my shoulder before saying, "You be good and take care of Grandpa while I'm gone, OK? I'll be back in a few days." I said I would of course and, after Dad boarded his flight, Grandpa and I drove back to the farm together.

That night I was very happy not to be at the campground. Even though it was still brutally hot in the farmhouse, I was right where I wanted to be, lying on the couch in the living room with Grandpa in his recliner, watching an episode of *Hogan's Heroes* together.

We weren't the only ones in the house that night though. My dad's older sister, Linda, and her youngest son, Kelly, were living with Grandpa during this time and Aunt Linda was in her room sleeping because she worked odd hours as a nurse and Kelly, who was in high school, was out with friends.

By the time I started to doze off to sleep that night, Grandpa had taken out his hearing aid and was sitting on the floor, directly in front of the TV, so that he could hear.

What happened next was, without a doubt, the single most important moment of my life.

I heard Grandpa let out a loud, boisterous laugh and then watched as his body started convulsing. When he slumped over onto the floor, completely still, I opened my eyes fully.

"Grandpa," I asked nervously, "Are you alright?"

When Grandpa didn't respond, I got off the couch to check on him. But when I reached him, his eyes were rolled back in his head, and he wasn't moving. I tried shaking him, but he felt stiff and rigid, as if all the muscles in his body were tightened.

When Grandpa wouldn't respond to my touch, I immediately ran to Aunt Linda's bedroom and banged on her door loudly before bursting in. I startled her awake and she gave me a hard look before asking what was wrong.

"Something's wrong with Grandpa." I said trembling. "He fell over in front of the TV and isn't moving."

Linda immediately got out of bed and went into the living room. As soon as she saw Grandpa on the floor, her pace quickened, and she checked his pulse. Then she screamed at me to call 911 while she began administering CPR. I remember watching Aunt Linda for what felt like eternity as she did chest compressions on Grandpa. I think she had to yell at me several times to call 911 before I snapped out of it and ran to the phone in the kitchen.

When I called 911, the operator asked me for the address, and I had no idea what to tell her. I was only 11 years old, and I didn't live there. The operator told me to look around for a piece of mail with an address on it. When I put the phone down to start looking for mail, I was saved when Kelly happened to walk in from his night out with friends. Through deep panicky gasps, I explained the situation to Kelly and, thankfully, he took over the 911 call and gave the operator the address to Grandpa's farm.

I still don't know the address.

I don't remember much after that because I'm pretty sure I went into shock. Everything that happened before I dialed 911 is crystal clear in my mind. But everything after is a blur.

I do remember walking back into the living room to watch Aunt Linda pound on Grandpa's chest, trying to get his heart to restart. But Grandpa remained unresponsive and never recovered. Between blowing air into his lungs and giving chest compressions, Linda cried and gave me a dreadful look that told me what I already feared. Grandpa was gone.

When the ambulance arrived, along with a fire engine, Grandpa's living room turned into a dizzy haze of flashing red and white lights. It felt like one of my surreal nightmares. When several large EMTs and firefighters burst into the house with medical equipment in tow, my shock intensified, and I closed off.

I remember being at the hospital later that night but have no idea how I got there or how I got back to Grandpa's farm. With Dad away on business and Mom, Carey and Cami still at Jellystone campground, I felt isolated and alone. I remember my cousins trying to talk to me at the hospital, but I couldn't respond because of the trauma. I had just completely shut down.

Later that night, when we were back at the farmhouse, I remember lying on the couch and unloading. I cried nonstop. Every time I tried to close my eyes, I would see Grandpa walking into the living room with a big grin on his face. It all happened so quickly and unexpectedly, my 11-year-old mind couldn't process it. In one second, Grandpa went from laughing to dead. One second.

The next time I saw my father was at the funeral home. I remember walking into the parlor and seeing Dad sitting across the desk from the funeral director. The first thing I noticed was that Dad was smoking again. I could see he was devastated because his hand trembled when he lifted the cigarette to his mouth. Seeing Dad like that made me feel ashamed. I felt like I had let my father down because, at the airport, he asked me to take care of Grandpa. And I didn't.

But Dad kissed me and hugged me tight when he saw me that day and, thankfully, I didn't carry that guilt around for too long.

A few days later it was explained to me that Grandpa died from a cerebral aneurysm, a blood vessel burst in his brain. They told me it was almost an immediate death and there was nothing anyone could have done.

It made me happy knowing that Grandpa didn't suffer when he died, but still, I missed him so much.

I remember my parents putting me in counseling when we returned to North Carolina, but I don't remember any of the sessions or if it helped. I think I repressed it all at first because my memory of that time, right after Grandpa's death, is spotty. Oddly, I remember that the song "Glory of Love" by Peter Cetera was popular at the time. The song played nonstop on the radio around the time Grandpa died, so I heard it all the time. It's weird, but every time I hear that song, it reminds me of Grandpa.

My nightmares intensified for several years after that. The *Shadow Man* visited me often, although my perception of him changed over the years after Grandpa's death. When I dreamed about the *Shadow Man* at the age of 6-7, he terrified me. But as I grew older, I came to identify the

Shadow Man as simply being Death itself, always within view. Not necessarily to take me that night, but to remind me that one day he will.

Watching my grandfather die was the single most defining moment of my life. After almost 40 years, not a day goes by that I don't think about it. Coming home to North Carolina in the summer of 1986, I was fundamentally changed. All I thought about was death. I kept thinking that I, too, would one day laugh and then die. Just like Grandpa. And it won't necessarily happen when I'm old. It could happen at any moment.

That's a lot for an eleven-year-old to process. For the next 6 years, until I turned 17, I was out of control. I became moody and distant from people, did poorly in school, got in a few fights, etc. But on the other side of those issues, I found a spark of self discipline and an aggressive determination.

Looking back on it all now, I think of it as a gift. I learned at the age of 11 that our time is limited and that you must live your life as if tomorrow doesn't exist. All the decisions I would make for the rest of my life would be based on that fundamental truth. While Grandpa's death was initially traumatic and confusing to me as a child, it has encouraged me to live my life to the fullest and not take anything for granted.

I may have overestimated the strength of my hand at times or folded too soon on a couple of hands, but I've also won some big hands. And most importantly, I've never walked away from the table.

Grandpa's death developed the courage I needed to take responsibility for my life. It took many years to process his death. It was tough because I also had to go through puberty and hormone changes during that fun ride. But by the age of 17, I finally accepted it.

I accepted that I was going to die someday and, oddly enough, it liberated me. I decided to be proactive and take my life a little more seriously, and not just in my studies, but also in my creative passions. I realized that if I wanted a unique and fulfilling life, I needed to start paying attention and putting in the work.

In short, I decided to start giving a shit and make a go at the life I wanted. I feel like I owe that to Grandpa, and myself.

Mama Bear

I've always been a mama's boy. Whenever I feel lost or angry at the world, Mom has always been able to help me find balance and perspective. She has a direct line to my soul and instinctively knows how to calm the rage that sometimes builds up inside me. After Grandpa died, Mom and Dad were both very supportive and patient with me while I worked through that trauma.

Mom is the quintessential archetype of a mother. Her children have always been her #1 priority in life. Through thick and thin, her love and support were unconditional. Whenever I got banged up from attempting ridiculous stunts on my bike, she was there with peroxide and bandages. Whenever we came inside from playing in the snow, frozen and snotty, she would have dry clothes and hot chocolate waiting. It doesn't snow very often in Charlotte anymore, but growing up in the 80s, we would get the occasional snowstorm.

Whenever I got sick, and wasn't faking it to get out of school, Mom would nurture me back to health. She would make me soup, get me medicine or, if needed, take me to the doctor. On my birthday she would make me pineapple upside down cake or apple crisp, which were my favorites as a kid.

Mom's nickname for me growing up was 'Baby Huey' because I had an insatiable appetite and would often eat everything in the house that wasn't tied down or purposefully hidden from me. 'Baby Huey' was a 1950s cartoon character, depicted as a giant baby duckling in a diaper, with an enormous appetite and a childlike innocence. Fair warning though, only my mother has permission to call me that.

I love my mother more than any words could possibly convey, but lord knows I drove her crazy as a child. Being the first born, I had to break through boundaries to gain my independence and, occasionally, I would push too hard. I got spanked a few times, but not too often. Usually only after I got mouthy and said something rude or snippy in defiance.

Growing up Catholic, my folks were firm believers in using guilt as their primary form of discipline, and I must admit it worked well. A guilt trip was far more effective on me than a spanking. I don't know how many times I heard my mother say, "Corey Paul, I'm disappointed in you." But whenever she did, it was far more agonizing to me than any form of corporal punishment. Believing that I'd lost my parents' love and support was just too much to bear.

In fact, I can remember a few times when I actually begged Mom to spank me instead of telling me that she was disappointed in my life choices. To me, a good old fashioned whoopin' was an immediate resolution and forgiveness of my transgressions. But Mom was smart and never caved in. She was patient and played the long game which, over time, helped instill a sense of restraint in me that made me think before doing or saying anything asinine.

Mom has always been the rock and stability in our family. She's the mediator of disputes and most often the voice of reason and temperance between me and my siblings. To most people, my mother comes off as being shy and reserved. But don't let her quiet nature fool you. She's highly intelligent and *always* paying attention. I think she would've made a damn good detective.

I credit most of my acting skills to Mom because, in my youth, I had to become quite adept at trying to pull one over on her. However, to this day, Mama Bear can always smell through my bullshit. She grew up playing cards with her daddy and learned early in life how to recognize a bluff. Whenever I did manage to get away with something, I'm pretty sure she knew about it and just let it slide. She was never overbearing or overly protective. She allowed me the space I needed to grow and learn.

Mom worked hard in providing for our family. On top of doing most of the cooking, cleaning, laundry and taxi driving for us kids, she also worked part time in the school system as a secretary while we were growing up. During lean times, she worked in a doctor's office as a receptionist to help Dad support the family. Both of my parents sacrificed a great deal of their lives for our future, and I'm tremendously grateful for that.

When I was young, both of my parents suffered from migraine headaches. When my father was drafted into the army at the start of the Vietnam War, he was medically discharged from duty because of his chronic migraines. His sensitivity to light during one of those headaches made Dad practically blind because he couldn't open his eyes. The light seared his brain and was debilitating. Thankfully though, when Mom and Dad got older, modern medicine cured them of their migraines using blood thinners and various other drugs.

Since she was a little girl, Mom has suffered through a variety of health problems. At a young age, she was diagnosed with "atrial fibrillation", which is just a fancy term for saying that her heart sometimes skips beats. Being in "A-fib" puts one at higher risk for a heart attack or stroke because it causes your heart rate to swing erratically. Recently, I experienced the same condition after suffering a traumatic physical injury. It's no fun.

Whenever Mom's heart rate drops unexpectedly, she's prone to dizziness and fainting. If she exerts too much physical activity, her heart will begin to race at dangerous levels. Mom has undergone two medical procedures to correct her heart rate, but neither of them worked. Apparently, a stubborn heart is just built into my family genetics.

In 2010, Mom got very sick with double pneumonia, which caused her heart rate to bounce around like a pinball machine. She was hospitalized for nearly two weeks while she recovered from the pneumonia. During those two weeks, I spent many hours in the hospital sitting with Mom. She gave all of us quite a scare.

In 2012, while we were vacationing in Ireland, Mom's heart began to race while we were walking to an ancient Celtic burial site to explore. She nearly collapsed in my arms unexpectedly, and I thought I was going to have to steal our guide's tour bus to race Mom to a hospital. Thankfully though, we were able to sit Mom down and get her heart rate to stabilize before I became involved in an international felony.

As an adult, I am still very close to my mother. She and I can gossip for hours while reliving old memories or venting at life's frustrations. We often play cards together, and she still kicks my ass every time, but I absolutely love it. I try to spend as much time as I can with my parents because, one day, I know I won't be able to. I hope that day is still a long way off because I will be devastated when it happens. It's hard for me to think about that.

I am very fortunate to have such wonderful parents. Their unconditional love and support gave me the strength and optimism to persevere through the most difficult periods of my life.

If you're lucky enough to still have your mother or father in your life, reach out to them and tell them that you love them. Tell them that you are grateful for what they've done for you. It lifts my heart and soul whenever I do.

Childhood Metal Mayhem

I was a bit of a social butterfly throughout grade school because I never really fit in with one particular group. I had a wide variety of casual friends and dipped my toes into a lot of different pies. I got along well with most people and mingled about in all the various social cliques in school, including the jocks, band geeks, weird theatre people, "popular kids" and, of course, metal heads. But my oldest and dearest friend is Britt Nichols.

I met Britt on the school bus in the first grade, right after my family moved to North Carolina in 1980. We hit it off immediately because we both have the same sense of humor. Our bus driver, Roger, would have to routinely separate us because we're both smart asses and feed off each other's antics. From the years 1980 to 1992, Britt and I were pretty much joined at the hip.

Thankfully, we never shared any classes together in school because Britt is a year older than me. I'm pretty sure we would have both flunked out if we had to sit next to each other during Algebra or English class. But after school and on weekends, I was usually at Britt's house because he lived only a few miles away from me and didn't have any younger siblings to deal with. Britt does have an older sister named Kelly, but she wanted nothing to do with us.

In our youth, Britt and I would watch movies and cartoons together before racing out of the house to do cannonballs off the wood deck surrounding his above ground pool. I would bet a large sum of money that we watched *The Empire Strikes Back* at least 200 times while growing up. Britt's folks would often invite me to stay for dinner, and I would unknowingly embarrass myself by eating everything in sight. Britt's parents, Walt and Barbara, were excellent cooks and never seemed to mind my insatiable appetite. They always treated me like family, and to this day, I consider them my second parents.

As we got older, Britt and I developed a love of zombie movies and horror films. Classics like *Return of the Living Dead, Friday the 13th* and *Nightmare on Elm Street* were in regular rotation on the VCR. We also howled with laughter at ridiculous, over the top comedies like *Kentucky Fried Movie, Ace Ventura: Pet Detective* or anything by Monty Python. Britt and I even made a few home movies of sketch comedy ourselves with his dad's VHS camcorder. *God, I hope those were destroyed!*

Not only did Britt and I enjoy horror movies growing up, but we also sometimes found ourselves in one. It was no secret that Britt's house and property were haunted. The area in North Carolina in which we grew up was originally inhabited by the Waxhaw Native American people. The township just south of where we grew up, named Waxhaw, was a popular trading post between Native Americans and European settlers. The area is rich in legend and ghost lore. Like many Native Americans, the Waxhaw people suffered serious population decline from diseases brought over by the Europeans, particularly smallpox.

The property on which Britt's house was built had many areas of hollow and sunken earth and was believed to have once been a Native American burial ground. Britt and his dad used to scour the property to collect arrowheads and other Native American artifacts carved from stone. Over time they collected several buckets of these items because they were everywhere.

Strange events would occasionally occur whenever I was at Britt's house. Lights and kitchen appliances would sometimes turn on by themselves or a door would slam in an empty room. Every now and then, while Britt and I were watching television, the hair on the back of my neck would stand up and a cold chill would run down my spine as I would intuitively feel someone watching me.

Growing up in the 80s, the predominant television for most people was a Cathode Ray Tube (CRT) television, which had a large, curved glass display. The heavy curved glass would often reflect light and shadows from within the room, acting as a mirror. Once, while Britt and I were watching a movie, a large and distinct human shadow slowly walked through the reflection of the television, passing between the TV and the couch on which we were sitting. Britt and I both saw it.

I was completely terrified when it happened and, for a brief instant, thought I was in one of my nightmares. Britt, however, was unaffected by the ghostly image and shrugged it off. He said it happened quite often, and you get used to it. I sometimes wonder if the *Shadow Man* entered my psyche through spending so much time at Britt's house. I started having those lucid dreams shortly after we moved to North Carolina after all.

Britt and I were your typical country boys growing up. We did some pretty stupid shit together. Britt's dad hunted pheasant and would pack his own shotgun shells, which meant Britt and I had access to gunpowder in his father's garage. We were thankfully smart enough not to fuck around with Mr. Nichols' guns. But sometimes, whenever Britt's parents were gone, we'd sneak into the garage and fill a toilet paper roll with gunpowder, then take it out into a field behind Britt's house to light and watch it burn.

From there we eventually graduated to having "firework wars" with other friends. We'd construct elaborate tube guns out of PVC pipe and find a secluded area at night to shoot roman candles and bottle rockets at one another. It's a miracle that I still have all my fingers and toes.

Sometimes Britt would raid his dad's coin jar of quarters so that we could walk up to the local gas station convenience store to play video games. When we ran out of coins, we'd both steal a candy bar on our way out of the store to snack on during our half mile walk back to Britt's house. I'm not exactly proud of that, but considering we pumped several hundred dollars worth of quarters into those video games, I think it can be overlooked.

Sometime in the late 80s, Britt's parents bought him a computer, and he became obsessed with it. I didn't really understand what the big deal about computers was at first. But after Britt showed me a picture of a naked woman on his computer, my interest piqued. Of course, at that time, it took about 30 minutes for Britt's computer to download one grainy picture. I remember both of us watching the monitor on Britt's computer as it slowly loaded millions of pixels, line by line, until it finished rendering a perfect set of boobs for us to ogle.

Much of my childhood was spent in constant fear of nuclear annihilation. Growing up in the 80s, my generation felt the tail end of the cold war between the United States and the USSR (Union of Soviet Socialist Republics). Total global destruction seemed to always loom in the background of my youth. Thankfully, I never had to endure the tremendous anxiety of something like the Cuban Missile Crisis of 1962. However, I do remember the beginning of the first Gulf War quite well. It began right before I turned 16 years old.

In January of 1991, I was at Britt's house when the United States and a coalition of other nations began Operation Desert Storm. Watching live footage of the conflict on CNN was a fascinating and very somber moment of my adolescence. It seemed like the entire world was glued to their televisions to witness death and carnage. It was surreal to say the least. Britt and I, along with his dad, watched in silence as our nation launched a barrage of Patriot missiles against Saddam Hussein and the nation of Iraq for their continued incursions into the neighboring nations of Kuwait and Saudi Arabia.

It was also around this time that Britt and I became huge fans of heavy metal music. The fast tempos, hard hitting beats, in your face lyrics and dark melodies appealed to us. The music seemed to personify the horror and fear of war that enshrouded our childhood.

We would watch MTV's *Headbanger's Ball* religiously on the weekends to discover new metal bands coming onto the scene. When *Beavis and Butthead* first aired on MTV in March of 1993, I remember laughing hysterically before realizing that Britt and I were those two idiots. But I didn't really care. Heavy Metal was a perfect release for all the anger, confusion and existential dread that I was going through at the time.

When I first heard the album *Master of Puppets* by Metallica, I became a huge fan of the band. When the band's video for their song "One" debuted on *Headbanger's Ball* in January of 1989, it became an instant classic that blew all other bands away. When Metallica's *Black Album* was released a couple of years after that, it solidified them as my favorite band of all time.

Music became a large part of my life while growing up. Going to concerts to see bands like Metallica, Iron Maiden, Megadeth, TOOL, Def Leppard, Black Sabbath, Pantera, Guns n Roses, and many others, became routine for me and my friends. This was of course long before online ticket sales. Sometimes we'd camp out at record stores overnight so we could get floor tickets to a show, ensuring a maximum metal experience.

Live music is all about creating and sharing energy, which has always resonated with me. Music is still a large part of my everyday life. In fact, my wife and I have tickets to see Metallica in a couple of months as well as tickets to see Billy Joel and Sting. While heavy metal is my passion, my musical palette is fairly diverse. After all, I am a child of the 80s and can shamelessly sing along with just about anything from that period.

In high school I decided that I no longer wanted to play the trumpet and needed to learn how to play guitar. Britt and I got our first guitars together and decided we were going to start a band so that we, too, could become rich and famous and tour all over the world. We were going to be Metal Gods in our own right, with millions of fans to worship us.

My parents bought me a cheap guitar and amp for Christmas in 1992, and I taught myself to play along to a lot of Metallica's songs. In college, I even started my own band and wrote original music, which was a huge creative outlet for me.

Although I never became the rock star I always wanted to be, music has been an integral part of my life that has helped me develop some important friendships.

Dungeons and Dragons

My most cherished memories from childhood are of playing *Dungeons and Dragons* with Britt and two other of my closest friends, Jason Kendlehardt and Tadd Wilson. The four of us would stay up all night eating pizza, listening to heavy metal and drinking sugary soda while role-playing. We would laugh and cut up on each other while adventuring through some crazy ass campaign one of us had designed. We all took turns being the Dungeon Master.

When the Netflix hit show *Stranger Things* first aired in 2016, I remember telling my wife, "That was my childhood". I, like millions of other kids in the 80s, used Dungeons and Dragons to escape from the mundane reality of life and the constant terror of the cold war. Role playing allowed us to enter a world where we could be heroes and battle monsters and demons, face to face.

The whole Dungeons and Dragons fandom started with Britt's mom who, on a whim, bought us the game to try. Britt's mom, Barbara, was a high school teacher and had heard that a lot of kids were playing the game, so she thought we'd enjoy it. Barbara even called my mom before buying the game, unbeknownst to me, to make sure my parents didn't think it was satanic or inappropriate. My mom had no problem with the game though because her younger brother, Tim, played Dungeons and

Dragons in the 70s. Mom thought it was a good idea to keep us out of trouble.

Britt and I read through the D&D manual and played only a little bit at first. I thought it was confusing and a little boring the first few times we played. The moment when we became full on Dungeons and Dragons nerds was when this guy named Todd, who was Britt's older sister's boyfriend at the time, showed us how to play the game. When Britt's mom found out that Todd played Dungeons and Dragons, she asked him to show me, Britt, Tadd and Jason how to properly play the fantasy role playing game.

So in the summer of 1988, poor Todd was obligated to spend his weekends being the Dungeon Master to a bunch of newbies so that he could get in good with his girlfriend's mom. I don't think Todd minded too much though because we all had an amazing time. Todd was an excellent storyteller and a very animated role player. We played on the front porch of Britt's house, nonstop, for many hours that summer.

Todd showed us that the real fun in the game was in the hands of the Dungeon Master and his or her ability to get players involved in the story and their characters engaged in the plot. As players, it was our job to give the Dungeon Master shit and make him work for our participation. If you've ever played Dungeons and Dragons, you'd understand that joke.

Todd was about 7 years older than us and in college and is not to be confused with my good friend Tadd. Tadd used to get seriously pissed off when people called him Todd.

I think having an uncommon name is what initially bonded Tadd and I together. People often called me Cody by mistake after first meeting me. Also, Tadd was the oldest child of four with two brothers and a sister, so we both felt the pains of fighting for our independence out of adolescence. Tadd's Mom used to routinely throw away his heavy metal tapes and CDs because she thought the album covers were satanic. They were staunch Catholics. Tadd's Mom particularly hated the artwork for the band Slayer. Naturally, disapproval from Tadd's mom only made us like the band more.

After the summer of 1988, Todd moved on with his life, left the campaigning to the four of us, and over the next four years, Britt, Jason, Tadd and I would play a lot of *Dungeons and Dragons*. Sometimes things got heated and tempers flared, usually between Britt and Jason. When we got into high school and all of us started getting jobs and girlfriends (*well, I got a girlfriend*), we still found time to play whenever possible. But by the end of the summer, in 1992, our role-playing days ended and I imagine it ended kind of like this:

Mage/Wizard: "*I cast Fireball.*"

Dungeon Master: "*Both the Ranger and the Barbarian are in the room with the ghastly fiend. They will incur damage as well if you cast it.*"

Ranger: "*Fuck. Don't Do It Tadd! I've only got 14 hit points left.*"

Barbarian: "*I can take it. Light the fucker up.*"

Ranger: "*Fuck you, Corey.*"

Barbarian: "*You're gonna die in the next round anyway, Britt. We can resurrect you. Light 'em up, Tadd.*"

Britt: *"I don't want to be resurrected. It's against my character's religion. I'm a Ranger and believe in the natural order of all things. Resurrection is unnatural and forbidden to my character."*

Dungeon Master: *"Jesus Christ, Britt, are you serious? Just let them resurrect you."*

Britt: *"Fuck off, Jason."*

Tadd: *"I cast Fireball anyway."*

Jason: *"OK. Roll damage. 6d6"*

Tadd: *"Plus 8 from my ring of enhancement."*

Britt: *"God Damn it."*

Jason: *"Britt, you're dead."*

Britt: *"No shit, Jason."*

Corey: *"Guys, please don't start."*

Jason: *"Don't get pissed at me, man. Britt's the one who chose to play a character that doesn't believe in wearing armor, heavy weapons or being resurrected. It's called "Dungeons and Dragons," Britt, not "Hippies and Unicorns".*

Britt: *"It's a ROLE-PLAYING game Asshole. I'm being true to my character!!"*

Jason: *"Just let them resurrect you."*

Britt: *"No. I'm going to roll a new character."*

Corey: *"C'mon man, that'll take another hour."*

Britt: *"I don't care. You should have thought of that before you told Tadd to cast fireball."*

Corey: *"I didn't MAKE him do it!"*

Tadd: *"Umm... Is the Lich King dead?"*

Jason: *"No, but he's on fire, badly injured and pissed. Now he attacks Corey with his rod of animation."*

Corey: *"I grab Britt's body to use as a shield."*

Jason: *"Roll a Dexterity and Strength check to block the attack."*

Corey: *"(rolls dice)... Hell Yeah!!!"*

Jason: *"Britt, you take another 27 points of damage and ... (rolls dice) ... are now reanimated under the control of the Lich King."*

Britt: *"I hate you guys."*

Jason enjoyed torturing us as the Dungeon Master. He's a bit of an asshole like that. The kind of friend you have to warn people about before they meet him. But he has always been a very loyal and trustworthy friend who, on more than one occasion, has gone out of his way to help me. When I began my journey back into peak physical conditioning, Jason joined me on many long mud runs and obstacle course races.

Jason's one of the most intelligent people I know and was accepted into the prestigious North Carolina School of Science and Mathematics for high school. He devours books at a phenomenal speed and somehow retains most of what he reads. When he got married, both Britt and I were groomsmen in his wedding and together gave a toast to Jason, which made him teary eyed. Jason lost his brash, hard plated exterior for a moment and showed genuine emotion. It was a rare occurrence.

Funny enough, despite his blunt and oftentimes rude mannerisms, Jason is still just a big kid at heart. He's 50 years old now and still goes to Comic Book and Fantasy conventions to cosplay. He plays role playing games into the wee hours of the morning. I gave up gaming after high school. It was just never the same fun for me after initially playing with Britt, Tadd and Jason.

As I look back on my adolescence, I realize how fortunate I was to have such great friends growing up. After Grandpa died, I was pretty closed off from the world and most people. I often found pop culture and casual friends to be fake and gravitated more toward counterculture trends and to friends who I thought were genuinely interesting and shared my rather dark view of the world.

Britt, today, is still like a brother to me, perhaps even more so than my real brother, Carey. He knows pretty much all my secrets, faults and failures. And he has always been there to listen to me rant and rave about whatever was rolling around in my busy little mind. He would always be truthful with me and give me his honest opinion, and I valued that.

Developing my friendship with Britt, Jason and Tadd helped me open up a lot after Grandpa's death and eventually helped me to develop similar friendships in the future. I still talk to those guys regularly. We text back and forth like we're still fourteen years old and rolling a 20-sided die.

49

Young Love and Chaos

Junior High was a shit show. But Junior High is a shit show for everybody, so I guess that's not saying much.

In 1987, while dealing with hormonal changes and being in a new school environment, on top of trying to cope with Grandpa's death from a year earlier, I was an emotional roller coaster most of the time. I had a lot of anger and anxiety building up inside of me and was in desperate need of a pressure release.

I went to Quail Hollow Junior High in Charlotte, which is about 10 miles from our house. That meant, to catch the bus, I had to get up at the ass crack of dawn every morning and ride my bike a half mile to the entrance of our neighborhood. That sucked ass, especially in the winter.

Going into Junior High in the fall of 1987, I was chubby and still holding on to a lot of baby fat. But by the fall of 1988, I had shot up 7-8 inches, was tall and gangly while sporting a mullet haircut. I have no regrets about the haircut.

I had trouble focusing in most of my classes, but thoroughly enjoyed my foreign language class because that's where I met my first girlfriend, Fran. She would pass me love notes during class that read *Ich Liebe Dich (I love you)*. I didn't really know how to respond to her and usually just smiled or winked. I couldn't respond to her in German because the only thing I studied in that class was Fran's tits. She developed early in life and was proud to show them off, much to the delight of almost every boy in school.

Fran was my first kiss and the first time I got to second base with a girl. It happened while we were watching the movie *Indiana Jones and The Last Crusade* together. Her parents had invited me over for dinner and I was a perfect gentleman in front of them. But not when they were in the next room while Fran and I were underneath a blanket in their bonus room.

I hesitate to call Fran my first love because, at 13 years old, I don't think it's possible to understand the difference between love and lust. I'm sure, at the time, I thought I was in love. But being 50 years old now, I think you first must take responsibility for yourself before you can understand love. And I was a long way from that at the age of 13.

My relationship with Fran didn't last long. I think she eventually found my moody disposition to be a buzzkill and ended up breaking up with me on my 14th birthday -- at my own party. The humiliation and rejection really tore me up, adding even more fuel to the raging fire building up inside of me. It was bad enough being dumped at my own birthday party, but to make matters worse, I spent that night at my buddy Chris Feathers' house.

Chris and I grew up playing baseball together and had known each other for years. I remember riding with Chris in the back of a flatbed pickup through the "Pineville Park Baseball Parade" to kick off the season in 1987. We were wearing our baseball uniforms and singing rap songs together. This was around the time when the Beastie Boys exploded on to the scene, so Chris and I sang songs like "Paul Revere", "Girls" and "Brass Monkey" throughout the whole parade. We also sang a few songs from Run DMC's album, *Raising Hell*.

Chris and I hung out a good bit through Junior High but kind of ran in different circles once we got into high school. We eventually lost touch when we went to separate Universities but thankfully reconnected around 2009 through social media. He lives just two miles from me right now. We still get along great.

I have a lot of happy memories with Chris, but the night Fran broke up with me is not one of them. I tried being tough about the breakup in front of Chris but still ended up crying like a baby on his couch that night when we went to sleep. That was, without a doubt, my shittiest birthday so far.

But Fran wasn't my only foray into young love. There were also the twins, Jennifer and Jeanna, whom I flirted with quite heavily. They were identical twins, but you could easily tell them apart because Jennifer was the athletic one and Jeanna was the more artistic one. Jennifer had my attention when she was in her volleyball shorts. Jeanna had my attention with her creative mind and artistic nature.

When Mom and Dad dropped me off at one of my first Junior High dances, Jennifer and Jeanna came up to me in the parking lot and both asked me to save them a dance. Mom and Dad saw it all of course, and I was totally embarrassed, but Dad just grinned and told me to have fun before driving away. That turned out to be a pretty good night.

As far as academics were concerned, I did the bare minimum in Junior High. I was bored in most of my classes, although I did enjoy learning to play the trumpet in Band class. I practiced regularly, usually in the back yard for all the neighbors to hear. Apparently, I've always been seeking an audience.

The most important thing that happened to me in Junior High was meeting my science teacher, Ken Waldron, who was also the school's football coach.

Coach Waldron was a tall, muscular man who wore thick glasses and looked like he belonged on both the football field and in the science lab. He was intelligent and mild mannered, with a deep voice that was well articulated and commanded your attention. Coach Waldron made science interesting, and I respected him in the classroom long before I ever walked onto the football field.

When Coach Waldron asked me if I was going to try out for the football team, I told him I was more interested in baseball and basketball, because that's what I grew up playing. But I think Coach Waldron sensed that I needed some discipline in my life, and he convinced me to try out for the team. I'm very grateful for that because it was on the football field where I was finally able to find some release for the anger and anxiety built up inside of me since Grandpa died.

In baseball and basketball, it's a foul to knock someone to the ground intentionally. But in football, it's encouraged. And I *really* enjoyed hitting people in pads and knocking them to the ground. Probably a little too much if I'm honest. During football tryouts, I kept tackling everyone in sight without understanding what else I was supposed to do. I didn't grow up watching or playing football, so I really didn't understand the game.

But Coach Waldron was patient and understanding with all his players and students. On the field, he took the time to explain the mechanics and fundamentals of the game. In the classroom, he would carefully explain the chemical reactions he was producing in the lab.

Whether in the classroom or on the field, Coach Waldron treated everyone equally and with respect. Sure, like all coaches, he barked and yelled at us while we ran drills and did conditioning exercises, but he also took the time to explain why the drills were important and how they were going to improve our performance on the field.

The most important thing I learned from Coach Waldron was how to get back up when I got run over or my ass handed to me. In doing that, I found the strength and discipline to pick myself up whenever I got knocked down. I learned to remind myself that the game's not over and that I had to get up and run the next play.

When football season ended, Coach Waldron encouraged me to try out for track and field, which he also coached. He took the time to show me the proper technique in throwing the shot put and discus and how to sprint by pumping my arms as fast as I could while maintaining pace and control. As a result, I broke the school record in shot put and was one leg of a seriously fast 400meter relay team which qualified for the state finals.

During the couple of years that Coach Waldron mentored me, my self respect and confidence grew, along with my Ego.

On the last day of school at Quail Hollow, I did something stupid and started a fight with a guy named Gary, who was Fran's new boyfriend. Gary had been taunting me about losing Fran throughout the school year. On the last day of school, my anger got the better of me and I took a swing at Gary, knocking him out cold. It happened in front of a lot of people, and I was immediately nabbed by the school administration.

My folks were livid, and the school threatened to hold me back a year as punishment. But in the end, it all smoothed over because, after he woke up, Gary admitted that he probably deserved the punch. I still felt terrible though and apologized.

It was from that experience that I learned to control my anger off the field and to stay away from women who create drama.

Coach Waldron would go on to coach track and field at South Mecklenburg High School the following year. He continued to have a huge impact on students and athletes throughout his career. They even renamed the track and field at Quail Hollow after him in 1998. I'm grateful for everything Coach Waldron taught me and the patience he had with me in Junior High.

While Coach Waldron went to South Mecklenburg High School to coach and teach, I wound up going to Providence High School, which proved to be another turning point in my life. Because while I really enjoyed football in Junior High, I seriously disliked my football coach in High School and ended up quitting before my senior year.

And it was one of the smartest decisions of my life.

Hoodlum Pirate Fashion

High School is when I started to get my shit together and take some responsibility for my life. Between school, turning 16, getting my first job, my first car and hanging out with friends, I was all over the place. It was a busy time, but I enjoyed it. I was looking for some direction and felt like I had something to prove to myself.

I played football for two seasons and was in both concert band and marching band but switched from trumpet to drum line my senior year. I made my acting debut and performed in the Theater Department's production of Shakespeare's "Much Ado About Nothing" my senior year as well. I was also the President of the 'Interact Club', which was a leadership and business development organization sponsored by the Matthews Rotary Club. I was even in the Physics Club, but only because they organized the "Battle of the Bands" every fall and I wanted to be a part of that.

During the summer of 1991, before my junior year, I attended a leadership development camp in Brevard, NC, a beautiful town located in the Blue Ridge Mountains. Tadd joined me on that retreat, as well as another good friend of mine, Karl Ruch. Over the course of that weeklong camp, Karl became good friends with Tadd and me. We shared a small cabin together and had a great time.

I first met Karl in band class, where he was the first chair percussionist. Karl was a naturally gifted musician who would sometimes sit in with the Charlotte Symphony Orchestra to play timpani. For all intents and purposes, Karl was a professional musician in high school. In addition to drums, he also played piano and was big into synthesizers and new age music. He loved the progressive rock band RUSH and idolized the great Neil Pert in the same manner that I idolized James Hetfield, the rhythm guitarist and heavy metal god for Metallica.

It was Karl who inspired me to keep practicing guitar whenever I got frustrated with it. Karl practiced all the time, and his talent showed it. He was a year older than me and would go on to study at Davidson College, in 1992, on a music scholarship.

When not practicing guitar or playing Dungeons and Dragons with Britt, I would usually spend my free time hanging out with Karl and Tadd, who were both hopeless romantics. They loved to read and write poetry and the three of us would often commandeer a table at a local coffee shop to wax poetic on topics ranging from philosophy, literature and religion.

Tadd and Karl aptly nicknamed themselves "The Poets" and would often engage in deep conversations while I usually sat quietly and listened, absorbing their insights and spirited debates. It was Tadd and Karl's love of classical education that inspired my own intellectual development. That inspiration led me to read one of the most influential books of my life, *The Art of Worldly Wisdom*, by the 17th Century Spanish philosopher Baltasar Gracian.

In the fall of 1991 I threw a big party at my parents' house for Halloween. I think I openly invited the entire school to come and was pretty amazed when over 100 people showed up, dressed in all manner of ghoulish and hilarious costumes. Britt's mom sewed me, Tadd, Britt and another friend of ours, Brian, matching wizard robes so that we could go as the four horsemen of the apocalypse.

The party was a huge success. We ate hot dogs and candy and then broke up into groups to carve pumpkins before smashing them off the second floor landing of our detached garage. Destroying some of those pumpkins felt criminal though because many of them were truly spectacular in design. There were some very talented artists in my high school.

Karl and his buddy, Jim, set up their keyboards and synthesizers to play techno music and everybody danced late into the night. It wasn't your typical high school kegger with kids throwing up and acting like idiots. It was just a great time with lots of fun and laughs. Nobody got hurt or sick thank God. At the end of the night, Tadd and Karl helped me clean up and then crashed at my house, where we slept in late the following day.

The morning after that Halloween party was a bit chaotic though because during breakfast, which consisted of leftover hot dogs, Karl had an anxiety attack when he realized that he had lost the keepsake ring that his high school sweetheart had given him. Karl kept his girlfriend's ring on a necklace he always wore and was convinced that it had fallen off somewhere while cleaning up the pumpkin massacre the night before.

After breakfast, as I busied myself cleaning up the rest of the house, Tadd and Karl began digging through multiple trashbags of pumpkin guts and god knows what else, searching for that ring. I thought for sure that their efforts would end in disappointment. But, in a stroke of brilliant luck,

Tadd found the ring buried deep in the pumpkin slush of one of those trashbags. Karl, of course, was elated and hugged Tadd tight for finding the ring. It saved him from a very embarrassing conversation with his girlfriend.

***

During my senior year, I got involved in student government and was on the Senior Class Council. By the end of my high school run, I was voted to be the student speaker at graduation, which made Mom and Dad quite proud. It was a lot to take on but, if I'm being honest, I did most of it because I needed to pad the shit out of my college applications because my grades alone weren't going to cut it. I needed to show some initiative to make up for the 'devil may care' attitude I had through my sophomore year.

When I entered High School, I took the opportunity to change my style. While my attitude may have improved and my discipline became a little more focused, I still wanted to be a rock star. I chuckle at how lost I was back then, so desperate for an identity and eager for attention. I suppose, in many ways, I still am. I still wear metal band t-shirts and have a couple from my high school days that are now over 30 years old. I'm trying to decide which one I want to wear at my funeral. It'll probably be a game time decision.

I asked my parents to buy me a black leather motorcycle jacket because all the metal bands I idolized wore leather jackets and I wanted to be a badass too. Dad wanted no part in dressing me like a 'hoodlum' and refused to buy me my jacket. He was afraid I was going to end up in the wrong crowd and start getting into trouble. After all, it was just a few months earlier that I let my emotions get the better of me, and I knocked out poor Gary on the last day of Junior High.

Looking back on it now, I can't blame Dad for refusing to buy me the jacket. He was only looking out for my best interest. He wanted me to wear khakis and collared shirts, like my brother. But for reasons I still don't understand, I have never wanted to conform. I've always wanted an authentic identity.

In the summer of 1990, I decided to join the Providence High School marching band for summer rehearsals and, somehow, got roped into playing at the grand opening of a new McDonald's opening about a mile from school. Apparently, McDonald's was making a play at becoming the new after school hang-out for kids and thought that John Phillips Sousa would bring in a crowd. I, of course, found playing at the Grand Opening of a McDonald's lame, but a lot of people showed up that day because they were giving away free food.

After the marching band finished playing, the manager of McDonald's started handing out employment applications to all the band members because they were in desperate need of staff. So, to spite my folks, I took the opportunity and filled out an application so that I could earn some money to buy my own black leather jacket. And, just like that, McDonald's became my first job.

Despite my rebellious motivation, Mom and Dad were very supportive of me getting a job and they shuttled me back and forth to work at McDonald's for a few months. Because I was playing football, I didn't really have a lot of free time, but I figured I could work on weekends to save up enough money to buy my jacket and then quit.

After a couple of months working at Mickey Ds, I was able to buy my motorcycle jacket, and it was everything I wanted it to be and more. It was a great feeling buying it with money I earned on my own. Mom and Dad hated the jacket of course, but they were respectful of my decision and told me it was my money to do with as I wished.

I wore that jacket all through high school and college and still have it in my closet today. It still fits, and every time I put it on, I am flooded with many fantastic memories. I even had the back of the jacket airbrushed with an eagle's profile and sewed on metal band patches to showcase my metal allegiances. I was really proud of that jacket, despite its vagrant, redneck style.

I didn't quit McDonald's after I bought the jacket though. I actually enjoyed working there at first because a lot of my coworkers were classmates and I got to flirt with a lot of the girls. Eventually I worked my way up to be promoted to the drive thru window, which is a coveted position in the hierarchy of fast-food employment. But I hated smelling like a grease trap at the end of every shift and usually had to shower two or three times after work to get the smell out of my hair.

When school started in the fall of 1990, one of my first classes was driver's education. By Christmas that year I had passed the class and was only a few weeks away from my 16th birthday. I was so excited, I could almost taste my freedom coming up on the horizon. All my close friends had already been driving for a year, and I was anxious to join them on the road. When I finally turned 16, I passed my driver's exam with ease on the first try and arrived home that day to find an amazing surprise waiting for me in the driveway.

While keeping me completely in the dark, my parents went out and bought me a used, 1984, candy apple red, stick shift, Chevy Camaro with t-tops. It was a beautiful car, and I loved it from the day I got it. I was absolutely shocked by the surprise and did not see it coming.

Dad enjoyed getting the drop on me and surprising me with the car, but he was also very clear about my responsibilities to hold on to it. He told me my grades had to maintain a 'B' average and that I had to stay in constant communication with him and mom about my whereabouts at all times. This was of course long before everyone had a cell phone in their pocket, which meant I had to use the phone, wherever I was, to check in.

Maintaining a B average wasn't easy for me at first but, thankfully, I held up my end of the bargain. Despite being given a red race car for my 16th birthday, I was responsible and didn't go drag racing or do anything like that. Dad taught me how to drive manual shift in our neighborhood and thankfully I didn't tear the transmission out while learning. Dad also warned me that the police would watch a teenager in a red sports car very carefully and, to my credit, I listened to him. I rarely drank alcohol while in high school and I never got a speeding ticket. I did, however, lock my keys in the car a few times and had to call AAA to get them to come unlock it for me, which was always embarrassing. I once did that with the car running. *<sigh>*

I loved riding around town in my Camaro with the t-tops off, blaring heavy metal and feeling the wind in my hair. I'm not sure what I did to deserve such a fantastic first car, but I will forever be grateful to my parents for trusting in me and giving me my freedom with some style. I think they've always understood me better than I know myself.

Shortly after my parents bought me the car though, I did do something silly and stupid that I regret to this day: I got my left ear pierced. I don't really know what I was thinking at the time. All the heavy metal bands that I idolized wore earrings and I guess I felt that I had to wear one too to be cool. It pissed Dad off to no end of course, but I eventually stopped wearing the earring shortly after I got it because it kept ripping out of my ear when I took off my football helmet.

After my brief foray into pirate fashion, I finally learned that I needed to stop pretending to be somebody I wasn't. This lesson came in useful when the tattoo craze started about a decade later. I have nothing against tattoos. There are some amazing tattoo artists in the world, and I do admire their work. But on the rare occasion that I considered getting a tattoo, I'd remember that damn earring and how much I regretted getting it.

I came to accept a lot about myself during my first couple of years in High School. In my search for identity, I came to understand that cultural trends and image were superficial, and that true identity comes from your actions, not how you look. Don't get me wrong, I still wore my black leather jacket, metal t-shirts and boots to school, but I wasn't going to let the clothes I wear dictate my path in life.

That realization helped me tremendously when I started my senior year because it helped me make a big decision that awakened a monstrous fucking drive in me.

Taking Control

I entered High School with the intent of focusing on football. My goal was to get a scholarship to play at a collegiate level. Coach Waldron's strong impact on me in Junior High helped motivate me, and I was excited to meet my next coach at Providence. I trained consistently over the summer before my sophomore year, and by tryouts, I was running the 40-meter dash in 4.4 seconds. We had to run it three times to get an average speed, and I hit 4.4sec every time. For comparison, the average time for the 40-meter dash in the NFL Scouting Combine is approximately 4.7 seconds. So, yeah, I'm proud of that and wanted to put it in this book.

Unfortunately, while I was fit, primed and ready to play football going into High School, I was woefully uninspired by my new coach. I found him to be nowhere near as inspiring as Coach Waldron and that disappointed me. In fact, I'm going to refer to my High School football coach as "Coach Meh" because I don't even want to mention his name.

Coach Meh barked and cussed at his players regularly and would demean them in front of the team. His coaching was more like a drill sergeant in boot camp, which I would have respected if he had the brains to back it up. But I found Coach Meh to not be nearly as intelligent or well spoken as Coach Waldron was. During school hours, Coach Meh sat in the weight room all day talking nonsense with his football cronies instead of inspiring others and educating in a classroom.

Despite my disdain for Coach Meh, I played football in my sophomore year and had a lot of fun. I played defensive linebacker, which was the best position for me because it meant my only job on the field was to kill the man with the ball. My fellow linebacker and partner on the field was a friend of mine named Ben Huff. Ben would go on to get a scholarship to the University of Michigan and be on the 1997 National Championship team with teammate Charles Woodson.

My junior year playing football wasn't as much fun. I found out quickly that pursuing a football scholarship meant devoting a lot of time in the off season in the weight room and kissing the Coach's ass for recommendations to college football programs. I loved playing football, I just didn't want to do it ALL the time, which is what continuing with a football scholarship would have meant. I had a lot of other interests and wanted to spend as much time with Britt, Jason, Tadd and Karl as I could because they all graduated a year ahead of me and were entering university in the fall. The summer of 1992 was probably the last time we would all be together for awhile.

The seal on my decision to quit football came during the off-season summer tryouts before my senior year. There were a lot of guys at tryouts that year and one way that Coach Meh liked to weed them out was by running Oklahoma drills until everybody puked. Oklahoma drills are basically when two players lie on the ground and, on the whistle, have to jump up and try to get past one another. It was hard hitting and exhausting, and I loved it.

But at tryouts that summer, Coach Meh lined me up in the Oklahoma drill with one of the new guys coming into school that year. He was half my size, but he had some energy and fire. I guess Coach Meh wanted to see what the kid was made of, so he lined him up against me. When we ran the drill the first time, I tried not to go full speed on the guy and embarrass him. I easily tackled him and put him on the ground. He practically ran right into me.

Evidently my going easy on the kid pissed Coach Meh off to no end because, after we ran the drill, he ran up to me, grabbed my facemask and started screaming, "God Damn It Maher, what the hell kind of pussy footed shit is that?! You show me you want to be on my team, or I'll find somebody else who does! Run it again!"

The second time we ran the drill I was so angry at Coach Meh that I hopped up and drilled my helmet into the new guy's chest, putting him down hard on the ground. Everybody whooped and hollered and Coach Meh patted me on the helmet in approval before walking away.

But the new guy didn't get up right away. He just rolled around on the ground in pain, groaning. When he eventually did get up, he limped out of practice and never showed up again. I found out later that I had broken two of his ribs.

Every time I saw the new kid in school that year, I felt ashamed of myself and tried to apologize. I felt like the Cobra Kai guy, in the movie *The Karate Kid*, who was told to sweep the leg and show no mercy. I felt like a brute thug who harmed someone by doing the bidding of a man I didn't respect.

I quit football about two weeks before school started my senior year. I walked into Coach Meh's office before practice and put my helmet and pads down on his desk and told him I didn't think I could give him everything I had anymore. I wasn't rude, but I didn't bother explaining to him why I was quitting. I disliked him so much that I didn't want to waste my time.

By this point, I could tell Coach Meh didn't like me either, because I didn't hang out in the weight-room all day and kiss his ass like a lot of the other seniors did. Coach Meh didn't try to change my mind at all. As I was walking out of his office, all he said was, "You're making a mistake, Maher." I wish I had come back with some quip, but I didn't. In fact, I don't even think I looked back at him.

***

My father was crushed when I told him I was quitting football, but he didn't get angry. He was definitely disappointed though. I promised Dad that I was going to get involved in other things and see what else was out there that interested me. Deep down, I know Dad thought I was making a mistake too. But like he's always done, Dad supported my decision and simply said, "You can do anything you want if you put your mind to it."

Dad's been saying that to us our entire lives, but it wasn't until I was 17 years old that I actually heard him. From that moment, my life path shifted. I decided that I was going to prove to myself and my parents that I really could do anything if I focused and worked hard enough.

It was six years between Grandpa's death and my senior year of high school. I dealt with a lot of anger, depression and struggles with identity during those years. But by working through that trauma and getting lucky in surrounding myself with quality friends, I found a profound sense of determination and took responsibility for my life. It was a major turning point for me.

Wendy

Growing up, Mom would often get Carey, Cami and I summer passes to a local entertainment park in Charlotte called Carowinds. With over 400 acres of roller coasters, restaurants and attractions, a huge water park and an Amphitheatre for summer concerts, getting summer passes to Carowinds allowed Mom to get some peace and quiet occasionally. It's basically a daycare for adolescents. Mom would sometimes drop us off for the day to meet up with friends while she took a break.

I have a lot of fun memories of Carowinds from my youth. It was a rite-of-passage for every pre-pubescent kid in my school to ride the Carolina Cyclone. That nasty roller coaster took a lot of courage to climb into for the first time. It had some serious corkscrew twists, hard turns and drops, but was a helluva lot of fun. Although I once rode it three times in a row after eating lunch and immediately vomited in a trash can upon disembarking. I despise vomiting.

In the summer of 1988, Chris Feathers and I went to see The Beach Boys at the Carowinds amphitheater, and we had a blast. I was a big fan of the Beach Boys in my youth and still listen to the songs "Sloop John B" and "God Only Knows" regularly. Sadly, Brian Wilson, one of the founders of the legendary California crooners, passed away today. *Thanks for the happy memories, Brian.*

In October of 1988, I went with a buddy of mine, Mike, to see Def Leppard on their Hysteria tour at the old Charlotte Coliseum, and my taste in music began to rapidly shift towards heavy metal. Laser light displays and dense fog machines running behind loud, chunky guitars and thumping bass drums were right up my alley. And, of course, all the young girls in tight jean shorts and crop top t-shirts singing along to lyrics like, *"I'm hot, sticky and sweet... from my head to my feet"*, helped tremendously.

Mike lived in my neighborhood and was viewed by my parents as being somewhat of a bad influence on me. During the summer, I would sometimes sneak out of the house in the middle of the night to meet up with Mike. He was a few years older than me and would often swipe a bottle of liquor or a few beers from his dad's stash whenever we'd sneak out together. We never really got into trouble though. Most of the time, we'd simply lie in the middle of the road and stare up at the stars, talking about music, girls and cars. I let Mike do most of the drinking because, as previously noted, I hate vomiting.

In February of 1989, right after my shitty 14th birthday when my girlfriend dumped me, Mike somehow scored two tickets to see Metallica on their Damaged Justice tour, and he asked me if I wanted to go. Although he wouldn't admit it, I think Mike was selling weed in high school and one of his pothead friends paid him with the tickets. I didn't tell my parents I was going to that show because I was afraid they would say no. I had a hard enough time getting them to let me go see Def Leppard. So, I told my parents that Mike and I were going roller skating that night and then sleeping over at his house.

My first Metallica concert was my baptism into heavy metal fire. I had never experienced such loud, raw and powerful energy at a concert before. Being in a particularly dark state of mind at the time, I gave in to my anger and turned to the dark side, becoming a metal head for life. In about six months I went from singing "California Girls" to screaming "DIE! DIE! DIE!" with 12,000 other raging metal heads. When I turned 15 the following year, I got my first job at McDonalds to buy my black leather jacket.

When the summer of 1991 approached, I decided I no longer wanted to work at McDonalds. I was sick and tired of smelling like French fries all of the time and my acne had gotten so bad, my face looked like a pepperoni pizza. So, I decided to get out of the grease trap and apply for a job at Carowinds. I figured working at Carowinds would be like a glorified babysitting job.

Every summer, Carowinds employs hundreds of people and would often hold job fairs for positions available for the upcoming season. So, using any excuse I could to drive my Camaro, I went to one. When I went to the Carowinds' job fair in the spring of '91, I told the hiring staff that I would work in any area of the park except food services or sanitation. I had no desire to clean toilets or vomit-covered trash bins at a roller coaster park over the summer. That would not have been better than working the drive thru window at McDonald's.

Carowinds hired me on the spot at the job fair to work in retail, and by the summer of '91, I found myself sitting in the "Old West" area of the park, selling personalized leather bracelets to kids. It wasn't a bad gig, but I did have to work outside at a small cart made to look like a stagecoach. Most days I cooked in the boiling summer sun. *It was so fucking hot.*

Like most entertainment parks, Carowinds plays theme music throughout the day, with each section of the park having a specific genre of music. Because I worked in the "Old West" section of Carowinds, I had to listen to "Spaghetti Western" music for 8 hours a day. I didn't mind the music too much though because Clint Eastwood is an idol of mine. I grew up watching his westerns and have enjoyed pretty much every movie he's ever made. His career and longevity in Hollywood are legendary. If I had the opportunity to work with anyone in showbiz, it would be Mr. Eastwood. Although, as of this writing, Clint Eastwood is 95 years old, so that may never happen.

That said, listening to the theme of 'A Fistful of Dollars' on loop for 8 hours would drive anyone insane. But it was still better than working at McDonald's. Plus, there were a lot of kids who worked at Carowinds who were my age, and I made friends with a few.

One of the first people that I met at Carowinds was a girl named Wendy, who worked in the puppet shop adjacent to my leather goods cart. She was cute and kinda nerdy, but easy to talk to. We had a lot in common, although she lived in South Carolina and attended Fort Mill High School.

I think what attracted me to Wendy the most was the fact that we were in different school systems, which meant that we didn't have any mutual friends or know any of the same people. That helped us connect more easily I think. We got to know each other organically, without having to devolve our conversations into high school gossip.

Early on in our courtship, Wendy and I talked at length about the struggles of being the oldest child. Like me, she was the first born and had a brother five years younger than her. Also like me, her parents were still together and happily married. We complained to one another frequently about how difficult it was to get our parents to loosen up and give us space. For Wendy it was especially difficult because her Mom was a school teacher. Wendy felt like she couldn't cut loose at all because her Mom seemed to have eyes everywhere watching her.

Wendy was also in the marching band, however she didn't play an instrument. She was on the color guard which, for those unaware, is the group of synchronized flag twirlers that performs while the band plays. Her high school had a very prominent marching band program that routinely won state championships in South Carolina.

Eventually Wendy and I started taking our lunch breaks together and, before long, we started dating. I liked that there was no drama with Wendy. After what I experienced in Junior High with my first girlfriend, Fran, I tried to avoid all that nonsense.

When Metallica came back through Charlotte on their "Wherever I May Roam" tour, during the summer, I started dating Wendy. I had floor seats, along with Britt, Tadd and Jason. That concert was even more spectacular than the show I saw them play in 1989 with Mike. The mighty James Hetfield and company played for a solid three hours that night and, once again, blistered the paint off the walls of the old Charlotte Coliseum. I thrashed, screamed and banged my head so hard at that show that I felt like I was in a serious car accident the following day. I had given myself whiplash from all the head-banging and could barely lift my head. I was a proper metal head by that point.

Unfortunately, I was scheduled to work the afternoon shift at Carowinds the day after that Metallica show. I barely managed to crawl into work that day. Luckily, it was a washout day in the park, with nobody in attendance. However, I still had to sit at my stagecoach cart, under a shitty little umbrella, getting soaked in the pouring down rain. All I wanted to do was go home and crawl back into bed.

Wendy worked the morning shift that day and we talked most of the afternoon, although in whispers because my head hurt so much. We talked about what we both planned to study in college. Wendy was a year older than me and was trying to decide which colleges she was going to apply to in the fall. She had stellar grades and could pretty much choose wherever she wanted to go. I, on the other hand, had no idea what I was planning on studying in college. At that point I was still hoping for a football scholarship, but that would soon change.

When Wendy's morning shift ended that day, she took pity on me and generously offered to cover the last 4 hours of my shift so that I could get some rest. I greedily accepted her offer, promised to make it up to her and then drove straight home to ice my neck, re-hydrate and sleep for 18 hours. I'm pretty sure it was then that I started to fall hard for Wendy.

Wendy was the first love of my life. I had dated and fooled around with other girls before her, but the relationship I developed with Wendy over the summer of 1991 was special. I didn't have to pretend to be someone I wasn't around her and felt like I could tell her anything. Again, I think it helped that we went to different schools because we weren't around each other all the time to smother one another, like most young relationships end up doing.

On weekends, Wendy and I would go out on dates, usually to dinner and a movie. The first movie we saw together was *Robin Hood: Prince of Thieves*, starring Kevin Costner as the worst actor to play an Englishman in the history of cinema. *It's 'Robin of Loxley' Mr. Costner, not 'Robin of Idaho'. You didn't even attempt an English accent.*

Despite Kevin Costner's portrayal of Robin Hood as an American Midwesterner, the movie was a huge hit, thanks in large part to the wonderful supporting cast, including Alan Rickman as the delightfully sinister 'Sheriff of Nottingham' and Morgan Freeman as the wise Moorish nobleman, "Azeem".

Wendy and I went to see "Robin Hood: Prince of Thieves" quite a few times in the theater, which meant the song "Everything I Do... I Do for You", by Bryan Adams, became "our song" together. I really liked that song at first, but it became so popular and was so overplayed on the radio that I eventually found it nauseating. I feel the same way about Metallica's song, "Enter Sandman". Don't get me wrong, I do like Bryan Adams. His album *Reckless* is a timeless classic. To this day, I enjoy playing my guitar and singing along with the hit song, "Summer of '69".

Even though "Everything I Do...I Do for You" was our song together, I think I best remember Wendy through Bryan Adams' song, "Heaven". Some of my best memories with Wendy are when we first started dating and we would ride around in my Camaro on warm summer nights, with the t-tops down, listening to music and feeling the wind in our hair. Whenever the song "Heaven" came on, everything just felt right in my world. *Jesus, I didn't realize how much of a romantic I am!*

When Bryan Adams announced that he was playing in Charlotte in July of 1992, Wendy said she wanted to go, and we bought tickets together. However, literally a week after we bought tickets to see Bryan Adams, Iron Maiden announced that they too would be coming to Charlotte in July of '92, touring on their amazing "Fear of the Dark" album. And, just my luck, it was the same fucking night as the Bryan Adams show. I was pretty pissed off at the ill timing of it all. *Like, what the fuck man!!? Really!?*

I briefly considered ditching Wendy to go see Iron Maiden with my friends, but ultimately, I couldn't do it. I loved Wendy and it would have been a dick move on my part. In hindsight, I've gotten to see Maiden many times in my life, so missing their show in '92 wasn't too bad, but it truly sucked at the time. Iron Maiden is one my favorite bands and, while Bryan Adams did put on a good performance that night, an Iron Maiden show is in a completely different league. Hell, it ain't even the same fucking sport.

***

Wendy and I would become High School sweethearts and would go on to date off and on for the next 16 years. She ended up going to Clemson University in the fall of 1992, ultimately wanting to work in marine biology. I would routinely drive down to Clemson during my senior year of high school to see her and even made the trip down from Boone when I studied at Appalachian State beginning in the fall of 1993.

Like all young lovers, Wendy and I had our share of emotional break ups and heartfelt reconciliations. One of our biggest fallouts occurred when I regrettably took another woman to my high school prom instead of Wendy. Wendy was a year older than me and I had gone to Wendy's prom with her. But during my high school prom, she was in college at Clemson, three hours away. I told Wendy that I wasn't planning on going to my senior prom because most of my good friends graduated a year ahead of me. I really had little interest in going.

However, that changed about a week before prom because a young woman in my English class asked me if I would go with her. I should have said no, but I suppose I was so delighted in the fact that someone actually asked me to go that I lost my moral compass. I didn't enjoy my senior year prom. The whole night I felt guilty about being there without Wendy. I tried to be as fun as I could for my date that night, but I think I was so conflicted with inner turmoil that I came off as standoffish. Going to my senior prom without Wendy was a mistake I regret to this day.

One of the most important lessons I learned during that period of my life is that, somehow, women will always find out if you do something you're not supposed to.

Wendy, of course, found out about my betrayal and our relationship blew up for the first time. We had a few breakups like that throughout our years, but somehow we always seemed to find our way back to one another. Usually through my groveling and sincere apologies.

When we were both out of college and I built my first house, Wendy moved in with me. I really thought for a long time that she was the one I would end up marrying.

Country Club Life

Working at Carowinds over the summer of 1991 was a lot of fun, but selling leather bracelets to kids wasn't exactly fulfilling work. Plus, I was pretty sure that if I had to listen to the soundtrack of "A Fistful of Dollars" everyday for another summer, I was going to lose my mind and start wearing ponchos. So, by the end of that summer, I started to think about what other jobs I would be interested in doing for the following summer.

As an employee of Carowinds, I got free admission into the park and would sometimes hang out at the water park with friends, but only on cloudy or rainy days. On sunny days the water park was too crowded and the smell of chlorine too intense. That's because whenever the water park was crowded, management would crank up the chlorine in the giant wave pool to mask the stench of urine. I know that's gross but, honestly, who hasn't peed in the pool before?

I made friends with a couple of the lifeguards at the water park and, after talking to them, realized that being a lifeguard was a sweet gig. All you had to do was pay attention and make sure nobody drowned. Everything else was essentially babysitting, like yelling at kids not to run on the pool deck and then bandaging them up when they didn't listen and would bust their asses.

Honestly though, what I think most piqued my interest in being a lifeguard was being surrounded by girls in bikinis all day. So, in the fall of 1991 I took both a lifeguard and a CPR course at the local Charlotte Mecklenburg Aquatic Center and got my certification for the summer of '92.

When we were growing up, Mom enrolled Carey, Cami and I in swimming lessons at an early age. Mom didn't know how to swim as a little girl, and she almost drowned once. She got caught in a rip current, and her Daddy saved her just in time before she was taken under for good. That experience traumatized Mom, so she made damn sure her children knew how to swim at a young age. I don't think Mom ever learned how to swim. I've never seen her in water more than waist deep.

After Grandpa died, Dad got a little money from the sale of the family farm and decided to put in a pool. Growing up, we had pool parties all the time for end of season baseball parties and summer sleepovers. The pool Dad put in was rectangular, sloped from the outside to the center, so that it was perfect to play water volleyball in. Mom wouldn't let Dad put in a deep end, so we couldn't dive. But cannonballs were fair game. It was always fun to walk outside and find someone napping by the pool because it was the perfect opportunity to wake them up with a kamikaze cannonball run.

When Hurricane Hugo decimated the city of Charlotte on September 22, 1989, our whole neighborhood was without power or water for a couple of weeks, so our swimming pool became the neighborhood bath house for a while. One of our neighbors, Lenny – who I'm pretty sure was drunk every time I talked to him – came walking into our back yard one day and stripped down, buck naked, before jumping into the pool. I thought it was hysterical and pretty ballsy.

But without the pool pump running for a couple of weeks, the pool eventually started to look like a swamp and the neighborhood bathers stopped coming by.

Because I grew up in pools, I thought getting my lifeguard certification would be a piece of cake. But I was wrong. Swimming requires a high level of endurance, and, at the time, I was certainly not built for that. I was never on a swimming team, so I never swam for distance or speed. I had to train consistently for a few weeks just to pass my lifeguard exam. Later in life, I would face a similar challenge when I decided to start running long distance in my late 30s.

After receiving my lifeguard certification, I had every intention of applying to work at the water park at Carowinds. But at the end of my lifeguard training course, the instructor gave everyone in the class a list of various country clubs, recreational parks and neighborhood pools in the area that hired lifeguards every season. Providence Country Club, which was only a couple of miles from our house, was on that list and I thought working there would be awesome because my commute would be only five minutes. I could sleep in a bit more and would be able to get home sooner after work. So, I applied to Providence Country Club and was hired for the summer of 1992. That pissed Wendy off because she signed back on to work at Carowinds again that summer, expecting I would too.

My first summer as a lifeguard was a breeze. Providence Country Club was a fairly new development and relatively small, so the pool wasn't a giant wave pool, like Carowinds, and there weren't nearly as many kids to watch over. All I did that summer was blow my whistle and yell at kids not to run. Because it wasn't a very big pool, there was usually only one lifeguard on duty at a time. So, I got pretty bored during the days by myself and missed being able to talk to Wendy regularly.

However, working at Providence Country Club was a big turning point in my life because it allowed me to see, firsthand, how the other half lived. I was enamored by the big, beautiful homes in the neighborhood, as well as the perfectly manicured lawns and new model sports cars sitting in the clubhouse parking lot. And I certainly noticed the trophy wives who tanned their toned bodies by the pool all day, after playing tennis that morning in their short skirts. I paid attention to what was going on around me, perched high in my lifeguard chair, and I became envious.

When the pool closed for the season at Providence Country Club, I was asked by the clubhouse if I was interested in working over the holiday season as part of their interior wait staff for corporate parties, wedding receptions and such. The pay they offered me was more than double what I had made as a lifeguard so I, of course, said yes. I needed the money for gas, food and concert tickets.

Working inside the Providence Country Club clubhouse was the most rewarding job I had while growing up. Time flew by when I worked there because it was nonstop work. I would help set up tables, chairs and place settings for an event, serve drinks and food during the event and then help clean up and break everything down, only to start over again for the next event. Sometimes I would be assigned to work at several events on the same day, at the same time. I would usually leave work late at night, exhausted but satisfied. While it was a lot more work than sitting by the pool all day as a lifeguard, I enjoyed working on the wait staff in the clubhouse far more than being a lifeguard.

The members of Providence Country Club were very generous to the clubhouse wait staff and I would often leave work with a wad of cash in my pocket from tips, on top of getting my hourly pay. But getting those tips didn't come easy because everything about working in a Country Club revolves around the details.

At most events, tables had to be arranged in a specific pattern, and 12-piece cutlery placement settings had to be arranged in a specific order. I learned quite a bit about dining etiquette, like when you serve someone a meal, you always serve from the left and when you clear a meal from someone, you always do it from the right. When the father of the bride stands up to give his reception speech, it was all hands on deck to be sure every guest in the room had a glass of champagne in their hands for the big toast. I bet I poured over a thousand glasses of champagne in the few months I worked in the clubhouse during my first season.

I feel very fortunate to have worked inside the Providence Country Club clubhouse at the age of 17. From my perch on the lifeguard stand by the pool, I was given only a cursory peek at how the upper class lived. But working inside the clubhouse, I got an up-close look at the people who owned those big, beautiful houses, and I paid attention. I would listen in on their conversations to find out what they did for a living.

I found that most club members worked in finance and banking and learned that Charlotte was a growing financial hub for the country, on track to eventually becoming as important as New York or Chicago. Several members of the country club were attorneys. One member was even a Federal Court Judge. A few others were entrepreneurs who owned their own businesses or were self employed.

Working in the Providence Country Club clubhouse inspired me and helped me begin visualizing a future for my own life. I decided that I, too, wanted a big house and new model sports car. It gave me the direction I was looking for, as well as a kick in pants to start giving a shit. My primary goal, of course, was to become a heavy metal rock star. But if that dream didn't pan out, I needed a back up plan. And that plan was pretty obvious to me after working in the clubhouse at Providence Country Club.

I decided that when I went to college, I would study finance and banking. I wanted to understand how money and financial markets worked so that I could achieve the future I wanted for myself.

At the end of the holiday season in 1992, the clubhouse management told me they no longer needed me because their busy season was over. But because I worked hard and was reliable, they made me an offer to come back the following holiday season to work again, and I did. In fact, I ended up working three consecutive holiday seasons at Providence Country Club while in college, and I enjoyed it.

Much Ado About High School

I kicked it into high gear my senior year at Providence High School with renewed focus and determination. Having finally found some direction while working at Providence Country Club over the holiday break in 1992, I knew that I wanted to study Finance and Banking when I went to college. But first I needed to get into college.

My hopes for a football scholarship were thrown out the window when I quit the team before the start of my senior year. I've never had any regrets about that decision. However, I do regret focusing on football more than my studies up until that point. Going into my senior year, my grades were only slightly above average and needed some improvement.

During my sophomore year I purposefully failed my A.P. Biology class *(A.P. stands for Advanced Placement)* and decided to take a make-up course during the summer because it would be easier. I'm not terribly proud of that decision but, in my defense, it's because I was talked into the collegiate level course by my guidance counselor. I had no interest in biology and the amount of homework that was assigned in that class every night was absurd. After just a month into the course, I was so far behind that I decided to call it quits and go to summer school.

My parents were righteously pissed off about me purposefully failing biology and threatened to take my car away as punishment. Even my A.P.

Biology teacher chewed me out six ways to Sunday when she found out about my plan. She told me that I would end up being a dead beat for the rest of my life. Thankfully I held my tongue and didn't say anything in response, even though I wanted to.

It wasn't exactly a high point in my academic career but, thankfully, my parents let me keep the car because I needed it to drive to summer school and work. I ended up passing the summer school Biology class with an A, but that's not much to be proud of. That's kind of like celebrating being "rash free" after taking prescription medication for a venereal disease.

Getting into student government in my senior year of high school is actually a funny story because, at the end of my junior year, a metal head friend of mine named Brad dared me to run for Senior Class Council, and I did. Brad didn't think I had the balls to give a speech in front of the entire school and said that I wasn't popular enough to win.

Running for office on the Senior Council required delivering a live speech, in front of the whole school, over a live video broadcast that would air during morning announcements. After the candidates made their speeches, the class would then vote on who they wanted to be on the council. It was a classic demonstration of democracy.

Naturally, I accepted Brad's challenge and with a chip on my shoulder and something to prove, I prepared a blistering speech to my classmates as to why I thought I should be on the Senior Class Council. Because I wanted to represent myself as authentically as I could, I even wore my black leather jacket during the live broadcast. I wasn't going to change who I was to curry favor.

I took my speech seriously and put as much thought and sincerity into it as I could because I didn't want to look like a joke. My goal wasn't just to prove to Brad that I could give the speech; I wanted to win and prove to myself that I could do it. Remarkably, my plan worked and I got elected.

After seeing my speech on TV, the High School drama teacher, Gene Kusterer, encouraged me to take his Drama class in the fall of my senior year. Mr. K said he was impressed with the delivery of my speech and thought I'd be perfect to play the lead antagonist in the drama department's fall production of Shakespeare's *Much Ado About Nothing*.

I had never really thought about acting before then. Music was what really interested me. By this point, I had ditched playing the trumpet and had made the switch to playing on the drum line. I played the big bass drum because I was the only guy strong enough in the marching band to carry it around. But my primary focus was on learning guitar and starting my own band. After begging my parents for a guitar for a couple of years, they finally broke down and bought me one for Christmas, and I was practicing daily.

Despite my prevailing interest in music, Mr. Kusterer's proposal that I take his Drama class my senior year piqued my interest because I was excited at the prospect of doing Shakespeare in front of an audience. Throughout most of grade school I thought English class was dreadfully boring, second only to History. But when I took Mrs. Williamson's English class at Providence High School my junior year, we studied Shakespeare extensively and I loved it.

It was in Mrs. Williamson's English class that I found an appreciation for classic literature. After reading *MacBeth* and *Hamlet*, I became an immediate fan of Willy Shakes, particularly his tragedies because I found the stories to be dark and foreboding. I also enjoyed reading "Beowulf" because it was very similar to the fantasy fiction I read on my own.

Because I played Dungeons and Dragons while growing up, acting and role playing came second nature to me. When we read Shakespeare's *Othello* aloud in Mrs. Williamson's class, I would ham it up and get into character for my scenes. Mrs. Williamson loved my enthusiasm, and like Mr. K, she encouraged me to pursue Drama as well.

The chance to perform Shakespeare in front of an audience felt like an opportunity I couldn't pass it up. Acting on stage seemed like a great way for me to explore another creative outlet and get used to being in front of an audience. After all, I planned on being a rock star, so I might as well learn a little something about performing on a stage. So, I took Mr. K up on his offer and signed up for his drama class my senior year.

My attitude about History also changed my senior year of high school when I took Mr. Curtis' American and European history classes. Sherill Curtis was a phenomenal lecturer and was widely considered to be the most overqualified teacher at Providence High School. He was a highly intelligent, very animated, southern scholar who taught history like he was giving a sermon from the pulpit. I'm not sure why Mr. Curtis was teaching history to high school students. He should have been at an Ivy League University, in a walnut paneled auditorium, captivating a room full of 200 brilliant minds with his colorful lectures and bravado. He inspired me as much as Coach Waldron did.

While I respected Mr. Curtis and enjoyed his history classes, they were tough. I considered myself lucky to get a 'C' in his American History class. By the time I took his European History class during my final semester, I was paying a little more attention and ended up getting a 'B'.

In the fall of 1992, I played the role of Don John in the school's production of *Much Ado About Nothing*. Overall, I enjoyed the experience. But on opening night, I thought I was going to puke. I remember standing backstage asking myself, "*What the fuck am I doing? Why the fuck did I agree to do this?*"

I would end up asking myself those questions quite a few times throughout my life.

I don't remember whether the show was sold out on opening night, but it didn't look like there were too many empty seats from backstage, where I was peeking out through the curtains. I was absolutely terrified of going on stage that night. I was shaking so badly that my voice took on a trembling tone when I spoke. I thought for sure I had embarrassed the shit out of myself.

The second night of the production was a little better, but I was still shaking like a leaf on stage. I think by the fourth night of the show, I had become a little more confident and was actually excited to perform.

Shortly after we closed the show, I received one of the most important compliments of my life. Every year at Providence High School, teachers were allowed to give out one "Award of Excellence" to any student they believed showed outstanding achievement in an academic field. It was considered a coveted honor to receive such a distinction.

When Mr. Curtis presented me with his one "Award of Excellence", for my performance in *Much Ado About Nothing*, I was completely blindsided by the honor. Mr. Curtis was an avid patron of theater and said that I had "a commanding stage presence" and a voice that "dripped with seedy undertones". Apparently, Mr. Curtis had come to one of our performances and thought I was a natural on stage. I thought for sure he must not have seen me perform on opening night.

By the end of my senior year at Providence, I had received a $5000 college scholarship from the Interact Club, was in student government and was voted to be the student speaker at my high school graduation. However, I consider receiving the "Award of Excellence" from Mr. Curtis as my highest achievement in high school. It was an award given freely, without campaign, from the most respected teacher in the entire school.

Unfortunately, I wouldn't think about acting again for over 20 years. But when I eventually did consider acting again, at the age of 38, Mr. Curtis' vote of confidence gave me the added courage I needed to give it a try.

How Not To Act

In the Spring of '93 I was accepted into Appalachian State University, located in Boone, North Carolina. It was a huge weight off of my shoulders getting that acceptance letter. Later that year, in June of '93, I graduated high school. Mom and Dad were so proud. Britt, Tadd and Jason, who were all home for the summer after their first year at college, came to my graduation and booed when my name was called. It was nice.

I had put in a lot of hard work during my senior year of high school and, come summer, I was ready to relax and sit poolside as a lifeguard again.

Providence Country Club did offer me a lifeguard position again, but I didn't take it because I got a better offer. My good friend, Karl Ruch, was also a lifeguard and he told me that he could get me a job at Carmel Country Club for the summer with pay that was almost double what Providence offered. So, I took the job at Carmel Country Club for the summer but left on good terms at Providence so that I could go back during the holiday season to work in their clubhouse again.

Working at Carmel Country Club was a much different experience than working at Providence because, at the time, Carmel was a much larger and older club. To put it bluntly, Providence Country Club was "new money" and Carmel Country Club was "old money". At Providence, I felt like I was working for self-made people, whereas at Carmel, it felt like working for trust fund babies and the super-rich.

Working at Providence, I was inspired by the club members and found them kind and easy to talk to. I got along well with almost everyone there. At Carmel Country Club though, I felt like the members regarded the staff with far less respect and their attitude to be more standoffish. For example, if I blew my lifeguard whistle and disciplined a child for running or horseplay at Providence Country Club, parents would generally accept my judgment and stand by my disciplinary action, which was usually making the child sit out of the pool for 15 minutes in time out. At Carmel Country Club though, parents would often get angry and confrontational about me having the audacity to discipline their child.

While working at Carmel Country Club I learned how not to act when I finally made my own money.

I worked for two summers as a lifeguard at Carmel Country Club and got to know, firsthand, the difference between the way people who are self-made act versus the way people who grew up with money act. When I left Carmel Country Club after the summer of 1994, I vowed never to treat people the way some of the members at Carmel treated me.

I feel like I should remind you that this was 30 years ago and a lot has changed since then. I've certainly changed in the last 30 years. In my youth I was heavily motivated to become successful so that I could one day be a member of a country club. Now, however, I have very little interest in joining a country club. I have very little interest in golf. I've really tried to enjoy the sport. I even bought a set of clubs about 15 years ago and forced myself to play. But in the end I simply accepted the fact that I found golfing to be boring and tedious. Maybe my outlook on that will change in the future, but for now I'll stick to being more active in my endeavors.

While working at Carmel Country Club, one of the members was George Shinn, the original founder and owner of the Charlotte Hornets, the original beloved NBA team of the Carolinas. George Shinn was actually a self-made man and did not come from generational wealth. I never met him while working at Carmel, but I did go to several Hornets games while in High School. I even got to see Michael Jordan play a couple of times when the Chicago Bulls came to Charlotte. That was when the Bulls dominated the NBA and won the national championship 6 times between 1991 and 1998.

Despite having to deal with some irritating members at Carmel Country Club, the summer of '93 was fantastic. Wendy and I saw each other a lot. She came home from Clemson that summer to work at Carowinds once again, this time in park management.

Wendy and I had a strong relationship by that point and were having sex often. I chuckle now at how bold we were. We'd often go to my bedroom to "watch a movie" and end up having sex while my parents were literally 30 feet away downstairs, watching TV. My folks thought that they could control us by insisting that we keep my bedroom door open while we watched our movie. But that didn't stop us of course. We also got daring and started taking overnight trips together, to the mountains and such, telling our folks we were with other friends for the night.

I don't really know why Wendy and I were being so sneaky about having sex. I guess to hide it from Wendy's parents, because my parents already knew. They're not naïve or dumb. I found out that my parents knew I was having sex like this:

DAD: *"I need to talk to you about something. Your mother and I know you're having sex."*

ME: *"Yeah, it's a little late to have 'the sex talk', but I've been safe and learned a lot. If you have any questions, I'd be happy to share some tips and techniques that I've...."*

DAD: *"Your mother found a couple of used condoms in the trash can in your bathroom."*

ME: *"Oh. Well, you told us a long time ago not to flush anything except toilet paper down the toilet because we're on a septic system and it could clog the drain line. Besides, those condoms aren't from me having sex. I put them on my fingers while practicing guitar. The lube helps me move around on the neck faster."*

DAD: *"...What?"*

ME: *"Nothing...Bad joke."*

DAD: *"Jesus Christ. How about you start taking your own garbage out to the bin, instead of making your mother do it?"*

ME: *"Right. I can do that. Do I need to apologize to Mom?"*

DAD: *"No, just... clean up after yourself. I'd tell you to stop but that would be pointless, so just continue to be safe."*

***

Life was pretty good in the summer of 1993. On one memorable evening, I worked an 8-hour shift at Carmel Country Club, sweating in the sun all day, before clocking out as fast as I could to meet Karl and some friends at the local Arboretum theatre to see a movie. We had bought tickets for the opening night of Steven Spielberg's little dinosaur film called *Jurassic Park*. Seeing that movie in the theater on opening night was spectacular. When the T-Rex made its iconic appearance in the film and roared for the first time, people were literally screaming in the auditorium.

By the end of that summer, I was anxious and ready to begin my college career at Appalachian State University. In August, Mom and Dad helped me move into my dorm room on campus, and I settled in quickly. App State is only a 3-hour drive from our home in Charlotte, which I thought was perfect. It was far enough away for me to feel free and on my own, yet close enough for whenever I got homesick.

I didn't go home too often though. The Blue Ridge Mountains are gorgeous in the fall, and I found tons of places to explore. I also met a few people to hang out with, but I mostly just kept to myself. I would drive around for hours on the Blue Ridge Parkway, listening to music in my Iroc-Z Camaro, with the t-tops off. Sometimes I'd park at an overlook with an amazing view and read for a while. It was a relaxing environment with few people and wide-open spaces, which is exactly what I prefer.

Leaving the Nest

I t was a bittersweet day when Mom and Dad moved me into my dorm room at Appalachian State University. Watching them get in the car to drive home without me was difficult. It was especially tough on Mom because I was the first baby bird to leave the nest. She cried of course, which made Dad and I shed a few tears, despite both of us trying to stay composed around all the other parents and students.

For most people, college is about keg parties, hooking up with random people and experimenting with recreational drugs while dealing with the annoyance of having to go to class for a couple of hours a day. And while I really enjoyed my college years, my experience was nothing like that.

For me, college was about growing up and taking responsibility for myself. I took my studies seriously and walked a narrow path so that I would remain focused. I didn't go to a lot of parties, drink my weight in beer, smoke weed and hook up with 100 different women. I studied my ass off, played guitar and stared at my computer most days.

Thinking about it now, perhaps I took college too seriously. Maybe I should have partied more and hooked up with a lot of chicks. If anything, it would have helped me develop social skills, which is what I desperately needed at the time. I've never been socially awkward in the sense that I'm afraid to talk to people. I just usually have very little in common with most people and, back then, the art of "chit-chat" eluded me. After 30 years of life experience, I'm much better at small talk now. But, when I was in college, I was rather rigid and woefully inexperienced in large social settings.

I have no regrets about the way I spent my college years, though. Mom and Dad paid for my higher education, and I owed it to them and myself to do the best that I could. When I graduated from college, what I lacked in general social skills I made up for, and much more, in the education I received. I developed financial acumen, became a more efficient writer and learned essential computer skills. Most of what I learned in college I've used consistently throughout my life.

I also learned to balance that rigid discipline with creative outlets, like playing guitar, so that I wouldn't get apathetic and bored. Maintaining a healthy balance between work and play is essential to me. I get depressed and angry when I don't have something creative to do.

Despite us being at separate universities, and about 4 hours apart, Wendy and I continued to date through college. She ended up joining a sorority at Clemson and I would drive down to go to socials and formals with her about once a month. During holidays and summer breaks we would spend a lot of time together.

I found a long-distance relationship to be the perfect situation for me. It was a clear separation between work and play, and that helped me to stay focused. It was difficult for Wendy though. We did the whole 'break up and get back together again' thing a few times. I knew she was dating other guys at Clemson, but she didn't tell me about them, and I didn't ask. I didn't want the drama or intrusive thoughts disrupting me in my studies.

When I wasn't studying, most of my free time at App was spent playing guitar, computer games or sports. For all four years that I attended Appalachian I lived in a dormitory called East Hall. It was one of the oldest dormitories on campus and widely considered to be haunted. I found that comical at first, but after living in East Hall for four years, I have to admit that it was pretty spooky, especially the basement.

The basement in East Hall was comprised of classrooms and offices for a small program within the university called Watauga College. During the days, those classrooms and offices were busy, but at night the basement in East Hall was empty. I'd often go down to the basement in East, at night, to find a quiet place to study. I could never study in my room because there were too many distractions.

Being in the basement of East Hall alone at night gave me the creeps sometimes. There was definitely an ominous presence down there. Sometimes you could just feel eyes on you, and it would get eerily quiet. It was the same feeling I got at Britt's house while growing up. I seem to have spent a lot of my youth in haunted spaces, now that I think about it.

At Halloween, the residents of East Hall would transform the basement into a Haunted House and hundreds of students from all over campus would walk through for a scare and thrill. We called it the "Dorm of Doom". One year, I was in charge of organizing it.

My freshman and sophomore years I took classes in the basement of East Hall through the Interdisciplinary Studies program at Watauga College. Essentially, the curriculum provided students with core course requirements through a teaching program designed to integrate the study of language arts, history and philosophy/religion together. The class sizes were relatively small compared to most other classes on campus, and group discussions and lively debates were encouraged by the faculty. My freshman year we studied the history, literature, religion and philosophy of what is now modern China.

I enjoyed the small class sizes, open discussions and professors at Watauga College immensely. Once a week, all the students in the Interdisciplinary Studies program would meet for a "town hall" type of gathering, which the professors called "Chautauqua". The term "Chautauqua" refers to an educational movement which started in various parts of the United States in the 1920s. The purpose of the forum was to present, discuss and/or debate any number of political, social or cultural themes.

Sometimes the professors would arrange for guest lecturers to give presentations on highly controversial topics at Chautauqua. Other times, students would present research assignments or perform music, dance or even poetry readings. Chautauqua was very engaging for the students, and the professors always made an effort to involve everyone in the discussions. It got heated at times because the Interdisciplinary Studies program had a very diverse group of students, from various ethnic, religious and socio-economic backgrounds.

Our weekly Chautauqua gatherings were held on campus at a place called "Legends", which was a medium size concert hall located across the street from East Hall. Legends was owned by the University and basically the only nightclub on campus. Most of the bands that came through town played there, although we didn't get a lot of big-name bands at App because it was a fairly small school compared to other state funded colleges in North Carolina. But there were a few bands that came through town who went on to make it big.

One warm evening, I remember walking by Legends and saw that it was packed out, with students sitting in the parking lot enjoying the music because the venue was at capacity. The outer doors to the nightclub were open and music was resonating throughout campus from the band playing inside. When I asked someone in the parking lot who was playing that night, they told me it was some guys out of Virginia named "The Dave Matthews Band". I replied, "Huh, never heard of them. They're pretty good." Within a decade of my first hearing them at Legends, "The Dave Matthews Band" would go on to become an international phenomenon and play for millions of fans around the world, selling out stadiums and concert halls.

***

The core classes I took through Watauga College during my freshman and sophomore years weren't too difficult and, for the most part, I enjoyed them. The first real test of my resolve to do well came during the second semester of my freshman year, when I took an 8 a.m. Business Statistics class across campus, in a building aptly named "Walker Hall".

Because I was a freshman, I didn't have a car on campus. Like most universities, parking was very limited, so my Iroc-Z was parked about 2 miles off campus in the freshman parking lot. That meant driving to my 8am class was not an option. However, even if I had my car available, I still wouldn't have driven because winters in the Blue Ridge Mountains were tough. During the winters, it was usually well below freezing in the morning with snow and ice on the ground common. The University rarely canceled classes due to inclement weather. Whenever it did, it was usually because the campus infirmary was overrun with students who had slipped on ice and injured themselves.

It took considerable effort in my freshman year to get up early and get to my Business Statistics class. I would have to bundle up in warm clothes and trudge for over a mile, sometimes through biting wind, icy sidewalks and snow, to get to that class. I still shiver remembering how cold it was some mornings.

Early on in my studies, I came to the realization that if I studied for two hours for an exam, I could pass with a "B". But if I wanted an "A" on the exam, I had to study for four to six hours. It was the difference between learning just enough to get by versus understanding the material completely.

I remember asking myself, earnestly, at one point, whether the extra time I put in for the "A" was worth it. At the end of that short, internal debate I decided to stick to my goals and put in the work necessary to get the "A". As a result, I graduated from Appalachian State University with straight "A"s and was on the Dean's list every semester. Well, technically I also got two "B"s, but I don't count those. I'll talk about why later.

Part of me regrets not cutting loose and having more fun in college. Maybe studying for only two hours, to get the "B", would have been enough. But another part of me knows that the discipline and goals that I set for myself in college were fundamental to the development of the strength and character I have today. When I graduated from college with honors, I was proud of what I achieved. The confidence I found in myself during that time gave me the courage to endure many other challenges that I would face later in life.

Music and Studies

I believe it was Carl Jung, the 20th Century analytical psychologist, who coined the term "synchronicity" in the 1950s. The term is derived from its Greek origins, "syn-", meaning "together" and "Chronos", meaning "time". Jung thought that seemingly random events or coincidences were not random at all but held a rather deeper connection between the mind and external world.

Really, though, it's just a fancy way of saying, *"Everything happens for a reason"*.

I was not a particularly spiritual guy in college. It would be another 20 years or so until I would have what I consider to be a spiritual awakening. But at the beginning of my sophomore year at Appalachian, I did have an experience that Mr. Jung would have classified as synchronicity. It was a chance encounter that fundamentally altered my life.

When I didn't have my head in the books studying, I was usually playing computer games or practicing guitar. I was the loud guy on the hall, blaring Metallica and various other metal bands while playing along with my guitar. I had been building my guitar chops consistently for about 2 years by that point and was trying to find the courage to seek out other musicians to play with. East Hall was filled with a wide variety of talented musicians, and I was pretty intimidated by most of them. Also, very few of them liked heavy metal, so I really didn't know where to begin to find someone I could jam with.

However, one afternoon, early my sophomore year, I was in my dorm room, playing guitar, when I was interrupted by a knock on the door. I was jamming out to the song "This Love" by the band Pantera and thought, for sure, that the knock at my door was the Resident Assistant (R.A.) on the floor coming to tell me to turn it down.

But when I opened the door, I found a guy with long hair and a scruffy looking baby-face standing in the doorway. He looked like he could have been a roadie for The Allman Brothers Band. He was wearing a "Misfits" t-shirt and had a wide grin spread across his face.

"Hey man. Was that Pantera?" he asked.

"Yeah," I replied, "Sorry if I was being too loud. I can turn it down if you need me to."

"Hell no, man. I thought it sounded awesome. I just wanted to introduce myself. I'm Chuck, and I play bass. We should jam sometime."

I've often wondered how different my life would be if I hadn't been playing Pantera at that exact moment, because meeting Chuck Feimster turned out to be a pretty important day in my life. From that chance encounter, prompted by nothing more than a mutual love of heavy metal, Chuck and I would go on to form a friendship that has now lasted for over 30 years. I consider him one of my closest and dearest friends and still see him often.

A few weeks after meeting Chuck on campus at Appalachian, I randomly ran into a friend of mine from high school, named Ryan

Johnson. I knew Ryan from the marching band at Providence. He and I were on drum line together my senior year. Ryan was a phenomenal drummer and had been playing since childhood. He was also a metal head and looking for people to jam with.

Meeting Chuck and reconnecting with Ryan, at just the right time, seemed to me like the universe was encouraging me to follow my creative dreams. The three of us started playing music and jamming together during my sophomore year at App State and continued playing together for several years after college. Playing music helped me keep my sanity through college, giving me the creative outlet I needed. Chuck, Ryan and I would play together for about 6 years, including writing our own original music, recording a couple of EPs and playing shows all over the Charlotte region.. We even got some local radio airplay. The name of our band was "Channel Black".

Towards the end of 1994, I was approached by the Resident Director of East Hall, Diane Porter, and asked if I would be interested in being a Resident Assistant (R.A.) in the building. For those unaware, R.A.s are basically the babysitters of dormitories. Their job is to be available for residents who needed help or had emergencies and to monitor the building for any illegal or inappropriate behavior.

The job paid $100 a week, which was like being rich to a college student like me at the time, so I accepted the offer. It seemed like the perfect opportunity for me to make some spending cash without getting too distracted from my studies. I was already in the building most of the time anyway. I might as well make some money while there.

Being a Resident Assistant in East Hall was the easiest job I've ever had. All I had to do was hang out with the guys on my floor occasionally and make sure nobody died or did anything too stupid. One night a week I had to sit in the front office and be on call for anybody who needed help.

The residents of East Hall were generally considered the "granola" crowd of the University. For some reason, the building attracted most of the misfits, bohemians, geeks, and counterculture types that came to Appalachian. During the four years that I lived and worked in East Hall, the most talented artists and brilliant minds that the University had to offer lived there.

East Hall also had the reputation of being a pothead's paradise. At any hour of the day, you could smell someone smoking a joint somewhere in the building as well as hear The Grateful Dead, Pink Floyd or Snoop Dogg being played. I never partook in wacky tobacky while in college, but I didn't care if other people did. In my experience, weed just mellows people out. It's the cocaine and intravenous drugs that would sometimes pop up in the building that I was uncomfortable with. Thankfully, I never had to get involved with too much of that shit as an R.A.

In fact, in the two and a half years that I was an R.A. in East Hall, I only wrote one citation to a resident for smoking weed. And that's because the dumb-ass walked right in front of me, lighting a bong, while my boss, Diane, and I were in the front office. I didn't want to do the paperwork, but I had no choice.

Whenever I was on duty in the office at East, I would bring my books with me and study. When I would hang the "ON DUTY" sign up on the door, I also hung another, handwritten, sign that read: "IT BETTER BE GOOD". Usually, when someone did knock, it was because they had locked themselves out of their room or somebody was complaining about a neighbor being too loud.

I guess it should come as no surprise to you to learn that I was the subject of many noise complaints myself while living in East Hall. One of the advantages to being an R.A., however, was that I got away with a stern look and a slap on the wrist most of the time.

The funniest noise complaint I ever received happened on a beautiful Friday afternoon in the fall of my senior year. I was done with classes early that day and thought I was free for the rest of the afternoon. It was glorious. I had my windows open to catch the refreshing breeze coming off the mountains, so I cranked up my guitar to jam out to Metallica's *Black Album*.

I think it was in the middle of the song "Sad But True" that the phone in my room rang. I cut my guitar, killed the music and answered it:

Caller: *"Yeah, is this the Resident Assistant on duty in East Hall?"*

ME: *"Uh... yes."*

Fuck. I forgot I'm on duty today.

Caller: *"This is Doctor So-and-So in the English Department next to your building. Someone is playing some god forsaken music obnoxiously loud, and I can't teach my class because of it. I'm giving you the courtesy of 5 minutes to get it to stop before I call campus security."*

I don't really know how I was able to do this so naturally, but I immediately responded with:

ME: *"Is the music still playing now?"*

Then I put the phone down on top of a pillow and cranked up my guitar and started playing for a few seconds. I immediately picked the phone up to hear:

Caller: *"...YES! YES, somebody's playing guitar. Very LOUD!"*

ME: *"Yeah, I hear it now. Sorry, I had headphones in and didn't hear it before. I'll tell them to stop right now."*

Caller: *"And write them up for being disruptive during class hours."*

ME: *"Don't worry sir, I'll handle it. I think I know who it is. I apologize for the disruption."*

Then I hung up, cranked up my stereo and guitar about 20% louder and continued to play "Sad But True" for another minute and a half before screeching to a halt as if I was suddenly interrupted.

Politics

B ecause I was involved with leadership and development programs in high school, I decided to give student government a try in college as well. My freshman year at Appalachian I volunteered to be the representative from East Hall and attend weekly Student Senate meetings. Nobody else wanted to do it, so I thought, *"What the hell, I'm here to learn. So, I'll go learn something."*

What I learned was that I do not like politics.

My short experience in the Student Senate at Appalachian was disastrous. It was nothing like student government in high school, where we sat around and openly discussed what events to organize for *Senior Week*. Student Government in college was run in strict parliamentary procedure and involved heated debates on how to allocate considerable funds that the University provided for student programs and campus events. You would think that would be easy to do, but you'd be wrong.

Almost every representative in the Student Senate was a political science major, except for me. It was a room full of future politicians, rehearsing for their upcoming careers. Most of the time it felt like everyone was arguing for the sake of arguing. It was a spectacle of lengthy grandstanding and party politics. Senators willfully divided themselves into liberal and conservative parties and would then fight, tooth and nail, over the most ridiculous topics. I found it to be tedious, exhausting and unproductive.

I know some people simply enjoy arguing, but I really think that a lot of the people in the student senate went home and masturbated to C-SPAN. They delighted in having a spirited debate over the dumbest shit, like arguing for two hours over whether the student cafeteria should buy a soft serve ice cream machine versus a frozen yogurt machine. Then they would argue for another hour over whether there should be a station for chocolate sprinkles and caramel syrup as well.

Despite my bad experience in the Student Senate, it didn't deter me from fulfilling my obligation. I attended every weekly meeting for an entire semester until my term ended. I did not, however, volunteer for a second term. I realized rather quickly that I'm not built for politics. I take it too personally. Sometimes, after a session was adjourned, some of the senators who attacked me would come over to shake my hand and act like it was all a game. It took serious effort on my part not to knock a few of those assholes on their butts.

Dad has wanted me to go into politics since grade school. "Someday you'll get pissed off enough to do something about it," he tells me.

What my father doesn't understand is that I stopped letting politics bother me a long time ago. I pay attention to what's going on in the country and the world, but I've learned to let go of any anxiety or anger that comes with staying informed. I treat politics like the weather. I have no real control over what happens, but it's important to know which way the wind is blowing and when a storm is coming.

Don't get me wrong, I understand the value and necessity of politics. I simply have very little interest in discussing my views with anyone because I've rarely found those conversations to be meaningful. I once had a terrible argument over politics with a good friend of mine named Brandon. I stormed out of the restaurant where we were having dinner to avoid saying anything that I would later regret. It's a good thing I did too, because when I got home that evening and cooled off, I realized that I was angry at Brandon for something neither he nor I had any control over. We simply had different perspectives.

***

I first met Brandon Padgett shortly after becoming a Resident Assistant in East Hall at App. Brandon was a second year R.A. when I got hired and, unbeknownst to be at the time, Brandon's the one who recommended me for the job.

Brandon and I are a lot alike and the two of us connected almost immediately after meeting. Like me, Brandon is a very creative person, with a deep love of music and movies. Brandon loves the progressive metal band "Dream Theater" and, like me, taught himself to play guitar. He's also a big guy who grew up playing basketball and football. Brandon's passion though is comic books and sketch drawing. Like Ryan and Chuck with music, Brandon is a natural born artist. *Why does everybody have natural talent except me? The only natural talent I seem to have is biting off more than I can chew.*

Like most of my friendships, Brandon and I first bonded over our shared love of heavy metal music. Shortly after we met, I went to Brandon's room one afternoon to talk about the ins and outs of being a Resident Assistant. When I sat down in a dirty armchair that he kept in his room, Brandon randomly put on Iron Maiden's iconic album *The Number of The Beast* and our conversation derailed into talking about music, movies, and comics for three hours. Other than Superman and Batman, I knew very little about comic books and superheroes back then.

At first, I found it a little strange how similar Brandon and I are. Being around him sometimes feels like being around another version of me - an uglier version of me of course, but still a good guy deep down. I don't expect he'll ever read this book because it doesn't have pictures in it. But if he ever does, he'll probably throw it at my head. *If you are reading this right now Brandon, I'm proud of you.*

When I found out that Brandon liked heavy metal, I introduced him to Chuck and, soon after that, the three of us started hanging out a good bit together. Some of the best memories I have in college are of going to concerts with those two guys. In the winter of 1996, the three of us went to see the band Pantera on their "Far Beyond Driven" tour. That show ranks as one of the top three concerts I've ever seen. The band sounded amazing, the crowd was rowdy and the energy in the coliseum was electric. By the end of the concert, there were police in full riot gear posted at every exit off the floor in case things got out of control. But things didn't get crazy or dangerous. They rarely do at heavy metal shows. I've seen more fights at a Jimmy Buffet concert than at any of the metal shows I've been to.

The scariest part about that Pantera concert was driving back to Boone after the show. The concert was in Winston Salem, NC, about two hours east of Appalachian, down the Blue Ridge Mountains. We had to drive through a heavy snowstorm to get back up the mountain and were in

Brandon's car at the time, which was an old Honda Accord he had delightfully nicknamed *The Millennium Falcon*. It was scary navigating through that blizzard. The snow was whipping the windshield so hard we could hardly see the road 20 feet ahead of us. It really felt like we were flying through hyperspace, with star systems rocketing past us at the speed of light. Thankfully though, Brandon took his time, and we made it back safely.

After college, both Brandon and Chuck moved to Charlotte and the three of us continued to hang out together. We'd have dinner regularly, go to concerts and movies and sometimes take weekend trips to the beach. We'd also go to NFL games to cheer on the Carolina Panthers. In 2006, when I took my entire family and Wendy on vacation to Germany, Switzerland and Austria, Chuck and Brandon tagged along.

When the band Tool toured on their iconic album, *Lateralus*, in the early 2000s, Chuck, Brandon and I went to several of their shows and had an amazing time. The first time that I saw Tool live, it was like a spiritual experience. Their performance and visual production stirred a visceral awakening within me. I rank the first Tool concert I ever saw in the top 3 shows of my life.

***

In 2003, shortly after George W. Bush invaded the nation of Iraq, starting the second gulf war, Chuck, Brandon and I were having dinner together. Brandon and I had a serious argument over the politics behind the conflict in Iraq, and by the end of the meal, I was so angry, I got up and left abruptly.

Eventually I realized that my anger at Brandon was not justified, and I decided that, from then on, I was not going to let politics have that much control over me. It's pointless arguing about something you have no control over. It does nothing but create stress and anxiety. I didn't want to lose a good friend simply because we had different points of view.

Since then, I've tried to create personal relationships with people based on shared passions, not shared politics. In my experience, a relationship based on a common passion is much more organic and fulfilling than one based on similar politics. I care more about what someone enjoys doing and why it brings them joy than I do about their political ideals.

I'm very grateful that Brandon and I remained friends, despite our minor political differences. We still talk to each other often and hang out when life permits. I consider Brandon to be family, like Chuck and my other childhood friends. Brandon calls my folks Mom and Dad, and I know Brandon's family very well. I met Brandon's wife, Jaimee, when they first started dating.

When Brandon and Jaimee got married in Rochester, NY in 2008, Chuck and I were both groomsmen at the wedding. My parents even attended the wedding, and we all had a great time. Chuck got completely smashed at the wedding reception and was cut off by the bar staff. But that didn't stop Chuck. He simply slipped into another wedding reception being held next door and kept drinking at their open bar. He even danced at the other reception.

Brandon is a good man, a fantastic father and a devoted husband. He works hard to provide for his family and has made a wonderful life for himself, despite his receding hairline. I'm grateful that he and I have remained good friends for over 30 years. My life has been better for having him in it. If my relationship with Brandon had ended 20 years ago over our political differences, I would have surely regretted it.

***

Don't let differing political opinions estrange you from your family and friends. Politics has polarized this country to an extreme level in recent years, and in my opinion, life is too short to argue about things out of your control. It's important to stay informed and voice your opinions when necessary but be mindful of what is truly important in your life.

Adopting this philosophy has saved me from many uncomfortable conversations. I have a few family members who are more conservative than me and who like to voice their strong opinions on social media and at family gatherings. I don't feel like I have to "unfriend" them for their political views. I simply respect their differing opinions and avoid getting involved in the conversation. I place a priority on finding peace and common ground in the moment.

It's not always that easy though. While out to dinner with family recently my mother-in-law, Maria, pressed me about my thoughts on immigration in this country, which is something that has garnered a lot of attention recently. To avoid that heated debate and prevent myself from saying something that I would later regret, I simply told Maria that we would have to agree to disagree on the topic to remain civil with one another. Thankfully, she accepted my response and left it at that.

I've found that turning up the heat on political soup with family and friends is a recipe for disaster. It often leads to an inedible dish and a loss of appetite. I humbly suggest you put it on the back burner to simmer and cool.

Brotherly Love

It's been difficult for me to write about the relationship I have with my brother. I've started and stopped this section of the book several times because I don't really know what to say. Or perhaps I don't know how to say what I want to say. I think a lot of people feel that way when talking about their family. The fact is, Carey and I have gone through many phases over the years and, in a way, we're very different from one another.

We hold the same core values and principles, of course. Like me, Carey is determined, disciplined and hard working, but our approach to life and where we've found value and meaning is substantially different. We've both taken some hard knocks along the road of life, but we've managed to persevere and keep our shit together, without losing our fucking minds.

Growing up, Carey and I played baseball in the summers and basketball in the winters. Being at the ballpark or on the courts all day on Saturdays was our life growing up. Dad was usually coaching, and Mom was working in the concession stand, selling nachos and soda. My sister, Cami, had plenty of other little girls to play with. Everybody had a good time, I think. We were a very typical family, living a very typical American life. And it was fantastic.

When not on the court or field, Carey and I played with all manner of toys, including Star Wars, G.I. Joe, the Transformers and He-Man. Video games were also a big hit, of course. Hell, even Mom got addicted to Super Mario Brothers when we got a Nintendo for Christmas one year. We would sometimes have to beg Mom to let us have a turn.

Mom and Dad did an amazing job providing for us. Christmas was always a big affair with lots of gifts. We weren't rich by any measurable standard, but we were never without anything. My folks were very good at stretching the budget and making the most of it. Sometimes our presents were toys Mom and Dad found at yard sales.

One Christmas, my folks found a huge pile of used G.I. Joe toys while at a yard sale. Most of the toys were pretty beat up. Some of the action figures were missing a limb or two and the helicopter was missing a blade on the propeller. But Dad took those beat up toys and set up a huge battlefield in front of the Christmas tree, to make it look like a bloody war zone. When Carey and I woke up on Christmas morning, we were both giddy over the display and played with those secondhand toys for hours. That was a great Christmas.

Mom has always had a nose for 'buy one get one free' sales, which meant that Carey and I got a lot of the same gifts at the holidays. If I got a green winter coat, Carey would get the exact same coat, but in blue. If Carey received a pair of gloves, I knew with 100% certainty that I would get a pair as well. Growing up, Carey and I would get the same brand of socks, underwear and t-shirts every year. We would get different sizes of course, because I was always a fat boy compared to my little brother when we were young. That lucky bastard has been skinny his whole life.

Growing up, I gave Carey a good bit of grief, which is the divine right of being the older brother. I gave Carey a lot of prank Christmas gifts, like giving him $10 in pennies or sending him on a scavenger hunt for his real gift, which involves him having to go underneath the house, into the crawl space. I hope he doesn't hang on to any anger over that. I may have crossed the line a couple of times, but I've never had malicious intentions. We only roast the ones we love.

Carey and I really started diverging not long after Grandpa died, primarily because I changed. My internal struggles in dealing with loss and my mortality altered my personality. I started hanging out with Britt, Jason and Tadd a lot more, playing dungeons and dragons and listening to heavy metal music. When I started dressing in a black leather jacket, Metallica t-shirts and jeans, Carey maintained a more sensible fashion sense, wearing khakis and sweaters. Carey was always more sociable than I am and had a more diverse group of friends growing up. He paid attention to the cultural trends of the day, whereas I never cared.

Junior High is when I started being out of the house a lot. I started playing football and basketball at school, as well as track and field. Carey never tried out for any school sports, and I'm not sure why. He was an athletic guy and had loads of talent. I remember one summer Carey went to an overnight quarterback camp for a week with one of his friends. When he got home from that camp, Carey had a tight spiral throw and incredible accuracy. I don't understand why he never tried out for QB. We've never really talked about it.

Carey and I got along well in high school, despite developing different personalities and running in different social circles. We had a few things in common. Carey likes heavy metal, he just didn't cling to that as an identity, like I did. Some of my best memories with Carey are of going to see Metallica shows together.

During my senior year of high school, I often drove Carey to school with me in the mornings. Unfortunately, Carey was also with me on the day that my beautiful red Camaro got totaled in front of Providence High School. It was a rainy, icy morning and the line to turn into the school was at a crawl. The car behind us didn't slow down fast enough and I remember glimpsing in the rear-view mirror one second before impact and immediately slinging my arm out to support Carey before we were hit. Carey and I became the inside car of a five car pile up that morning and my Camaro didn't survive. Thankfully, neither one of us were hurt. We were both wearing our seatbelts. But man, I was beyond pissed off and emotionally traumatized at losing my car.

However, with the insurance money we got from the accident, and a little extra financial help from Dad, I was able to buy a 1986, Iroc-Z Camaro as a replacement. That car had a V8 engine and *Holy Shit* was it a fun car to drive. During my freshman year of college at Appalachian, I would zoom by everybody while going up the mountain. The only problem I had with my Iroc was the severe lack of trunk space. It usually took 5 or 6 trips for me to get everything I needed up to school. When I eventually bought a large speaker cabinet for my guitar amplifier, I had to sell the Iroc and buy an SUV, so that I could have some space to haul all my shit around. I gave up the sports car so that I could play in a band. But I figured I would just buy a new model corvette when my band hit it big, so I wasn't too bummed about that tradeoff.

In the fall of 1995, as I was entering my junior year in college and driving a Ford Bronco, my brother started his freshman year at Appalachian State University as well. It was nice having Carey on campus with me, but between my busy class schedule, band practice with Chuck and Ryan and working as an R.A., I really didn't have a whole lot of free time to hang out with him. I felt bad about that because when Carey started school that year, I think he felt a little lost.

Carey had gone through freshman orientation with a good friend of his and the two of them were planning on being roommates together. Sadly though, Carey's friend was tragically killed in an automobile accident on the way home from orientation and Carey was depressed when he started school. I had never seen Carey like that before, and I felt terrible for him. I know how tough it is to deal with unexpected death.

I tried involving Carey with me and my friends at App. We had dinner often and he hung out at a few band rehearsals with Chuck, Ryan and I, but nothing really helped. Carey was depressed, and I could tell he was getting tired of hanging around with my boring ass all of the time. Carey and I ran in different social circles back then. Basically, I was a nerd who kept a small group of close friends while Carey was in with the popular crowd, and more of a socialite. I don't know why we're so different in that regard. I guess I have trust issues with most people and only care to spend time with those that I truly know and feel comfortable around.

In our year at App together, Carey discovered that, underneath my large frame and heavy metal exterior, I was, in fact, a fuddy duddy. Carey wanted to enjoy his college years more and socialize, and I can't fault him for that. Carey went to visit a couple of fraternities that year and decided he was going to pledge. I remember how happy and excited he was when he told me about his decision, which is why I regret telling him that he shouldn't.

Carey was in his freshman year and still in shock from losing his friend over the summer. I advised Carey to wait and pledge a fraternity during his sophomore year. I thought he should use his freshman year to get into good habits and maybe find a direction for his studies before joining a social club. I was afraid he would start drinking a lot at frat parties to fight his depression and lose sight of the big picture. My intentions have always been honest with both of my siblings, but I realize now that I may have played the role of big brother too hard while growing up.

Carey, of course, got royally pissed off when I advised him to wait on joining a fraternity, and he pledged anyway. It's definitely in our genetics. Our family has a very long history of stubbornness.

Unfortunately, Carey's pledge week did not go well because he got hazed pretty hard by the fraternity brothers. They made Carey sit outside all night, in the freezing cold, to "guard" the Appalachian State Flag flying over the football stadium. The fraternity brothers claimed that another fraternity would attempt to steal the flag, and it needed to be protected. As a result of sitting out in the cold all night, Carey got the flu as well as righteously pissed off. Another strong genetic trait in our family is that we don't take shit.

Carey withdrew from pledging the fraternity after that incident and I was proud of him for his decision. But, as expected, his mood went dour again and his depression took over. At the end of his freshman year, Carey decided to transfer out of Appalachian State to start fresh somewhere else. He enrolled at the University of North Carolina at Charlotte the following year and, ironically, would end up getting a degree in theater. His mood greatly improved after that transition, but I could tell he was still wrestling with his identity.

I've tried to talk to Carey about his emotions many times throughout life, but I don't think he and I have ever communicated very well in that regard. I take my share of the blame on that. I know that sometimes I don't listen to Carey enough. For a long time, I was stuck in big brother mode and would offer unsolicited advice instead of just being a sounding board for him to vent. Unfortunately, I didn't learn that lesson with Carey soon enough because, in our 30s, he and I had a pretty bad falling out. It was a terrible time for me, and I should've kept my mouth shut.

But I'll get to all of that later.

Dad

In the Spring of 1997, I was angry and without direction. After all the hard work that I had put in at App State, the only job offer I had after graduating was working as a financial advisor in the First Union building in Uptown Charlotte. I couldn't understand why I wasn't in some think tank at a capital investment firm, crunching numbers and running cash flow analysis on businesses under acquisition. I wanted to be Gordon Gekko, from the movie "Wall Street", where multi-million-dollar deals are done over lunch and I could say, "I'll have my attorneys send over the paperwork in the morning."

Instead, I felt like a life insurance salesman, pushing tax deferred annuities and whole life insurance policies on people who needed some direction on where to put their leftover $200 every month. I know there is value in being a financial advisor. Many people need help with basic finance and planning for the future. I guess I was just expecting something more exciting.

In my disappointment, I sank into a depression and began to eat my way through it. I would arrive at work around 9am, sit down in my gray dungeon of a cubicle, and immediately think about what I was going to eat for lunch that day. At the end of lunch, I would start thinking about what I was going to have for dinner. As a result of my emotional eating, by the end of 1997, I weighed almost 300 pounds and looked like the Pillsbury Dough Boy.

Dad was busy with his private appraisal practice during this time. He had gotten his appraisal license when I entered college and worked his apprenticeship under a supervising appraiser while I was working my way through finance courses at App State. By 1997, Dad had achieved enough credits to become a certified appraiser on his own and no longer needed a supervising appraiser to sign off on his work, so he opened his own private practice. With Dad's skills as a salesman, he quickly developed a large list of clients at local banks and mortgage companies and was working long hours in his cramped little office over the detached garage at my folks' house.

Dad could tell I was not happy at my job Uptown, and when I told him I wanted to quit he didn't argue with me. He simply said, "Would you want to become an appraiser?"

I hadn't really thought about being an appraiser, but I figured anything was better than what I was doing, and I agreed to help Dad with his work and learn about the business of appraising to decide if it was something I wanted to pursue. To be honest, I never thought appraising would become my career. I considered it as something to give me some income while I figured out my next steps.

By the spring of 1998, I had taken my 90 hours of classroom training to become an appraiser trainee, and Dad became my supervising appraiser. I didn't realize it then, but about a decade later I would find out just how lucky I was in becoming an appraiser under my father. I will forever be grateful to Dad for that, along with so many other things he did that had a positive impact on my life.

My relationship with my father really strengthened after college. Not only did I start working with him on a daily basis, but we also played together on weekends. We would ride motorcycles all over back country roads and go kayaking on the Dan River in Virginia or on small lakes in the area.

When I was in High School, I begged my parents for a motorcycle. I was obsessed with the 1991 movie, *Harley Davidson and the Marlboro Man*, starring Mickey Rourke and Don Johnson. It wasn't a great movie, but it oozed with cool machismo I thought. I particularly loved Mickey Rourke's character, Harley, and wanted to be just like him.

At the end of the film, Harley pulls up to a pretty woman in cut-off jeans and asks her, "Where you headed?" The woman replies, "Nowhere special," and Mickey gives her a knowing smile. He then says, "Hop on and I'll take you there," and the beautiful woman gives Mickey a coy smile before hopping on the back of his bike and riding off into the sunset. End Credits.

The writing was crap of course, but Mickey Rourke delivered his lines with such cool bravado that I was hooked. I wanted to be cool like that and decided that I had to have a motorcycle to ride off into the sunset on. But my folks, being rationale and levelheaded, understood that I would probably kill myself on a motorcycle at 17-18 years old and said "No".

In a strange twist of fate, I would eventually end up working on a film with Mickey Rourke in 2015 on a film titled *Ashby*. The film was a dark comedy, and my role was a CIA assassin sent to kill Mickey's character at the end of the film. I spent one long day with Mickey, chit chatting between takes about all things Hollywood. I thought he was a down-to-earth guy and took his acting seriously. I never mentioned my love for the film *Harley Davidson and the Marlboro Man* to Mickey. It's kind of an unwritten rule not to be a "fan boy" on a set with celebrities. It's considered unprofessional.

In the scene that Mickey and I were in together, I get the drop on his character, and he accepts his fate by falling to his knees in tears, asking God for forgiveness. I thought Mickey played it brilliantly. To get into the right head space to play the scene, he used a photo of his beloved dog, Loki, who had passed away years earlier, as a trigger to bring on the tears for his scene. It was impressive watching him work. They say don't meet your heroes, but meeting Mickey Rourke was a pleasure.

When I was out of college and making my own money, I told my parents that I was going to buy a motorcycle. Mom tried to talk me out of it saying it was too dangerous, but I wouldn't listen. Dad, knowing he couldn't stop me, asked me if I would at least take motorcycle lessons so that I could be properly trained to ride. Dad even offered to take the lessons with me.

Dad had never ridden a motorcycle before and took the classes with me because I think Mom wanted him to, to ease her mind that I was being safe. Mom was secretly hoping that I would end up not enjoying the classes and decide not to get a motorcycle. But the plan backfired. Dad fell in love with motorcycle riding while taking the classes with me and bought his own bike, a Honda Goldwing, before I bought mine. Needless to say, Mom lost her shit for awhile.

I couldn't afford a Harley and ended up buying a new Honda Shadow, which was still a big, mean looking bike. I had a pair of custom pipes put on it so that it sounded just like a big gurgling Harley though and was happy that I looked and sounded cool.

Dad and I rode motorcycles almost every weekend for several years and would sometimes even ride together to do appraisal inspections. We loved to cruise around on empty curvy roads and feel the wind on our faces. Sometimes we'd stop for lunch at one of the small towns we'd ride into. I eventually bought a big open trailer that we would use to take our bikes up into the mountains to ride.

My relationship with my father became especially strong after college. While he did love riding his motorcycle and kayaking, I could tell his real love was in doing these things with me. He never wanted to stop being in my life, and I will always be grateful to him for that.

But it was really hard to be cool around Dad. Riding around on my big gurgling motorcycle, I felt like a stud and took pleasure in the moments when people would glance at me after getting a whiff of my alpha stench. But then Dad would pull up next to me on his Honda touring bike, loaded with a cassette player, blaring "Annie's Song" by John Denver.

It wasn't exactly Mickey Rourke, *"Hop on, I'll take you there,"* cool, but it means a lot to me now that I got to spend that time with Dad during those years.

The Bat Cave and Maximus Zorch

I lived with Chuck Feimster for several years after college. When Chuck moved to Charlotte after graduating in 1998 to continue playing in our band, *Channel Black*, we got an apartment together at The Fairways at Piper Glen in south Charlotte. During the days, Chuck was working as a customer service rep at a cellphone company while I was starting my appraisal career, working with Dad out of a cramped office space above the detached garage at my parents' house.

Dad and I called our office over the garage the "Bat Cave" because, while working one day, we heard scratches and movement in the ceiling above us and started noticing guano (bat poop) all over the driveway. Somehow, the attic to my parents' garage had turned into a roost for a colony of bats. Dad eventually had to pay an exterminator to get rid of the bats without harming them. They're protected in North Carolina and considered vital to the ecology because they eat disease spreading mosquitoes and other insects.

In the evenings and on weekends, when I wasn't working in the "Bat Cave" with Dad, Chuck and I would try to rehearse with Channel Black as much as we could. But motivating Ryan, our drummer, to get off the couch at his parents' house and stop playing video games was becoming harder and harder to do. Ryan had dropped out of college and was now living with his parents. Percussionists. They just march to the beat of their own drum apparently. *Ba Dump, Diss*

When we did manage to get Ryan off the couch, the three of us would write songs and rehearse for hours, holding marathon weekend rehearsals. We started off rehearsing in my parents' garage (the main level), serenading the neighborhood with our hard-hitting heavy metal for hours. But we would shut it down by 10pm to avoid the neighbors calling the police, although we probably should have been more concerned about being shot by a few of those neighbors because I'm quite sure they were driven mad by the repetitive nature of our songs and practicing.

By the end of 1998, after having worked with Dad in his appraisal business for a year, he and I decided to finish the lower level of the garage and turn it into our office for some much-needed space to work in. The small, cramped space above the garage was not heated or cooled and we were both uncomfortable working long hours up there. That's when Chuck, Ryan and I relocated our rehearsals to a powered storage unit just a mile away, which also didn't have heat or air conditioning. But we didn't care about that. Sweat and heavy metal go hand in hand.

Chuck and I lived very well together and became like brothers during that time. We were both respectful, cleaned up after ourselves and kept the same hours for the most part. If one of us was up late or had friends over, we kept the noise to a minimum. It wasn't your typical metal band lifestyle I suppose. We didn't have scantily clad chicks hanging out with us all night, smoking weed while listening to Black Sabbath and Iron Maiden. Why the hell DIDN'T we do that?! Youth is wasted on the young.

Instead of living the rock and roll lifestyle we thought we wanted, Chuck and I lived like an old married couple. We often went out to dinner together and had a rotation of Mexican, Chinese, Japanese and Steakhouse restaurants that we would frequent. At 10pm every night, Chuck and I would watch The Simpsons together.

Sometimes, after Chuck had a rough day, he would come home from work and play bass in his bedroom with the door closed for hours. But at 10pm, no matter his mood, I would hear Chuck turn off his amp and come out of his room to watch Ned Flanders say, "Howdy Hoe, Neighbor". Chuck and I can still quote *The Simpsons* to one another after 25 years.

Chuck and I also became excellent at speaking Zorch with one another. "Zorch" is what we call diving down a rabbit hole and having conversations about all things philosophical, metaphysical, controversial, conspiratorial and bizarre. It wasn't "drunken philosophy" though because we were usually stone sober when we had those conversations. And they always ended up at some ludicrous rationalization or point of circular logic and we'd end the discussion by nodding and saying, "Good Zorch" to one another.

***

In the fall of 1998, while I was doing an appraisal inspection on a doublewide mobile home out in rural Cabarrus County, I unwittingly became the owner of my first fur baby, Maximus Achilles Kahn. That's what Chuck and I would eventually name him. Max was just a little orange tabby kitten at the time I found him, no more than a couple of weeks old.

When I rang the doorbell of the doublewide to let the owner know I was there, Max was sitting on the front stoop, rubbing all over my legs, looking for some love and attention. I gave him a few scratches behind the ears. He was so tiny and soft back then.

But when the owner opened the door to greet me, he saw Max and angrily kicked him off his porch. The owner explained that Max had shown up to his house a few days earlier and that he didn't want anything to do with him. Despite his lame excuse, my face grew stern at the owner's behavior towards Max and, to clear the air, he jokingly said that if I wanted Max, I could have him. The guy was a real piece of work.

When the owner went back inside, I walked around the house to complete my exterior appraisal inspection and Max followed me through the tall, unmowed grass and meowed constantly for my attention. It was obvious that Max needed help and was not getting any from the asshole who owned the home.

After I completed my inspection, I got into my car to leave and Max sat down outside my driver's side door, staring at me with his big green, sad eyes. He was so pitiful looking. I'd like to say Max reminded me of Puss In Boots from *Shrek 2*, but, technically, that movie wouldn't get released for another 5 years. <sigh> Why am I so damned old?

As I sat in my car, Max stared up at me from the driveway with desperation etched beneath his dirty little face. His eyes pleaded with me to save him and give him a life to be grateful for.

"I don't need a damn cat", I told myself confidently as I started my car.

Then Max let out a soft, high-pitched meow that, somehow, I heard through my window and over the engine. After I heard Max cry, my steadfast decision turned to ash. Since the owner of the doublewide had made it clear to me that he had no interest in caring for him, I scooped Max up off the gravel driveway and put him in the car with me. Max immediately curled up in my lap and slept blissfully the entire ride home. He had suckered his way into my life, and I'm so glad he did.

On my drive home from that inspection, I called Chuck. "Hey man, how are you with cats?" I asked him nervously. Thankfully, Chuck grew up with animals too and had no problem with me bringing Max home. Max would eventually live with me for 18 years before he passed, but both Chuck and I raised him together from a kitten in our apartment.

I consider Max to be my first child. He was a feisty little guy and loved to play. He would surprise me and Chuck regularly by hiding somewhere and then jumping out to chase us around the apartment, trying to attack the heels of our feet. We would, in turn, chase him around until he was too exhausted to play anymore.

We named him "Maximus Achilles Kahn" after the movie *Gladiator*, which came out in 2000. It was obvious to Chuck and me that Max, himself, was a former gladiator of the great arena in a past life. "Achilles" was his middle name, due to his penchant for attacking the back of your feet. We added the "Khan" because it had a nice ring to it and suited his personality.

One Big Regret

In late 1999, my band *Channel Black* disbanded. I had reached a point of frustration with all of it and decided I'd had enough. I was tired of getting nowhere after 5 years of playing, writing, promoting and gigging. I had my fill of long road trips, crammed into a borrowed, beat-up van full of gear, only to play a 30-minute set in front of a crowd of 12 people.

Ryan's attitude was also intolerable to me by this point. I was the only one promoting our band and would work hard to find us gigs. But after I'd get us one, Ryan would say he couldn't play because he'd missed too many days at work and couldn't afford to take the time off. Like Chuck and me, Ryan worked a day job but pretty much used all his sick days and paid time off to sit at home, play video games and smoke weed.

With our band now dissolved, Chuck and I planned a trip to Hawaii in February of 2000 to visit my buddy Jason over my 25th birthday. Jason was in residency at the Army hospital in Honolulu at the time. John Blackman, a friend of Jason's from the NC School of Science and Math, also met us in Hawaii, and the four of us had a great time sightseeing for a week.

The NFL Pro Bowl was being played in Hawaii the week we were there, and for the few days that we were in Honolulu, we saw American football stars everywhere as well as a ton of beautiful women. Jason, of course, convinced all of us to check out a popular strip club while we were in Honolulu and the four of us drooled over the amazingly talented strippers who had flown in from all over the world as entertainment for the Pro Bowl fans. But we were poor guys just out of college compared to the football players and couldn't even afford a smile from any of the pretty ladies.

Taking that trip to Hawaii was great fun, but it also created one of the few big regrets I have in my life.

About a month before our trip to Hawaii, I received notice that Channel Black was invited to perform in a Battle of the Bands showcase at the Hard Rock Café in Orlando, FL. I had submitted our demo tape and promotional materials to the organizer at Hard Rock a few months before we disbanded. The invitation said we were one of ten bands selected for the showcase out of over two hundred submissions.

The problem was the night that the Battle of the Bands showcase was scheduled for was also during the week Chuck and I were booked to go to Hawaii. We discussed canceling Hawaii to do the gig, but Chuck and I both figured Ryan would drag his feet and not be able to go on the long road trip, so we declined the invitation.

I often wonder what would have happened if Channel Black had gotten back together to play that gig. There were going to be record labels and concert promoters at that Battle of the Bands, and it would have been an amazing opportunity for us to finally showcase all of the hard work we had done. Maybe we would have hit our big break at that show. If we had, my life could have ended up going in a completely different direction than it did.

My big regret isn't that we didn't play the show though. I eventually became OK with having given up the rock and roll lifestyle. I now know for a fact that I am not built like a rock star. I couldn't handle life on the road for very long.

My regret is that I stopped playing guitar altogether in 1999. Not only did Channel Black disband, but I also pretty much packed up all my guitars and gear in frustration and didn't play again for decades. I feel like I gave up on music too soon. It's fascinating how your perspective changes over the years. I usually end up looking back on my mistakes and failures and feel grateful that they happened, because if they hadn't happened, I wouldn't be where I am today.

But with guitar, I feel like I gave up something that I loved to do by putting too much expectation into it. That's what I really regret. That understanding would come in handy when I started working as an actor fifteen years later.

Thankfully I would end up diving back into my guitars during the pandemic and rekindle my passion to play. But I would be an incredible guitar player today if I had kept playing through the last 25 years.

Youth is so wasted on the young.

Day of Days

In 2001, the appraisal industry, like most industries, was rapidly changing. With the surge of work in the housing market bearing down on all appraisers nationwide, more and more lenders began to require that appraisals be streamlined and submitted online in digital format, directly to underwriters. The average age of an appraiser during this time was about 60, and most appraisers couldn't or wouldn't keep up with the technological changes that lenders were pushing. But because I was young and competent in using computers and navigating the online world, I found it easy to evolve with the changing times. This resulted in Dad and I staying very busy with our appraisal business.

Change is a fact of life and naturally inherent in any organizational system. If you want to stay relevant and competitive in this world, you have to accept change. It's the very essence of Darwinian evolution. Most people mistake Darwin's theory to be, "Survival of the Fittest", which is a bit of a misnomer. "Survival of the most Adaptable" is a more accurate conception of Darwin's theory in my opinion.

When I first started appraising, Dad and I still used traditional film for our appraisal reports. I can remember dropping film off at a one-hour photo lab after an appraisal inspection and waiting impatiently for it to get developed so that I could finish my report. Digital cameras at the time were considered new technology and expensive. But eventually I bit the bullet and bought myself a digital camera to keep up with the changing times. The memory card that came with my first digital camera was 64MB and could hold 24 photos. Nowadays, a modern 128GB cell phone can store up to 38,000 photos.

As a result of staying relevant in the appraisal industry and all its rapid technological changes, I was working full-time as an appraiser by 2001 and making great money. The housing market in Charlotte was growing tremendously fast at the turn of the century and there was plenty of work coming down the pipeline. Because I was living well below my means and had managed to save up quite a bit of money, I started to think about buying a house. I was getting tired of apartment living and dealing with thin walls and noisy neighbors. Plus, Wendy was pressuring me to get my own place so that she and I could move in together.

But before I decided to simply buy a home, I had an idea that proved to be both brilliant and, ultimately, disastrous for me. It was an idea sparked by a line in a television show that set me on a path that would ultimately end in heartbreak and failure by 2010.

One evening in my apartment, while watching an episode of the iconic television series "Band of Brothers", produced by Steven Spielberg and Tom Hanks, I heard a line that inspired me to build my own home instead of buying one. In the episode "Day of Days", which depicts the Allied forces' invasion of Normandy on D-Day, Lieutenant Dick Winters, played by the incredibly talented actor Damien Lewis, looks out over the unbelievable carnage and loss of life on the beaches beneath him and says to himself:

"That night, I thanked God for seeing me through that day of days and prayed that I would make it through D plus one. And if, somehow, I managed to get home again, I promised God and myself that I would find a quiet piece of land someplace and spend the rest of my life in peace."

Hearing that line, so eloquently delivered, inspired me to want to move to the country and build my own home to live out the rest of my days in peace. Dad and I had been riding our motorcycles throughout the countryside for a few years by this point and I knew plenty of places to start looking for a piece of land. From all the appraisal work I had been doing over the last three years, I was confident that I could design my own home and build it. I knew plenty of mortgage brokers and how construction loans worked. I simply need to put in the work, put all the pieces together, and make it happen.

So, in the summer of 2001, I designed my first home and bought an acre of land in a newly developed subdivision called Walnut Crest, in the small town of Waxhaw, NC, about 18 miles south of my parents' house. I designed the floorplan and elevations of my home to resemble a stone cottage, reminiscent of something you'd see in a beautiful Thomas Kincaid painting. The home had a tall cathedral ceiling in the living room with a big stone fireplace and exposed wooden cross beams. It included three bedrooms and three and a half baths as well as a big bonus room over the two-car garage for me to work out of.

I hired an Architect and friend of the family, David Wood, to draw up the structural plans for the home and my cousin, Patrick Granson, signed off as the General Contractor, so that I could get loan approval and the financing to build it. Even though I was only 26 years old at the time, Dad supported my rather ambitious decision to design and build my own house. He even helped me find a project manager to construct a budget and oversee the day-to-day construction of the home while I continued to work on appraisals and make money.

The project manager Dad recommended was Lester Brackage. Dad had worked with Lester extensively during his days selling and installing bridge systems throughout the southeast. Lester had even built the detached garage on my parents' property several years earlier. Dad trusted Lester; therefore, so did I.

By the middle of August 2001, when all the pieces to build my home were in place, I applied for a loan and was quickly approved to begin construction on my first home in Walnut Crest. I had every confidence that what I was doing made sense, and I was excited when we hired a grading subcontractor to clear my land of scrub brush and prepare the site for my home's foundation.

However, my hope and optimism for the future would quickly change to fear and uncertainty because within a month, the entire landscape of civilization would change and the whole world would be set on fire.

On the morning of Tuesday, September 11, 2001, I woke up early and eagerly hopped out of bed to make my way down to Walnut Crest to meet the grading subcontractor who would begin clearing my one-acre lot for the foundation of my first home.

It was Day 1 of construction and, admittedly, I was a little nervous. It would have been naïve and foolish of me not to expect any problems during the 6-7 months it would take to build the home, but I felt confident that between me and Lester, my project manager, we could handle any issues that happened to come our way. I was just hoping that there would be no problems on Day 1.

While watching the grading contractor roll his backhoe onto my lot and begin cutting in the driveway for my home, I felt elated that my hard work was finally coming to fruition. For a creative person like me, watching something that I created in my mind begin to take physical form is euphoric.

After watching the grading contractor work for an hour, I decided to leave the site and head back to my office to work on appraisals for the rest of the day. During the drive back I was beaming with pride and optimism. I couldn't believe that I was building my own home at the age of 26. It felt like a dream come true.

When I arrived at the office shortly before 9am though, that dream turned into a terrifying nightmare as I found both Mom and Dad glued to the TV, watching live footage of a skyscraper on fire in New York.

"What's going on?" I asked as I walked into Dad's office.

"A plane just hit the World Trade Center a few minutes ago," Dad said with deep sorrow in his voice. "Those poor people ... Can you imagine?"

At 8:46am that morning, American Airlines Flight 11, a commercial airliner carrying a total of 92 people, crashed into the North Tower of the World Trade Center.

For a few minutes, Mom, Dad and I watched in silence as the chaotic scene in New York unfolded. Tom Brokaw, news anchor for NBC Nightly News, captured our full attention that morning, along with at least a hundred million other people around the world.

"How does an accident like that even happen?" I remember asking. "The plane must've been malfunctioning to be flying that low and so close to those buildings. Why would the pilot turn into the city if they were having..."

But before I could finish my thoughts, we watched in utter disbelief as American Airlines Flight 175, carrying 65 people, collided into the South Tower of the World Trade Center at 9:03am.

At that moment, the entire global landscape of civilization would change. My heart sank into my feet as the realization of what was happening set in.

"This isn't an accident. Dad," I said softly. "It's an orchestrated attack."

I don't remember much about the rest of that day to be honest. I do remember going into my office to try and get some work done. But, like everyone else on the planet, I was too stunned and shocked to get anything accomplished.

By the end of that terrible day, 2,977 souls would die horrifically, in an unimaginable display of radical terrorism. It truly felt unbelievable at the time.

A Labor of Love at Gunpoint

As the weeks and months following the attacks on September 11 crawled by, the world seemed to fall deeper into darkness and uncertainty. Talk of large-scale military action by the United States was the top story on every news station 24/7. But I had more personal and immediate problems to worry about, like building my first home.

Through the end of 2001, work on my home in Walnut Crest progressed at a fast pace. Every morning, I would wake up early and drive down to the house to meet Lester. We would discuss the hiring of various contractors and what I needed to do to keep things moving. During this time, it was my primary job to watch the budget and pay Lester and his subcontractors for their work. Easy enough, right? *Wrong.*

By the time the house was framed and the brick siding was installed, I got very concerned about how we were going to be able to finish the home within Lester's budget. We had eaten away at least 70% of the budget before we had even started on the interior finishing of the home. Being an appraiser, I had a good understanding of the costs involved in building a home, and I didn't see how we could do it.

Lester kept telling me to relax and to have faith in his abilities to finish the project, but that did little to placate my fears, and I grew increasingly skeptical of Lester. At his core, Lester was a good man, but he was old and out of touch with the construction world in my opinion. He was also nasty to be around.

Lester was a heavy smoker and very unhygienic. He would wear the same clothes for a week before washing them and he smoked two to three packs of unfiltered cigarettes a day, which explained his persistent, throaty cough. His hands and fingers were permanently tanned brown from all the tar he consumed, and he was missing at least half of his teeth. Whenever Lester smiled, he reminded me of a dirty pirate.

By the time the front door was installed on my home in January of 2002, I had had enough of Lester and sent him home in frustration. It was clear to me by that point that Lester drastically underestimated the budget to build my home. I was afraid that if I kept Lester on board and allowed him to choose the remaining contractors, he would have finished the house in poor quality, and I wasn't going to let that happen.

It was a terrifying time for me. With Lester gone, I had to finish the home myself with very little money left in the budget and no experience in hiring contractors. I felt like I was in over my head and lost a lot of sleep during that period of my life.

"Why the hell did I do this?" I remember thinking to myself repeatedly. *"I should have just bought a damn house months ago, not build one. Why do I need to go over the top with everything I do?"*

Ultimately, I had to make a Hail Mary pass and try to refinance the home to get the necessary money to finish it. That's when I first met Gary Macleod, a mortgage broker who specialized in helping people like me in tough situations. I thank the Gods that I met Gary because he was able to work out a loan to help me get the funds I needed to complete the house at a level of quality I wanted.

Finishing construction on my first home was a painful learning experience. I could probably write an entire book on all the lessons I learned and mistakes I made. The hardest lesson I had to learn was that you can't trust everyone. But I suppose everyone learns that lesson at some point in their lives.

One subcontractor I hired flat out robbed me. *I'll refer to this piece of shit as 'Dick'.*

I had hired Dick to install the interior trim in my home after he came recommended to me by another contractor. But after a couple of days into his work, Dick casually brandished a nine-millimeter pistol in front of me and, with a smile on his face, asked me if I could pay him the remaining $2000 of his contract upfront. He never pointed the gun at me, but Dick's threat was unmistakable. I played it cool of course and paid him that day, but I never saw that Dickhead again. After that, my faith in humanity was permanently diminished.

I'm not sure why, but I never reported the incident to the police. Because he never actually pointed the gun at me, I guess I felt like the end result would be nothing more than a logistical nightmare of paperwork and statements. Plus, I had more pressing matters to deal with, like finishing my home.

Despite all the struggles, I went through the process of finishing my first home, and on April 1, 2002, Wendy and I moved in. Because I had gone way over my initial budget, the mortgage on my home was significantly higher than I had originally anticipated, and I was worried about how I was going to be able to afford the payments. I was making good money as an appraiser, but it's definitely a cyclical business. Some months I made more than enough money to cover the bills, but some months I barely scraped by.

Unfortunately, Wendy couldn't provide any meaningful financial support to help pay the bills. Despite her being out of college for five years with a degree in Biology, she still had no direction in her life and was working as a travel agent at AAA, earning little money. I tried to encourage Wendy to find a career path or a more lucrative job in her field of study, but my advice always fell on deaf ears. I couldn't understand why she wasn't working in a medical lab or a veterinarian's office making better money. It sure would've helped me out. This would later become a major issue and be one of the primary reasons why I ended my relationship with her.

Thankfully though, Chuck agreed to move in with me and Wendy to help us out by paying the same rent we were paying in our apartment together. I will forever be grateful to Chuck for that. Chuck living with me during those first few years really helped me stay afloat.

In the Spring of 2002, after we had all moved in, I spent the remainder of that year working outside in the yard. I became completely consumed by a vision of creating the perfect landscape to frame my stone cottage. After the struggles I went through building the home, I was very happy to be doing manual labor, as opposed to being robbed and cheated. I spent practically every weekend planting shrubs and flowers and putting down lime and seed for the yard.

By the following Spring, I was overjoyed with the fruits of my labor. The yard and house looked amazing, and I was proud of my home. It was a helluva journey getting to that point, but somehow, I managed to keep my sanity and see the project through to the end.

Cats and Dogs

I've always loved big dogs. When I was 9 or 10 years old, I befriended a stray dog in our neighborhood that I named Bozo, after the 1970s TV personality Bozo the Clown. Don't bother looking Bozo the Clown up on your phone. It'll just give you nightmares. While I vaguely remember watching and enjoying Bozo when I was young, I'm a bit horrified when I look at him now. He looks like a pedophile that drives around town in a van with *Free Candy* spray painted on the side of it.

I'm not sure why Mom and Dad let me watch that weirdo at such a young age, but I suppose every generation has some sort of strange toddler fandom. I remember when the Teletubbies burst onto the scene at the turn of the century and young kids everywhere went apeshit for those creepy, little, bulbous bastards, who talked in gibberish and had antennae on their heads.

My dog, Bozo, was a large black Labrador and, because of that, Mom and Dad insisted that he remain an outside dog. But Bozo and I quickly became best pals, and we would run around all day together throughout the subdivision and surrounding woods to play and have fun.

One day, while Bozo and I were out in the neighborhood, a kid named Carlton, who used to bully me, threw a rock while I was riding my bike and hit me on the head. It caused me to fall off my bike, hit the ground hard and gave me a nasty bit of road rash. When Carlton came up to taunt me further, for falling off my bike, Bozo laid down next to me in an act of protection. When Carlton started throwing rocks at both me and Bozo again, the little prick got what he deserved, and Bozo bit him.

Carlton cried foul play of course and told his parents, conveniently leaving out anything about him throwing rocks at me and Bozo in provocation. Carlton's parents, who were no better than their demon seed of a child, threatened to sue, and my folks were forced to find Bozo a new home.

That incident was probably my first taste of how unfair life can be. Losing Bozo for no other reason than that he was protecting me was devastating. I begged Mom and Dad for another big dog, but it wasn't in the cards. We did have other dogs while we were growing up, but they were all small lap dogs. One of them was a small shih tzu named Sassy, whom we got from Britt's family after one of their dogs had puppies. Britt's family always had dogs in the house.

One of the first things on my to-do list after I moved into my home in Walnut Crest was to build a fence in the back yard so that I could get a couple of big dogs. Max, the orange tabby I rescued from the Doublewide Dungeon a few years earlier was still living with me, but I really wanted the companionship of dogs so that I could once again hike around the wooded areas of my property and play with them.

It was exhausting work installing a fence around my half acre back yard, but luckily, I had a lot of help building it from Carey and Chuck. When the fence was completed, I started to look around on Animal Control websites for dogs up for adoption and fell in love with my second fur baby, Shep.

Shep was estimated to be only a year old when I adopted him from the pound in 2002. He wasn't a pure breed German Shepherd though. Shep was a lovable mix of German Shepherd and Chow, with a black tongue and curly little tail that he used to wag feverishly whenever I scratched his butt. Shep also pranced when he walked, like a little ballerina prances across the stage.

Because I had such a big yard and knew I would be gone a good bit during the days doing appraisal inspections, I decided to get a second dog to keep Shep company. As luck would have it, Wendy had a friend who was trying to find a new home for his dog, Caesar. Caesar was a Great Dane/Labrador mix and weighed about 100lbs. Wendy's friend had adopted Caesar as a puppy and severely underestimated how big Caesar would get. After a year, Caesar's original owner realized that he had made a huge mistake in getting such a big dog to live with him in his tiny one-bedroom apartment. Big dogs need space to run. And, man oh man, did Caesar like to run.

When Wendy and I took Shep over to her friend's apartment complex to see if Caesar and Shep would get along, those two 'Dumb Dumbs' ran like the wind together and played nonstop. And that's how I became the father to my third fur baby, Caesar.

By the time we adopted Caesar, he was as big as a horse and had a menacing bark that sent shivers down the spines of anyone who heard it. But the fact was, Caesar was a big baby. He must have been abused by his former owner because Caesar cowered away from everyone he didn't know. Whenever someone would come over to the house to visit, Caesar would bark once and then run to hide under the nearest desk or chair. It took some time for Caesar to trust me, but eventually he became as lovable and loyal to me as any of my dear friends or family members.

In the fall of 2003, Wendy and I decided to throw a Halloween housewarming party. We invited friends and family and had a great time doing the Monster Mash and other fun activities. I was proud to show off my new home and would recount to anyone who would listen the many trials and tribulations I had gone through in building it. I'm sure I bored a lot of people to tears.

At the end of the Halloween party, Wendy and I heard a faint meow coming from the front porch. Upon investigation, we found a small calico kitten desperately looking for love. I admit that I initially did not want to take in another animal. I felt like two dogs and a cat were enough. But being the sucker that I am for an animal in need, we ended up feeding the kitten that night and eventually brought her inside when it started getting cold outside. And that's how I came to have my fourth fur baby, Pumpkin – aptly named for being found at Halloween.

Pumpkin was a tiny little thing, with a scrunched face and short stubby tail. The fact that we never found any other cats in the yard probably meant that Pumpkin was left behind by her Mama for being the runt of the litter. But you wouldn't know that by the way Pumpkin acted because she was a demanding little Prima Donna. Whenever you sat down, it would take Pumpkin exactly 2.4 seconds to hop into your lap and demand cuddles. This was new to me because Max was not that way at all. Max was very much an independent cat who liked to play and chase me around the house, attacking my feet. Pumpkin, on the other hand, would watch patiently for the play to end and wait for somebody to sit down so she could hop up and get all the attention.

By the end of 2003, I had a full house with Wendy, Chuck, Caesar, Shep, Max and Pumpkin all living under the same roof, but I loved it. I would do appraisal work during the days, ride my motorcycle with Dad on the weekends and take long walks through the woods surrounding our neighborhood with Caesar and Shep. In the evenings we would all huddle in the living room, with the stone fireplace burning, and watch movies or read. Caesar and Shep would lie on their beds, Max would perch somewhere high to keep a watchful eye on all and Pumpkin would curl up on somebody's lap. We had a happy little family of fur babies.

In 2004, my appraisal business got busy as new home construction in Charlotte and the surrounding areas soared. Making good money again helped alleviate any financial concerns I had because I was able to once again build up some savings. Eventually I found myself getting bored and started to feel a creative itch for something new to throw my energy into.

With money coming in again, the struggles I had endured while building my first house seemed to fade away and I started to view that period of my life as a positive experience. In fact, I had learned so much in building my first home that I started seriously thinking about using the money I was saving to start my own construction company to build custom homes to sell. I had a good understanding of the costs associated with building a home and felt like I had a decent shot at making it as a home builder.

In early 2005 I decided to take some classes at a local community college to prepare myself to take the North Carolina General Contractor's licensing exam. The GC exam had only a 50% pass rating among first time takers at the time but, by the summer of 2005, I had passed the exam on my first attempt.

With my GC license now in hand, I then created my construction company, Drakestone Construction, and embarked on a journey to create my legacy in the world.

Unfortunately, that turned out to be a big mistake.

A Career in the Making

I've been a residential real estate appraiser for over 25 years now and, for the most part, I've enjoyed the work. But like any job, it comes with its ups and downs.

I never thought I would end up appraising for this long. I got into the business shortly after college to help Dad get his appraisal practice up and running and to make some money while I found a direction with my life. But after a few months of helping Dad, I ended up getting my own appraiser license because I like the freedom that the job gives me.

Being an independent appraiser, I am self employed and responsible for my own clients and work. I don't have sick days or paid time off, but I also don't have a boss. I've found that I work best in that environment as I don't respond well to being micro-managed. I'm just too independent, hardheaded and stubborn, I guess.

The job of a residential real estate appraiser is to find the market value of a home by inspecting the house for its condition, quality and location, then finding similar homes to that property which have recently sold. Most of my work is done for banks and lenders. When somebody buys a house or borrows money against their home, to buy a car or pay for college tuition, banks need to know how much money they can lend on that home as collateral. Obviously, banks don't want to lend out more money than the home is worth. That's where I come in.

The business is very cyclical though, tied almost directly to mortgage interest rates. It can sometimes feel like feast or famine being an appraiser. When interest rates go down, people buy homes or borrow money against their house because the money is cheaper. That means demand for appraisals increases, and I have work. When interest rates go up and people stop borrowing money, demand for appraisals goes down. I won't go into the economics of it all because I know it's incredibly boring to most people.

Appraisals are also used outside of lending in divorce settlements, estate planning, tax appeals and the like, but the bulk of my business is lending work. I know it's not a sexy profession, like being an A list actor, but being an appraiser has paid the bills and funded all my creative endeavors and travels throughout the last 25 years, so I can't complain.

Besides providing me with financial stability and income, being an appraiser has also given me quite a bit of perspective on life.

When the housing market crashed during the "Great Financial Crisis" in 2008-2011, most of my work was foreclosure appraisals. Banks needed to know the value of all the homes they were re-possessing, and I would be sent out to take pictures of those homes from the street and estimate their value. On a few occasions I found myself taking a picture of a house with children playing in the front yard and my heart would grow heavy knowing that those kids would soon have to move when the bank foreclosed on their home. *How will the parents explain that to their children?*

So many people lost their homes during that period that appraising became depressing work. But it gave me some much-needed perspective when I lost my own home in 2010. I didn't have hungry mouths to feed and had a job making money when so many others didn't.

Coming out of college, I was socially awkward and maybe even a little agoraphobic. I've never been paralyzed in fear while in large groups of people. I've just always kept a small circle of friends and never really learned the art of social conversation, like "chit-chatting". Because I'm a rather large guy, people often mistake my quiet nature as being aloof or unapproachable. That's probably why my job prospects coming out of college were so limited. I simply didn't communicate with people very well face-to-face.

I've always admired how Dad can just walk into a large room of people and openly communicate with anyone. It just comes natural to him after being a salesman for so many years. Working as an appraiser eventually did the same thing for me because being a quality appraiser requires a high degree of effective communication.

Part of my job as an appraiser is to do a physical inspection of the home I am appraising. This usually includes both an exterior inspection and an interior inspection of the house. Most of the time, the owners of the property are home when I complete my inspection. People let contractors into their homes all the time, but when you let a plumber into your house to repair something, he or she usually works at a specific point in the house, like the kitchen or bathroom. They have no reason to walk through every room of your house.

But as an appraiser, it is my job to walk through your entire house and inspect every room, looking for any signs of structural damage or repairs needed. I have to open closet doors, peek behind shower curtains and look at every aspect of the home. When I inspect a house, I typically have to invade someone's personal space. Because of that, I had to learn to become very casual and open with people to make them feel comfortable with my short intrusion of their privacy.

Over the last 20 years, I have averaged one appraisal inspection a day, or about 250 appraisals a year. So, I have literally walked through thousands of homes in my career as an appraiser and, in doing that, I am now quite adept and comfortable at communicating with people.

You can learn quite a bit about someone when you enter their personal space at home. I've walked through multi-million-dollar estate homes that were furnished and decorated in exquisite fashion. And I've walked through homes people were living in that I thought should be condemned because they were structurally unsafe.

I've been in the homes of hoarders, with people who've held onto so much junk that I was seriously concerned at how the house was still standing under the weight of it all. I've also been in homes that were so filthy that I felt like I needed a shower when I left. I don't understand how some people can live like that.

On one occasion, I walked into a small home to find an elderly woman lying comatose on a hospital gurney in the living room. The owner of the home was the elderly woman's daughter, and she was trying to refinance her home to get some money so that she could care for her mother. The daughter explained that the hospital kicked her mother out when she could no longer afford care.

When I got into my truck after that inspection, I started crying because I knew that my appraisal wouldn't support the loan that the woman needed to continue caring for her mother. I ended up calling social services to advise them of the situation but, regrettably, I never followed up.

Early in my appraisal career, a woman once tried to seduce me during my appraisal inspection. Not because she thought I was attractive, but because she needed my appraisal to come in at a certain value to make her loan work. I politely turned her down.

More recently, I did an appraisal on a beautiful, multi-million-dollar home for a couple going through a nasty divorce. The husband and wife were both present during my inspection, and as I walked through the home, they screamed at each other the entire time. I minded my own business and didn't eavesdrop, but when I left, I couldn't help but wonder what went wrong in their relationship. Thankfully, my wife and I have never screamed at each other like that, and I hope that we never do.

It's easy to assume that life is blissful for people who have money. But being an appraiser has provided me with quite a bit of perspective on life and the various struggles that all of us go through. Not everyone who lives in a mansion is happy. Money can certainly provide you with comfort and some measure of peace of mind, but it can't provide you with sustained happiness. True happiness comes from the love you have with friends and family, as well as with yourself. *I know that I promised early on in this book not to make superficial statements of the obvious, but in this case, I'm going to make an exception because I think it bears repeating.*

It's important to surround yourself with reminders of the love you have in your life. My wife and I have many photos and memories hanging on the walls of our home to remind us of all that we have to be thankful for. Sometimes, when I'm having a tough day, all I have to do is walk through the immense gallery of photos in our house to be reminded of all the wonderful people and memories that I have to be grateful for. I would encourage you to do the same.

I Don't Want To Talk About It

It has been very difficult to write about one of the biggest failures of my life, primarily because it happened through no fault of my own. Like so many others, I simply got swept away in the massive turbulence which occurred during the global financial crisis of 2008-2011. Equity markets around the world sank like stones, easy money became hard money virtually overnight and the United States housing market went from robust and healthy to weak and dying – all in a matter of months. Nobody saw it coming, except maybe Michael Burry, the investing guru who famously shorted (betted against) the housing market several months before the whole thing started.

If you want a full explanation of what happened during "The Great Recession", I suggest you watch the 2015 film *The Big Short*, starring Christian Bale as Michael Burry and a slew of other fantastic actors, including Steve Carell, Brad Pitt and Ryan Gosling. The film won an Academy Award for best writing and a Producers Guild Award for best motion picture. Ironically, I don't think I've ever seen the whole movie in one sitting. Every time I try to watch it, I get so goddamn angry that I want to throw something at the TV. I have to turn it off and walk away. I have seen the whole movie in pieces though.

In 2002, I finished building my first home in Walnut Crest. It was a painstaking process, and I made a lot of mistakes, but I also learned quite a bit. So, in 2005 I decided I was going to be a custom home builder and put what I had learned to productive use. It felt like a smart move at the time.

Having been a real estate appraiser for seven years by 2005, I had extensive knowledge of the housing market and knew what consumers valued. I also had plenty of connections to lenders and understood the process of obtaining construction loans. Having worked my ass off in college, I felt that I could easily handle the accounting and finances of the company. And because I had built my personal home just a few years prior, I had a good understanding of the costs involved in residential home construction. With the skills and knowledge I had, I felt like it would have been foolish not to start building homes.

I had no interest in building "cookie cutter" homes that all looked alike. I wanted to be a true custom homebuilder and personally design every home that I build. For me, the initial designing of the home was the most enjoyable part of the process. Building a custom home is like composing an original song. I view it as an art form. Perhaps I missed my calling in not becoming an architect.

The ultimate satisfaction in building a custom home was when I completed it and could marvel at how I took an idea in my mind and brought it into reality. It's the same feeling I get while playing guitar and losing myself in the music. I think I may have initially started building homes to fill a creative void in my life. I had walked away from playing guitar years earlier and was in desperate need of a creative outlet again.

Artistic motives aside, I was also seeking fortune and glory. I was 30 years old at the time and wanted to make a name for myself in this world. I felt invincible at that point in my life because I had yet to experience true failure, at least not at anything I had put genuine effort into. Life had yet to kick me squarely in the nuts. When it eventually did, the mutha-f'ker wore steel-toed boots.

After passing the North Carolina licensing exam for General Contractors on my first attempt in 2005, my confidence soared. I just knew that my company would succeed. In fact, I remember telling Dad that the only way I could fail was if the entire housing market collapsed. We laughed at the odds of that happening, but, as fate would have it, that's exactly what would occur 3 years later.

It wasn't easy building my first few homes. I anticipated there would be challenges of course, but I did not expect them to come crashing down on me all at once. On the first home I built with my company, I had to drill a well on the property to obtain a source of water because there was no city water available. My well contractor used every drilling rod on his rig and dug almost 900 feet before he had to call it a dry hole. Getting that news was like putting $10,000 on the ground and setting it on fire. It gave me a panic attack thinking I wouldn't be able to find a suitable water source for the home. Thankfully my well contractor moved to a different site on the lot and found an adequate water supply on the second hole he drilled. But I was puckered up for a few days until that happened.

I worked with all manner of individuals while building homes. Most of the people I hired were decent and hardworking, but on occasion I would have a bad experience. The first brick mason I ever hired turned out to be completely incompetent, despite being highly recommended by a couple of builders I had spoken to. I met the brick mason at the jobsite on the morning his crew started work and gave him the foundation plans for my home. I then left so that I could continue to do appraisal work and line up other contractors to keep progress going on the home.

When I returned at the end of the day, to check on the brick mason's progress, there wasn't one fucking pier properly placed within the foundation. It was as if the mason didn't even look at the building plans I had given him that morning. He just randomly placed piers wherever he thought best. When I confronted the mason about his error, the prick got agitated and claimed that his foundation was better than my engineered plans. It was then that I realized he didn't know how to read a set of building plans. In fact, I was skeptical whether he could read at all.

After working with that brick mason, I realized that I needed to vet my contractors better, so I made it a habit never to hire someone for a job without first observing them working on a jobsite.

Before I hired my roofer, Jeff, I first met with him on an unrelated job that he was working so that I could watch his crew and feel confident that they knew what they were doing. When I arrived at the site, Jeff climbed off the roof to talk to me but continued to help his crew out by running shingles up the ladder for them. I liked that about Jeff and it gave me the confidence I needed in hiring his crew.

By doing that kind of legwork before hiring my subcontractors, it kept my stress level down. Plus, I met a ton of good people and started some great working relationships. The effort I put in on the front end of hiring skilled labor was worth the time involved. It brought quality craftsmanship to my homes and peace of mind to me.

Eventually though, I hired a friend of mine from college, named Dillon, to be my project supervisor. I was working 40 hours a week as an appraiser and then another 40 hours a week hiring contractors, ordering building supplies and managing the finances of the company. I was burning out fast and needed help. I couldn't stop appraising because I needed to continue to bring in money until I got my company off the ground and profitable.

Dillon lived with me, Wendy and Chuck in my Walnut Crest home for about a year while we got Drakestone Construction off the ground. Chuck and Dillon were already good friends from college and had lived together before, so it wasn't awkward. We were a happy little family during the year Dillon lived with us.

Unfortunately, neither Chuck nor I was aware that Dillon was an alcoholic when I hired him. Dillon hid his addiction incredibly well and lived with us for almost an entire year before I figured it out. I had no idea Dillon was drunk while working on my homes. Eventually, Dillon's excessive alcohol consumption made him very sick, and he could no longer hide it. He was literally coughing up blood before I made the connection. I was blindsided by the realization at first. However, looking back on it now, I should have seen it coming. All the signs were there. But, as always, hindsight is 20/20.

Dillon left Drakestone shortly after I discovered his addiction. Thankfully he joined Alcoholics Anonymous and, to my knowledge, has been sober for the last 15-20 years. I really like Dillon. I thought we worked well together and that he was a great friend and housemate. I hope he is doing well. I haven't spoken to him in quite some time.

Losing Dillon as my project supervisor wasn't exactly a terrible loss though because, shortly after he left the company in late 2007, I started to see warning signs in the real estate market that a downturn was on the horizon. Banks began pulling back significantly on lending due to a substantial rise in defaults on mortgage-backed securities. I knew that spelled big trouble for everybody in the housing market. I just had no idea that it was going to be a Category 5 hurricane.

Nobody did.

Deliciously Ostentatious

While my first couple of years with Drakestone had their frustrations, the business was quite successful. I sold five spec homes and was also contracted to build two custom homes for customers, using my unique designs. "Spec home" is short for *speculative home,* or a home that is built to sell in the open market. I financed the construction of my first few spec homes with my own capital and put up my personal home as collateral. It was the cost of doing business. But in building those spec homes, word got around that I paid attention to detail and was easy to work with. I started to get calls from prospective customers who were looking for a quality homebuilder. My confidence soared, and I felt ten feet tall. I was exhausted from all the work I was putting in but felt very optimistic about the future of the company.

By the start of 2007, I had built a terrific team of subcontractors whom I could trust. They got their jobs done on schedule and did quality work because I paid them on time. The fastest way to lose a quality subcontractor is to not pay them right away after they've completed a job. Like all business ventures, cash talks and bullshit walks. I knew some builders, my competitors, who would go several months without paying their subs. Those builders would spread themselves too thin and be unable to pay their bills until they sold a home.

I was smart though and always maintained enough working capital to pay my crew. I ran a tight ship on my finances. I wrote all the checks and kept the books clean and balanced. I learned my lesson about watching the budget while building my first home, in 2001, with Lester. That dirty pirate blew my budget out of the water and caused me to get into a financial hole.

I reinvested the profits from the sale of my first few homes into buying more land to build homes on. I bought three beautiful lots on the Stonebridge Golf Course in Union County, NC. Each of those lots cost about $125,000. One of the lots I purchased overlooked the 18th green of the golf course, which also had a small pond with a beautiful spray fountain at its center. The view from that lot was gorgeous.

The house I decided to build on that lot was my favorite house design. It looked like a medieval keep, complete with a turret and spires. It was a Provincial style home, which was very popular around the turn of the 21st Century. I thought it was deliciously ostentatious.

I liked the floorplan of that Provincial home so much that I decided to build myself a new home using that same design. While I loved the first home I built in 2001, I thought it was vastly inferior to the quality of homes I was building by 2007. I needed a model home which I could showcase year-round to potential customers. So, at the beginning of 2007, I started construction on two ostentatious homes at the same time. One spec home on the golf course as well as my new personal home.

I did not build my personal home on the golf course in Stonebridge though. I preferred to have some privacy in my backyard and instead found a beautiful, wooded lot in a nearby subdivision called Hickory

Hollow. It was a small, quiet little development located about a mile from Cane Creek Park in Union County, NC.

Cane Creek is a gorgeous public park, with over 1000 acres of forest land as well as a 350-acre lake. I would often take my boys, Caesar and Shep, there to hike and do some trail running, which the dogs loved. Dad and I would also go kayaking on the lake at Cane Creek and I was excited to be building a new home so close to the park. Mom and Dad even bought a lot in Hickory Hollow, right across the street from me. They wanted me to build them a new home after finishing mine. Unfortunately, that would never happen.

I built my personal home in Hickory Hollow at the same time as I built the Stonebridge home so that I could save as much money as I could during construction. Contracting two homes of the same design, back-to-back, was a great cost savings strategy. I had been doing business with my subs and suppliers for a couple of years by this point and had given them a lot of work, so most of them gave me a break out of professional courtesy. I ended up building my personal home for about 15-20% less than the home on the golf course by doing that.

Unfortunately, starting work on those two ostentatious homes, in early 2007, was the beginning of the end for me. When I took out the loans to start building both of them, the money was easy to get, and everything seemed status quo in the market. There were homes being built everywhere and demand was high.

However, nine months later, when I had finished building those homes, the market seemed precariously fragile, and credit was nowhere to be found. Demand in the housing market had plummeted and everything had turned upside down.

Unbeknownst to me at the time, those two homes were the last I would build with my company.

Panic at the Disco

The year 2007 was supposed to be a great year for me. But, in actuality, it was a chaotic year that felt like being sucker punched in the mouth. It wasn't just the economy and housing market that turned sour on me in 2007. The whole year was plagued with confusion and frustration in my personal life as well.

Those personal issues started in January, before I began construction on those two ostentatious homes that would eventually become my demise. To celebrate the success of my hard work up to that point, I organized a big group of friends and family to take a weeklong Caribbean Cruise together. I was flying high and felt optimistic about my future and wanted to share that joy with the people I loved. I invited everyone close to me on the cruise, including Wendy, my parents, Carey and Cami, Britt, Jason, Chuck and Brandon, as well as a few other friends. It was a fantastic vacation – until the last day.

The real reason I invited everyone on that cruise was because it was my intention to surprise Wendy and propose to her on that trip. I had decided that it was time for me to stop shuffling my feet and make a commitment. I wanted her and I to be officially engaged when we moved into the new home I was building in Hickory Hollow.

On the last day of the cruise, our entire group gathered at the ship's bar in the disco to have drinks before dinner. I think everybody except Wendy was anticipating my proposal that evening. Perhaps Wendy did know my intentions, but she never acted like she did, and we never talked about it afterward.

I had the ring in my pocket when we walked into the disco. Wendy had an heirloom ring from her grandmother that she wanted to use as her engagement ring, and I had sneaked it into my suitcase while packing for the trip.

But, at the last minute, I couldn't pull the trigger. I froze up and shut down. I remember being petrified of sticking my hand in my pocket and reaching for that ring. It was one of the most awkward and confusing moments of my life.

There was no specific reason why I didn't propose to Wendy that day. She did nothing in particular to upset me on that trip. We didn't have a fight or anything like that. In fact, we rarely fought. I had a great time all week until I walked into that disco bar. That's the confusing part of it all.

All I can say is that when I walked into that disco room and saw everybody staring at me, my gut turned to rot and I heard an inner voice, deep in my subconscious, scream *"Don't Do This!"* It was, without a doubt, one of the most uncomfortable feelings I've ever had. Nothing felt right about it at all.

My mind went blank, and I started to sweat. My vision of a marriage proposal, in front of friends and family while overlooking the beautiful blue Caribbean Sea, was nowhere to be found. The very reason I had taken the time and effort into planning the cruise and encouraging all my friends to come along had vanished. Something within me was trying desperately to get my attention and it demanded to be heard.

I thought I was being a coward, at first, and was angry at myself for having such cold feet that evening. Wendy and I had been living together for nearly four years and dating for almost 16. I couldn't understand why I was having so much trouble committing to her.

Wendy and I met in the summer of 1991, when I worked at Carowinds for a summer. She lived in South Carolina while I lived in North Carolina. The state line was only a couple of miles from the house that I grew up in. It was actually a shorter drive to Wendy's house than it was to my high school. But because we technically lived in different states, we went to different schools and in-state colleges. Such is the magic of imaginary lines.

Because of that imaginary line, for the first 11 years of our relationship, Wendy and I didn't see each other every day or hang out all the time. I spread my time around a lot through those years, hanging out with my friends and working. I didn't have a lot of free time to see Wendy in college because we went to different schools, about four hours apart. I studied my ass off in college, started playing in a band and worked as an R.A. Wendy and I saw each other every other weekend, at best, during those four years. When I got my first apartment after college, I moved in with Chuck to keep our band together.

My relationship with Wendy had a lot of space in it for most of our years together, and I guess I preferred that. Perhaps that was selfish of me, but I didn't force her to stay. We had a few periods of "on again, off again", but we always reconciled and came back to one another in the end.

Wendy and I dated for 11 years before we officially lived together. In 2002, she moved in with me at my home in Walnut Crest. That's when the dynamic of our relationship changed, and I started seeing her as a life partner. But even then, we didn't live alone. To help me pay the mortgage on the house, Chuck also lived with us, as well as Dillon for a year.

So out of our 16-year relationship, Wendy and I lived alone together for only a few months before we went on that cruise in January of 2007. And in those few months, I realized that, while I loved her, I didn't feel like Wendy was the person I was supposed to spend the rest of my life with. We had both grown into different people and I felt like we had very little in common anymore.

That realization came crashing down on me when I walked into that cruise ship disco.

When it came time to leave the disco bar, I decided not to propose. I just put on a big smile and told everyone that we should go to dinner. I remember my family and friends giving me confused looks and quietly asking me if I was OK. I guess the inner turmoil I was feeling was obvious to everyone. But, true to my nature, I simply masked my insecurities and told everyone that I felt great. But deep down I felt like my entire life had just taken a hard right turn.

I should have ended my relationship with Wendy after that cruise. It was on that boat that I realized that I was never going to feel comfortable marrying her. But instead of ending the relationship when we returned home, I threw myself into my work and started building those two fucking houses.

I placated my fears by telling myself that I was just stressed about all the work I had ahead of me. I thought for sure that I would probably feel more comfortable about marrying Wendy when I finished those homes. But that didn't happen either. It would be another two years before I finally found the courage to end my relationship with Wendy.

Sadly, I never got to dance to "Saturday Night Fever" in the disco.

The Devil's Summer

In the summer of 2007, the devil came to roost in my backyard. The drought began in early spring but, by the summer, it was disastrous. North Carolina experienced its driest calendar year on record. Water reservoir levels dropped to critical lows across the region. By October of 2007, over 70% of the southeastern United States was in the worst classification of drought possible.

Rain is typically your worst enemy when building a home. Work gets delayed and progress slows down, which ultimately eats into profit. If it rains early in the construction of a home, before the roof is installed, the entire work schedule has to be revised. You have to push all of your subcontractors off for awhile, which causes more delays in the long run. Getting a lot of rain during the first month of construction on a home is a logistical nightmare.

But in the summer of 2007, I prayed for it to rain.

Due to the drought conditions, Union County issued water restrictions to conserve resources. As a result, the Stonebridge Golf Club had to minimize their watering of the golf course to avoid heavy fines. The beautiful, lush green view I once had on the golf course slowly turned into a bleak desert landscape. The shimmering pond that my home overlooked evaporated into a puddle of mud. There wasn't even enough water in it to run the fountain.

I remember being astonished at how starkly different the view from my spec home had changed in just 6 months. It had gone from a vision of Paradise to a portrait of Hell. It truly felt like the devil had come to town.

One ridiculously hot day, while looking over that brown, barren landscape on the golf course, I made a promise to God that I would never again complain about the rain. I'm reminded of that moment every time I hear someone bitch about the weather. I learned never to take the rain for granted during the drought of '07.

Despite my prayers, it didn't start raining heavily again until the winter. However, water restrictions in Union County remained in effect well into 2008, which meant that I couldn't finish landscaping my homes for nearly a year after they were finished. There was no point. The ground was so hard and dry, nothing could take root.

The excitement and hope that I had started 2007 with vanished. Between the increasingly bad news developing in the housing market, the inner turmoil I was feeling about my relationship with Wendy, and the drought conditions plaguing the area, I became a pressure cooker of angst and tension. Unfortunately, it was while in this state of mind that I had a conversation with Carey that created a rift between us that exists to this day.

I was in the final stages of construction on my new personal home in Hickory Hollow. Carey had come out one day to help me move some cabinetry from the garage into the house. The moronic crew that dropped off my kitchen cabinets just left them in the garage overnight, sitting in an uncontrolled environment for anyone to steal. The garage doors had not yet been installed, but the interior of the house was locked up and secure. I had given my cabinet supplier a code to the key box in the garage so that they could get into the house. But apparently those instructions were too complex for the delivery crew. *Idiots!*

Carey and I had a fairly good relationship up until the Fall of 2007. At least, I thought we did. We'd had a few falling outs and reconciliations before that, but nothing that didn't mend itself over time. But on the day that Carey helped me move those fucking kitchen cabinets, our relationship fundamentally changed.

Carey was in a good mood to start the day, but I wasn't. I was under a lot of stress at the time, and I'm sure I just bitched about my problems at length to Carey.

Eventually, Carey revealed to me the reason for his good mood when he told me that he was going to propose to Brandy, the woman he had been dating for over a year. Brandy had two little girls from a previous marriage, Keira, who was 4 years old and Savannah, who was 6.

I should have said, *"Congratulations! That's amazing news, man! I'm so happy for you!"* and left it at that. But I didn't. My mistake was in also telling Carey that I thought he should wait to get married until he had a steady job and enough income to support a family of four. I was worried about the responsibility he was about to take on, especially providing for two children.

I want to be clear that I never told Carey not to marry Brandy. I like Brandy. She's got a wry sense of humor, which appeals to me. I simply suggested that Carey wait to get married and instead focus his energy on first becoming financially stable. At the time he was 30 years old and still jumping around from job to job, looking for direction and stability.

I realize now that what I told Carey was a reflection of my own insecurities at the time. I was dealing with some very uncomfortable feelings about marrying Wendy. I was telling myself that I had to wait to marry Wendy until I was financially stable. I was waiting for it to feel safe. I was feeding Carey the same bullshit that I was eating.

As you can imagine, Carey was deeply hurt by my words and left the jobsite pretty upset. I couldn't understand why he got so angry at first. I knew what I said hurt him, but I didn't say anything cruel or malicious. I simply told him to think about the responsibilities he was taking on and prioritize his financial footing first.

Carey and I have never talked about that day. He stopped talking to me completely for almost a year after that. I think we grumbled *"Merry Christmas"* to each other during the holidays that year, but that's about it.

Mom and Dad eventually became my liaison to Carey. If I wanted to know how he was doing, I'd ask them. I felt like he didn't want to speak to me ever again, so I never called him. When I talk to him now, I tread carefully with what I say and avoid trying to give any form of advice. I miss the big brother relationship I had with Carey. When he left angry that day, it felt like he stopped being my little brother.

I eventually came to understand why Carey got so angry with me. He was in love and knew that Brandy was the one he wanted to spend the rest of his life with. He was sharing that joy with me and I threw it back in his face.

I don't regret what I said to Carey. I did believe what I told him to be true, and I still do.

What I regret is that I said it to him on that day. I should have celebrated with him at that moment and saved my opinion for a later day. I understand that now.

Carey and Brandy got married the following year, in October of 2008. Thankfully, Carey and I reconciled enough to be civil by his wedding date. But the tension has always remained between us.

Carey and Brandy have been married for almost 17 years now and have two children together, Quinn and Lorelei. Strong Irish names in the family. Carey adopted Keira and Savannah and raised them as his own. He has worked hard to provide for his family and is an excellent father and husband.

Carey followed his heart and took on the responsibility of fatherhood rather quickly. He has devoted his entire life to his family and done everything he could to give them the best life possible. There were challenges, of course. Carey, Cami and I all had some rough years after 2007. But Carey's devotion to his family and his tireless work ethic conquered every obstacle in his way.

Carey's heart and strength come from the love and dedication that he has for his family. He deserves every bit of love and joy he gets from them. I'm proud of him.

Hindsight

A s the bad news continued throughout 2008, and it became obvious that the country was heading into a serious recession, I became angry and blamed myself for my predicament.

I should have waited one year before starting construction on my new personal home and the Stonebridge home. I would have seen the warning signs sooner. I pushed it too far, overextended myself and got caught with no chair to sit in when the music stopped. A smarter businessman would have kept a better eye on the market and seen the slowdown coming. I should have scaled back considerably at the start of 2007, not gone full speed ahead.

Hindsight. Always 20-fucking-20.

It's true that I didn't want to stop building. I kept pushing because I was doing remarkably well at the start of 2007 and wanted to keep momentum going. I had a reliable crew of contractors that took me a few years to put together and they were hungry for work. I wanted to feed them and continue my creative passion for designing and building beautiful homes.

When the house of cards started to fall in 2008, the foreclosure rate on homes in the United States tripled. Unemployment doubled. The collapse of Lehman Brothers in September of that year started a chain reaction which nearly crippled the entire global economy. The S&P 500 and the Dow Jones Industrial average both lost 50% of their value. Wachovia Bank, the fourth largest bank in the country at the time, with over $800 Billion in assets, nearly collapsed before Wells Fargo stepped in to save it from insolvency.

By the time I was standing in bankruptcy court, to seek protection from my creditors, I had stopped blaming myself. I knew for a fact that building those two houses in 2007 was not the cause of my demise. I didn't overextend or push anything too hard. There was nothing I did or could have done that would have changed the outcome. Failure was inevitable for everyone.

Even if I had never built those two ostentatious homes, the outcome would have been the same. I would have just prolonged my agony before having to make the same hard decision to dissolve my company. It took me a long time to accept that fact and make peace with it.

The worst part about running my company was the overwhelming amount of accounting involved. Running a home construction business requires an enormous amount of bookkeeping – buying materials, paying for building permits and attorney fees, paying contractors, creditors, marketing and advertising fees, real estate fees, etc., etc., etc. It felt endless sometimes. But whenever I sold a home, I was overjoyed to watch my business account refill with more money than I had started with. So, the hard work felt justified.

However, towards the end of my company, all I did was write checks to creditors and slowly watch my working capital drain to $0. I survived for about two years doing that, and it was agonizing. To this day, I have anxiety about paying bills. It doesn't matter if it's a $40 water bill or a mortgage payment. Writing a check for anything triggers tremendous anxiety in me. I always feel like I'm on the verge of losing everything again. I have some serious residual trauma about writing checks and paying monthly bills. I wish I could say I was kidding about that.

To this day I have a deal with my wife that if she takes responsibility for paying our bills every month, I will do most of the grocery shopping, meal prepping and cooking in the house. She happily accepted that arrangement.

When I eventually ran out of my working capital at the end of 2009, the banks foreclosed on all my homes. They took the first home I had built in Walnut Crest, the home I had built on the golf course as well as my new personal home in Hickory Hollow. They also foreclosed on my remaining two lots on the golf course. The bank sold those vacant lots at auction for $35,000 after I had bought them just a few years earlier for $125k. Their value had dropped by 75% due to the disastrously imbalanced housing market and critically wounded financial markets.

The stress that I experienced during that period of my life was tremendous. My physical and emotional health deteriorated. I was only 33 years old, yet it became obvious to me that I was headed down the path of some serious medical issues, including the risk of heart attack or stroke. I realized that I needed to take action to avoid spiraling out in a cyclone of anger, self pity and depression.

Thankfully I made the effort and reclaimed my health, but it wasn't without considerable effort.

A Sober Courtroom

In May of 2010, I stood before a panel of judges in bankruptcy court, dissolved my company, Drakestone Construction, and asked for protection from my creditors. My case took only 5 minutes for the judges to rule on. As soon as they heard that I was a home builder, they simply shook their heads in unison and sighed. They understood that my financial position was not my fault. I was just one of many builders that had stood before them under the same circumstances. And so, with a very unceremonious bang of a gavel, I was released from my debts and granted reprieve.

While it took only 5 minutes for the judges to hear and rule on my case, I had to wait for three hours in the courtroom that day for my case to be called. I was astonished at how many other people were in the courtroom doing the same thing. I even recognized a couple of them as fellow home builders.

Almost everyone in the courtroom was seeking bankruptcy protection from mortgage lenders. We had all lost our homes and were fighting for our financial future. The air was stagnant, and it was depressingly quiet. It was one of the most sobering rooms I've ever been in.

But when I walked out of that courthouse and into the crisp spring air, I stood underneath a beautiful blue sky and smiled as I felt the immense weight of it all lift off of my shoulders.

I was still angry and felt like a failure. But I didn't have to think about it anymore. I was released from all financial obligations to creditors and could ignore all mail addressed to my company because it no longer existed. Of course, I had to forfeit all my financial assets in obtaining bankruptcy protection, but by that point there wasn't much left anyway.

It has been fifteen years since I stood in that sobering courtroom. Writing about my failure as a homebuilder has been laborious. I honestly didn't know what I wanted to say at first because I haven't thought about that period of my life for some time. I literally stopped thinking about it all on the day that I walked out of the courthouse. But as I started writing, the memories and moments started flowing and I was able to piece my thoughts together into a cohesive framework. It has been an exercise in temperance.

I have no regrets about anything. I still have feelings of bitterness and resentment, but I'm grateful that it happened early in my life. I was able to start over and get back on my feet. Dad sometimes asks me if I have any interest in building homes again and I immediately respond by saying, "No". I don't want the stress. I would be constantly worried that the rug would be pulled out from underneath me again.

My life took a turn for the better in the decade that followed my bankruptcy. I found strength and healing through reclaiming my physical and emotional well-being. I fell in love with a beautiful woman and married her. I also found creative release in the form of acting, writing and producing films. I started playing the guitar again.

My perspective on life, and what happiness means to me, has evolved substantially since that period of my life. The last 15 years have been the best years of my life so far. Except for the last six months.

But I'll get to Humpty later.

From Fat Boy to Meat Head

When I was young, I idolized actors like Christopher Reeve as Superman, Sylvester Stallone as Rambo and Arnold Schwarzenegger as Conan the Barbarian because they were big and strong and always ended up saving the day. I also liked that they didn't take shit from anybody. I told myself that one day I would be big and strong and wouldn't have to take shit from anybody either.

I was a chubby kid growing up. Mom always kept candy and sweets hidden around the kitchen and I was an expert at uncovering her hidden stashes. I had a nose for sniffing out Little Debbie fudge rounds, oatmeal cookies and Swiss cake rolls.

Growing up, we ate your typical Midwestern fare. Mom would make pan fried chicken, corn on the cob, greens beans with bacon and carrots, fried potatoes, sweet cornbread, ham and beans, meaty chili, country style steak, mashed potatoes, etc. For dessert, it was usually banana pudding or pineapple upside down cake. On my birthday, I would always ask Mom to make Apple Crisp, which was basically brown sugar, butter, flour and a couple of apple slices. During the holidays, Mom would make lemon bars, butterscotch balls, peanut butter blossoms, fudge and, of course, sugar cookies.

We would go out to eat as a family about once or twice a week, usually after a long day at the ball field or on the basketball courts. We'd typically go to a buffet restaurant because it was cheap, and everybody could eat whatever they wanted.

Whenever I was at Britt's house, his folks would often invite me to stay for dinner, and I'd feast like a king on steak, barbeque and cheeseburgers. When we played Dungeons and Dragons into the wee hours of the morning, my diet would consist of Doritos, sugary soda and pizza.

Looking back now, I cringe at how poor my eating habits were while growing up. It's a miracle I was never diagnosed with diabetes. I got teased regularly in elementary school about being chubby, but I tried not to let it bother me too much. I was a big boy and not afraid to throw my weight around if someone really got under my skin. Plus, playing baseball and basketball regularly kept me from getting too fat. My brother, Carey, stayed skinny throughout childhood, which pissed me off to no end. I guess he had more self control than I did back then.

In Junior High, I hit a growth spurt and shot up 6-8 inches, which made me skinny for the first time in my life. That's also around the time I started playing football and lifting weights to put on muscle. As a result, I stopped getting picked on and girls started to pay attention to me, which was a nice feeling.

At the start of high school, I hit the weight room pretty regularly and became a follower of the holy trinity of strength exercises – the bench press, squat and dead lift. My cousin Kelly, who is about 7 years older than me, would sometimes take me to the gym with him to show me various exercises and how to use proper form and technique. I'm very grateful for everything Kelly did for me.

Before my senior year of high school, I quit football and eventually got fat again. Between schoolwork, hanging out with friends, working a part time job and being involved in various after school activities, my time in the weight room dropped significantly, but my eating habits remained the same.

Going into college, I started to obtain some discipline. I hit the books pretty hard but also made an effort to stay active and got to the campus gym a few nights every week. On weekends, I would play football and basketball with Brandon and some of the guys from East Hall. But by the time I started working on my finance and banking courses, my free time went out the window and I started to put on some significant weight again.

Despite coming out of college with stellar grades and a strong work ethic, I was fat and depressed. I just couldn't seem to find discipline in my eating habits or consistency in my physical conditioning. Like most people, I yo-yo dieted frequently and would lose 20 pounds in one year only to gain 25 pounds the following year. I did this for about a decade after college.

In 2008, I made the decision to stop screwing around and take my health seriously. This decision came during a very stressful period in my life, when I was building custom homes. From the stress I was feeling from my construction business, I ended up getting terrible acid reflux, which gave me a severe sore throat that kept me up at night. As a result, I began popping acid reflux pills like candy.

I could feel myself in danger of going into a downward spiral and knew that if I didn't act, I would eventually end up on a daily regimen of pills for all manner of health-related issues like high cholesterol, high blood pressure and God knows what else.

As the global financial markets began to freeze in 2008, I found myself with a lot of free time. My appraisal and construction businesses were both dismally slow, and I realized that I had one of two choices. I could sit on the couch, watch TV, play video games and eat my depression away, or I could find something to focus on and be productive with my time. Thankfully I opted to do something about my declining health.

I started to read articles online and in health and fitness magazines to educate myself on proper nutrition and specific exercises to target major muscle groups. I began to pay attention to everything I ate and even set up a spreadsheet to calculate everything I put in my mouth to get a better understanding of my daily caloric intake.

It was a shocking revelation to me how much I was eating and how poorly I was treating my body. I became fixated on changing my lifestyle and getting into peak physical form. I stopped going out to eat with friends and family and, instead, started prepping my meals everyday, based on a high protein diet and avoiding refined sugars and processed foods. Whenever I got hungry and wanted to cheat, I made a conscious effort to ask myself, *Am Am I eating because I'm bored or stressed? Am I eating because I think it will make me happy? Or am I hungry because my body legitimately needs fuel?*

For this to work, of course, you must be willing to be honest with yourself. Having the strength to call yourself out on your own bullshit is vital in creating change. If you can't be completely honest with yourself and take responsibility, it's unlikely that you will ever find fulfillment in life. I truly believe that.

While I was growing up, my parents and friends would placate me and tell me that I wasn't fat, just "big boned". As I got older, I would tell myself that my weight and size were a result of my genetics and there was nothing I could do about that. But the more research I did about nutrition and the more stories I read about people who successfully took control of their eating habits, the more I realized that I needed to call myself out on my bullshit.

I eventually had to admit that I had a very unhealthy, emotional connection to food. For the first 33 years of my life, I viewed food as a source of happiness and motivation. To motivate myself to work out, I would think about having a big bowl of ice cream afterwards. In college, after studying for four or five hours for an exam, I would reward myself with a large pepperoni pizza and a two-liter bottle of sugary soda.

Many people in the United States struggle with their weight. The CDC estimates that 40% of the U.S. population is obese. And while a lot of that is due to our culture, I also believe some of that gluttonous behavior stems from evolutionary biology. For the first 30,000 years of human evolution, food was scarce. Our survival instincts told us to eat whenever we had the opportunity. It's only been in the last 200 years, since the industrial revolution and advancements in agricultural science, that the global food supply has substantially increased. I think many people still eat from a subconscious fear that it may be their last meal.

They say the first step in fixing any problem is admitting that you have one. Once I came clean with myself about my unhealthy relationship with food, it was not difficult to control my appetite and change my eating habits. I simply had to be mindful of my actions and maintain discipline. Whenever I was tempted to eat a sleeve of Oreo cookies crushed into a tub of vanilla ice cream, I would instead visualize a specific image of me that I wanted to turn into reality. That image was of me in a Superman shirt, with the "S" spread broadly across my chest and shoulders and big, beefy arms bulging from my sleeves. I wanted a chiseled jaw that you could cut marble with and no overhanging gut.

By visualizing the reality that I wanted to create, I was able to change my eating habits and significantly diminish my emotional attachment to food. Over time, I reprogrammed my mind to not use food as my primary source of happiness. That's not to say I don't occasionally reward myself with food anymore. Life's too fucking short not to eat cookies and ice cream occasionally. I simply learned to control my indulgences and to consciously think about what I was eating 90% of the time.

To get that broad chest, big arms and chiseled jaw, I set a goal to go to the gym everyday and gave myself no excuses. On days that I didn't feel like working out, I would tell myself that I had to at least drive to the gym and park in the parking lot. I could at least do that.

Once I was in the gym's parking lot, I would then tell myself that I had to at least go inside and do 15 minutes of strenuous activity to make the trip worthwhile. I kept a gym bag in my truck at all times, with shoes, headphones and clean workout clothes in it. I gave myself no excuses. When I worked out, I kept my headphones on and focused on my goals. I didn't chit chat or socialize too much; however, the little old ladies at my gym loved to gossip with me and I obliged. It was quite adorable, and I loved it.

Doing that consistently for a few weeks really helped me set a strong routine, which eventually became a change in my lifestyle. It didn't take long for me to become a gym rat. I found the daily physical activity to be an immense stress relief and began seeing rapid results.

By the fall of 2008, I looked like a completely different person. People who hadn't seen me in a while almost didn't recognize me. Between my carefully monitored diet and daily workout regimen, the extra fat I was carrying melted off me, and I began to put on significant muscle mass. I felt better than I had ever felt in my life. I started thinking more clearly and my attitude improved as I felt balanced and in control of my life.

Reclaiming my physical and emotional health was an empowering feeling and my confidence soared. I needed that in 2008 because my professional world was falling apart, and I had no control over it. While my financial troubles continued to mount over the next couple of years, my ability to manage that stress became easier. My acid reflux eventually dissipated, and my overall mental and emotional health skyrocketed.

I tried to get Wendy to join me on my journey to a healthier lifestyle, but I don't think she was ready to take it seriously, no matter how much I encouraged her. I told her how great I felt with the changes I'd made and tried to motivate her to do the same. I didn't berate her or throw "bro speak" at her to motivate her. I understand how difficult it is to change. You must want to do it. I don't think Wendy really understood what I was going through though and that hurt me.

It was at that point that I finally accepted that I didn't want to spend the rest of my life with Wendy. I wanted more from the person I spent the rest of my life with. I did love Wendy still, but I had to accept the fact that we had grown into two different people.

My relationship with my sister, Cami, developed heavily around this time because I reached out to her to talk about how I was feeling in my relationship with Wendy. Cami was tremendously helpful about how to handle the situation and was never judgmental. I learned a lot from her and began to understand her better. She always listens to what I have to say, and I'm happy that we developed a strong relationship during that period of my life.

In November of 2008, I broke off my relationship with Wendy and asked her to move out. It really tore me up inside because I knew that she loved me. But I could no longer ignore what I was feeling inside.

I had Cami reach out to Wendy almost immediately after breaking up with her so that she could help Wendy get through it all. I don't know if that was inappropriate or not, but I did it with only good intentions.

If ever there was time in my life when I needed to turn things around and get a boost of optimism and hope, taking responsibility for my health in 2008 was it. My life changed dramatically at the age of 33. It put me on a much more positive and rewarding life path. Learning to be honest with myself was fundamental in helping me navigate through the next few years, while I rebuilt my life. I lost most of what I had worked for in my bankruptcy a couple of years later, but with the confidence and strength I found in 2008, I was able to let go of it all and step into a more satisfying life.

Over the last 17 years, I've maintained a relatively clean diet and gone to the gym everyday. I can't imagine going back to my former lifestyle now. I began to push myself further and challenge myself to find my limitations. I entered mud runs and obstacle course races with friends and eventually took up long distance running. In 2014, I set a goal to run a full marathon before my 40th birthday, and I did. The following year, I ran 50 miles a week, every week, for a year. I also learned to pay attention to what my body needed, including rest and recovery.

I also went searching for love again. And found it rather quickly.

Cammers

I love my brother and sister very much, but sometimes I feel like there is a great divide between the three of us. We've all gone through some serious struggles in the last 20 years. The highway of life has left each of us with emotional scars and road rash. Carey struggled for many years to find a lucrative career after he got married. Cami went through a divorce soon after her daughter, Nora, was born and has been a single mother for the last decade.

We don't talk about those stressful periods in our lives very often. For some reason, it's difficult for me to have deep, meaningful conversations with Carey and Cami. I've made no secret of the fact that I often have trouble communicating with Carey as an adult. He and I were close growing up but drifted apart in our 30s. And although my relationship with Cami is stronger now than it was in our youth, I still feel like my connection with her is strained.

Don't get me wrong, we don't fight or despise each other by any means. In fact, when you put the three of us in a room together, it usually takes less than two minutes for the laughter to start. Sarcasm and dark humor are our native tongue. We reminisce about our childhood and swear like we're still teenagers. When we're all in a good mood, it's fantastic. But unfortunately, it's been a while since we've been able to do that.

Somewhere along the way, we all put up emotional walls to avoid talking about the hard moments that have shaped our lives. I take my share of the blame in that. It is admittedly difficult for me to think about the years 2007-2010, let alone want to discuss them with anybody.

As previously discussed, the wall between my brother and I went up in the Fall of 2007, after I advised Carey to wait on getting married until he was financially stable. After that fallout with my brother, I realized that if I wanted to maintain a relationship with Carey and Cami as adults, I needed to listen to them more and dial back my role as big brother. I had to stop offering unsolicited advice and simply offer unconditional love. It was hard coming to grips with that. Sometimes it still is.

In coming to that understanding though, my relationship with Cami blossomed in 2008, during one of the most tumultuous periods of my life. My company was on the brink of going under and I was terribly anxious about my future. I had very little love for myself back then and was terrified to let go of what little security I did have. Talking with Cami made me realize that the reason I was having a hard time letting go of Wendy was because I was afraid no one would ever love me again. Cami helped me identify that insecurity, which allowed me to face it and move on.

Both Carey and Cami received their masters' degrees in counseling, however Carey did not pursue it as a career. Cami, however, has been working as a counselor for over 20 years now and is currently a therapist for cancer patients at a hospital in Charlotte. She's very good at her job because she is passionate about the work. When she first started, Cami worked as a counselor for abused children. Some of the stories she's shared with me over the years have made my soul ache and my blood boil. One of Cami's former patients was a pre-teen girl whose mother had sold her to a motorcycle gang for drug money. The level of depravity in that act is truly inconceivable to me.

I could not do what my amazing sister does for a living. The emotional weight of her job would be too heavy for me to bear. Cami is, without a doubt, much stronger than I am in that regard, and I'm incredibly proud of her.

As adults, Cami and I have developed a fairly strong relationship together. We have pet names for one another now. She calls me Co-Co, and I call her Cam-Cam, or Cammers. In our youth, my relationship with Cami was typical and less intimate. Like all big brothers do, I teased her occasionally but was never cruel or malicious. I once told Cami that if she drank too much apple juice, an apple would grow inside of her, and she might die. It was my way of securing the last bit of apple juice in the fridge. Cami later confessed to me that she was terrified of drinking apple juice for many years after that.

Growing up with two older brothers, Cami learned to stand her ground rather quickly. She developed a nasty little temper in her youth and eventually started throwing punches whenever she got teased. I thought her reactions were a bit excessive at times, but I can't deny that it worked. I stopped messing with Cami after I shot her with a water pistol, and she responded by drawing blood.

Because I'm five years older than Cami, we didn't have much in common growing up. When I turned 16 and started driving, she was only 11. When I went off to college, I wasn't around much to talk to Cami as she went through high school. Regrettably, I didn't make much of an effort to connect with her back then. I was just too busy with my studies, working, and playing in a band. That's not an excuse, just the facts.

I know Cami had a rough time in high school. Despite having plenty of friends, I think she was depressed and felt very lonely. Cami and I are very similar in that we're both highly creative people who get bored easily. Also, like me, she had trouble finding her identity and often felt like she didn't fit in anywhere. We both wore masks to hide that discomfort.

Carey, on the other hand, seemed to have his shit together throughout grade school. He did well in his academics, was heavily involved in student government and other leadership groups and had a different girlfriend every time I came home from college.

Carey's search for identity didn't begin until he entered college. A few weeks before he started his freshman year, Carey lost a good friend in an automobile accident. I tried to talk to him about his feelings, but I'm not sure I was of any help. In my free time Carey and I would hang out, but I could tell he felt very isolated and alone. He eventually transferred to the University of North Carolina at Charlotte to get a fresh start.

Cami also attended Appalachian State when she graduated from high school. Although when she started in the fall of 1998, I had already graduated. So, once again, Cami and I didn't see each other very often. I moved back home, and she moved out. Although when I did get to see Cami, I could tell she was happier and more comfortable in her skin. I think gaining her independence on a college campus gave her the opportunity to reinvent herself. We've never really talked about that period of her life though. It's just how I remember her then.

When Cami came home from college on weekends, she would sometimes go cruising with me on my motorcycle. She'd hop on the back of my bike, and we'd take a long ride through the countryside together. I enjoyed that time with her. It was especially fun when Dad could convince Mom to get on the back of his bike and ride with us. Mom never liked being on a motorcycle.

When Cami is genuinely happy, she radiates an infectious joy to everyone around her. She has a beautiful smile, a wry sense of humor and a quick wit. She's also highly intelligent and well-spoken, with an eccentric sense of style. Like me, she constantly needs some form of artistic endeavor to focus on. It's how we both find balance in our lives.

Cami has made me many custom Christmas gifts over the years, and I cherish every one of them. After I built my first house in Walnut Crest, Cami gave me a homemade scrap book titled, *The House That Corey Built,* with pictures of the home throughout its construction. She also wrote a hilarious poem chronicling the struggles I went through in building it. It meant so much to me that Cami took the time and energy to show her love like that. She's given me many wonderful gifts like that over the years.

***

Towards the end of her college career, something happened to Cami which seemed to radically change her state of mind. She altered her appearance and developed a 'devil may care' attitude almost overnight it seemed. She became uncharacteristically moody and would go from being happy to miserable in a matter of minutes. If you asked her what was wrong, she would put on a forced smile and reply, "Nothing". She closed herself off to almost everyone.

Cami was later diagnosed with bi-polar disorder, which is characterized by dramatic mood swings between manic highs and depressive lows. It can cause hyper anxiety, loss of sleep and decreased clarity of thought. My father says that his mother struggled with similar mood swings, which makes sense because bi-polar disorder is also reportedly high in genetic predisposition. Grandma Maher was never diagnosed with bi-polar disorder though because it wasn't an official diagnosis until 1980.

The first time that Cami intentionally hurt herself, it was incredibly hard for everyone in my family to process. It devastated Mom and Dad of course, and it shocked both Carey and me. To this day, I have a hard time understanding what Cami is going through. She doesn't like to open up about that side of herself too often, and I respect that boundary. But it pains me to see her suffer the way she does sometimes. I hope she knows she can always talk to me, even if it is just to cuss, rant or rage. I have a lot of experience with that.

I think my biggest hope in writing this book is to use it as a steppingstone to re-connect with my brother and sister again. I want to understand them better and talk about our internal struggles over the last 20 years.

I hope to connect with my siblings on a more intimate level because, in the coming years, the three of us are inevitably going to share a significant amount of emotional trauma when we lose our parents. If I can begin to develop a better understanding of Carey and Cami now, maybe the three of us will be able to support one another more comfortably when life becomes inevitably unbearable.

The *Shadow Man* is always standing in the corner of my room, ever present in my mind.

Starting Over

At the start of 2009, shortly after I broke up with Wendy, my high school sweetheart, I found myself wading into the confusing waters of dating. I was on a quest to find my one true love. Although, to be honest, I don't think I thought of it that way back then because I don't think I really believed in true love by that point yet.

I knew that I didn't want to start my dating journey by being set up on blind dates through friends or family. I wanted to find someone outside of my inner circle so that if things didn't develop with someone I was set up with, I wouldn't have to explain why. I was hoping to enter the dating world without too much drama, if that was possible. But I was confident in knowing what I wanted in a partner, and I was certain that it would take some time to find her.

The woman I was looking for had to be intelligent, well spoken, fitness oriented and attractive. She had to be self-sufficient and gainfully employed without being too uppity and posh. And it would be fantastic if she liked heavy metal music and would go to concerts and shows with me. I didn't really care if she had been previously married but was admittedly wary of dating someone who had children from a previous marriage. Again, I wasn't looking for drama.

My ideal mate would also have to be comfortable with my financial situation, which was dismal at best, at the start of 2009. My construction company, Drakestone, was sinking so far into debt by that point that my impending bankruptcy looked almost guaranteed.

Being self-employed, I really didn't have a typical office environment in which to meet potential partners. And I've never been a "player" to frequent bars and clubs to pick up women. I never really had an appetite for casual sex or "hooking up". I don't judge people who embrace that lifestyle. I just prefer intimacy and companionship. I need someone who will sit beside me and be my ride or die, able to take the wheel whenever I lost control or wanted to drive off a cliff.

At first, I thought maybe I was setting my bar too high and that I was looking for a unicorn. But I compromised for far too long with my ex on a lot of issues and, when I decided to end that relationship, I vowed to stick it out in the dating world for as long as it took to find my perfect fit. I thought for sure I was entering into a long dating war that would take years.

But what the hell do I know? It only took 6 days!

On January 6, 2009, the Day of Epiphany as celebrated in Christianity, I met my ride or die future wife, Rebekah Leann Bowen.

Because I was comfortable with computers and the Internet from a young age, I started my journey back into the dating world by first taking my chances in the world of online matchmaking. So, technically, I guess Rebekah and I first met online a week earlier through Match.com, the internet dating website founded in 1995. I don't know exactly how many users there were on Match back then, but I remember there were hundreds of women with profiles in my area when I started looking. And, remarkably, Rebekah was the first woman I met.

After scrolling through dozens of profiles of women, I came across Rebekah's profile and was immediately captivated by her beautiful smile. So, I nervously sent her a message. I'm not sure what I said, but I'm sure it was awkward and full of typos. Thankfully though, Rebekah responded, and we talked through message boards for a couple of days before setting up our first date on 1/6/2009 at a small, boutique restaurant called The Cajun Yard Dog, just a few miles from my office.

I've always been a jeans and t-shirt kinda guy, but for some reason, when I went to my first date with Rebekah, I decided to treat it like a job interview and wore a button-down shirt and khakis. I knew she had just returned to Charlotte a few months earlier, after having lived in Raleigh for a few years out of college and was now working as an executive assistant in a large accounting firm in Uptown Charlotte. So, I figured business casual was the best approach to take for our first face-to-face.

But when I arrived at The Cajun Yard Dog, Rebekah was already there, wearing jeans, black boots, a t-shirt and a black leather jacket. It was the first thing I noticed about her when I walked in, which made me immediately regret my choice of wardrobe.

Despite my failings in choosing clothes that evening, the date went spectacularly well. Rebekah and I ate dinner, drank a few beers and talked nonstop for three hours. It was amazing to me how well we communicated so quickly and how much we had in common. Although Rebekah is seven years younger than me, she grew up in Charlotte just 10 miles from my childhood home and went to Providence High School, same as me. She even knew my sister and had taken the same trip to

Seattle, WA with the Women's High School Choir that Cami had been on in 1998 and that my mom had chaperoned.

Rebekah's first job was at a Chic Fil A – a fast-food joint – across the street from the very McDonald's where I got my first job. We had a lot of rather abstract commonalities like that because we both grew up in the same area and came from similar socio-economic upbringings.

I guess that all sounds kind of lame and unromantic though, so I should probably add that I was also strongly attracted to Rebekah on our first date. Her smile, in person, was even more beautiful than the one on her dating profile, and she looked pretty hot in those black leather boots she was wearing. Rebekah's always had great legs.

I wouldn't call our first date a "love a first sight" moment though. It was obvious to me that, despite how well we got along, Rebekah did have her walls up pretty high. She had gone through a bad break up in Raleigh in 2008 and had moved back home in the summer of that year to get a fresh start. She was living with her parents at the time and commuting Uptown to work everyday to save up some money and pay off some debt.

Rebekah had also gone on a few dates with some other guys she had met on Match before me and had some terrible experiences. She had to ghost one guy at a sushi restaurant when he began to berate the waiter because he thought his vegetable tempura was "too greasy". *It's beer-battered and fried, dude. Of course it's fucking greasy.* Rebekah politely excused herself to go to the bathroom and never went back to the table.

So, I could understand why Rebekah had her shields up on our first few dates. But I can't say that she was the only one with walls up high. I was shocked when I left the restaurant after our first date and drove home wary about getting too excited on how awesome I thought it went. After all, Rebekah was literally the first woman I met on my dating journey. How could I possibly believe that I would find my perfect fit in the first woman I meet? That's just absurd.

But I still went home that night and messaged her to see if she wanted to hang out again sometime.

A Deal with the Devil

Despite both of us being relatively guarded, Rebekah and I had our second date the very next night. Again, we drank a few beers, had some dinner and talked for hours. This time I wore jeans and a t-shirt.

We talked about music and movies, and we discovered how similar our childhoods were growing up. Like me, Rebekah has two siblings and grew up in a loving home with parents who worked and provided every opportunity for them. Our core values and work ethic appeared to be similar, and despite the seven-year age gap, our cultural roots were also fairly aligned.

Rebekah idolized her older brother, James, who is my age, and much of her taste in music and movies originated from him. She loves heavy metal and was even singing in her younger brother, David's, metal band at the time. David plays guitar too and was still in high school at this point. Their band had a very European, symphonic metal sound, like the Finnish metal band Nightwish, whom Rebekah also idolized.

The more I learned about Rebekah, the more I liked her. But I also began to grow increasingly suspicious. Things that are too good to be true usually are. I kept waiting for the other shoe to drop and reveal something to me that would turn me off to her.

"How does the first woman I meet be a hot, intelligent woman who sings in a metal band and appears to have her shit together?" I thought to myself cautiously.

I was waiting for Elizabeth Hurley to show up in her skintight red leather outfit from the movie Bedazzled and make me an offer to have Rebekah fall in love with me in exchange for my soul. To be honest, I was partially inclined to accept that arrangement at the time. If Elizabeth, herself, was unavailable to fall in love with me, that is.

Rebekah and I continued to see each other regularly over the next several weeks and had a wonderful time getting to know each other. She did stand me up a few times though. She had started working at an accounting firm in the summer of 2008, so the start of 2009 was Rebekah's first experience of "tax season". Those are the months between January and April in the United States where accountants put in long hours to count all of the beans their clients had made in the previous year and then calculate how many of those beans had to be given to the government. Because Rebekah had to routinely work late in her office during busy season, she had to cancel a few of our dates at the last minute.

I didn't mind getting stood up by Rebekah for work, though. The way I saw it, Rebekah was simply prioritizing things that mattered in her life and chose her job and future employment over hurting my feelings. I suppose some guys would get upset at that, but I didn't. It attracted me to her even more. She was hard-working, independent and gainfully employed. That's exactly what I was looking for.

But on the nights when I didn't get ghosted because of her busy work schedule, Rebekah and I continued to connect perfectly. She was informed and well read, spoke intelligently and held to her opinions if challenged, which I found very sexy. She wasn't afraid to talk *Zorch* and have meaningful philosophical discussions. For the most part we landed on the same side on almost all major issues. When we talked about sex, politics and religion, we both agreed on the same fundamental ideology: *Enjoy your life and examine all possibilities. Do no harm but take no shit. Help others when you can.*

We were candid with one another from the start like that. It really was like we were two old souls who had met previously, in a past life, and were re-connecting again to pick up where we left off. Our senses of humor aligned almost perfectly. We both have a penchant for subtle, juvenile jokes and being sarcastic wise asses. We can have fun for hours in each other's company, like two kids in a candy store.

One of the things that I love about Rebekah is her ability to quote movies. Like me, she's a film buff, and can pretty much quote *Ghostbusters* in its entirety as well as *Empire* and *Raiders*. When the movie *Deadpool* came out in 2016 and we both heard Ryan Reynolds proclaim his love to Morena Baccarin by saying, "Your crazy matches my crazy", Rebekah and I immediately looked at one another and grinned. It summed us up completely. We say that line to each other all the time now.

We once went to a party at a friend's house and, while on a tour of their home, the host casually said, "That's the bedroom", which made Rebekah lean into me and whisper, "But nothing ever happened in there". To which I immediately replied, "What a crime." Then we both giggled like 14-year-olds while everyone else looked at us confused. *That's from Ghostbusters, BTW.*

Although we got along famously from the start, Rebekah and I didn't have our first kiss until our third or, maybe, fourth date. I may be wrong about that though and, if I am, I'm sure she'll correct me. I do know for a fact, however, that our first kiss was after we had gone to see the movie *Australia*, starring Hugh Jackman and Nicole Kidman.

My God, that was a long and tedious movie. I'm sorry Hugh but, if you're reading this, it was my least favorite of your films. I love everything else you've done though.

Enduring *Australia* for 2 hours and 45 minutes wasn't all that bad though. Whenever Hugh had his shirt off, which was most of the movie, Rebekah would get a little handsy with me, which was a first in our blossoming relationship. So, after the movie, I walked Rebekah to her car and took my shot. I'd like to say it was a deep and passionate kiss, but I honestly remember it as being sweet and comforting. Again, like two old souls reuniting with one another.

When things eventually moved into the bedroom after a few weeks, we were both fairly clumsy at first, but the connection was definitely there. I don't like to kiss and tell, but our sex life did eventually get pretty hot and spicy. After about a year of dating, we did it in the bathroom of a municipal building while attending my cousin's wedding. We snuck out like two teenagers after the ceremony and took care of business before returning to the reception smug and satisfied.

I hope her parents don't read this.

The Bar Fight

R ebekah was raised in a devout southern Baptist home, and her parents hold on to very traditional values. She was required to go to church every Sunday while growing up and was raised in a rather strict household relative to mine. Rebekah's parents wouldn't let her watch MTV because I guess, to them, it was just hedonistic nonsense. I, on the hand, watched Headbangers Ball religiously and was allowed to gobble up all the devil horn action I could stomach.

But what Rebekah wasn't permitted to do in her youth was made up for and more by the strong discipline and classical education that her parents provided her with. She was taught to read at a very early age, and her mother, Maria, would take her to the library to find books that interested her and to rent VHS tapes of classic films like *Gone with the Wind* and *Fiddler on the Roof*. Maria also made Rebekah take piano and vocal lessons at a young age. When Rebekah turned 14, she told her parents that she wanted to get a job and they supported her by driving her to and from work for many years. As a result, Rebekah learned the value of a day's work and to take responsibility for herself.

Rebekah's father, Jim, never missed one of her Choral Recitals and was a family man, like my own. They took regular family vacations and drove all over the country during her youth. When Rebekah was 18, Jim bought her a car, which allowed Rebekah to get to and from work and her after-school activities, like working on the stage crew in the Theater Department at Providence High School.

I've known Jim and Maria now for 16 years and, in that time, I've grown to love and appreciate both of them dearly. They've always been supportive of me and Rebekah and are always there for us when we need a hand with something. I'm happy that my parents and Rebekah's parents get along so well. We've taken many family vacations together and have always had a blast. So, I hope you don't misunderstand me for what I'm about to say next.

The only real problem that Rebekah and I ever had was while she was living with her parents during those first few months that we dated. Rebekah would often ask me to pick her up at her parents' house whenever we'd go out. She was living under her parents' roof after all and wanted to keep up that 'good girl' image for them. I didn't mind picking her up for our dates though. I could tell that Rebekah wanted a proper courtship from me, and I was OK with that. It told me that she respected herself and her parents and that she expected me to be a gentleman. Who could be upset with that?

The problem I had was that Rebekah was 27 years old and still had a relationship with her parents like she was 17. Because of her parents' conservative nature, Rebekah wasn't "allowed" to stay overnight with me, even after a few months of our dating. I'd have to drive her back home at the end of every date to appease her parents and save her from the hassle of being chastised. It felt really odd to me.

I was 34 years old when Rebekah and I started dating and had been on my own for well over a decade. I was living an adult life, going through very serious adult problems, like dealing with the realization that my construction business was going under. Taking Rebekah home to her parents' house every night after one of our dates made me feel like I was dating a high school girl again.

I understood the necessity of Rebekah living with her parents to save money, but her relationship with them had yet to evolve to a point where they respected her as an adult, capable of making her own decisions. And Rebekah didn't seem ready to set her own boundaries and evolve into an adult relationship with her parents. It started to bother me a lot, and I think Rebekah started picking up on it.

The only come to Jesus moment that Rebekah and I have ever had was on Saint Patrick's Day in 2009 when Rebekah told me that she wanted to get engaged, just two months after we first met. *She's gonna kill me for writing about this. Don't bother looking for my body. You'll never find it.*

Rebekah and I went to some Irish pub to have a Guiness for the sake of the day, and I broached the subject about Rebekah getting her own apartment.

"We've been dating for a couple of months now and we haven't really spent a full night together like normal, adult couples do. I get that you don't want to disappoint your parents by staying over at my house, but if you had your own apartment they wouldn't know."

Rebekah's response to me was, *"My parents wouldn't be disappointed if we were engaged."*

ME: <blank stare>

And that's how the fight started, Your Honor.

I'm not going to go into the details about that fight because Rebekah and I buried those bones a long time ago and there's no need to go digging into that grave. But that's the way I remember the fight starting, and if she doesn't agree, she can write her own damn book.

I came close to walking away from her after that fight. I just wasn't going to put a ring on her finger because she couldn't find the courage to set boundaries with her parents. Too, I had lived with my ex for many years before I met Rebekah, and I was certain that I wasn't going to get engaged to anyone before living with them for at least a year. You find out a lot about someone when you live with them for a year. I lived and worked with Dillon for almost a full year before I realized he was an alcoholic and needed some serious help.

But Rebekah's parents were more traditional. Her older brother, James, got engaged within six months after meeting his now ex-wife, Courtney. They got married within 1 calendar year of their first date. That was the kind of conservative ideology that Jim and Maria expected Rebekah to adhere to. But, as much as I liked Rebekah, I wasn't prepared to do that.

Thankfully though, before I could make a bad decision and leave the relationship, Rebekah stepped up and took the judgmental hit from her parents by starting to gradually stay overnight with me at my house on the golf course. By the summer of 2009, Rebekah found a one-bedroom apartment for herself, and I helped her buy furniture and move in. From that point on, our relationship was smooth sailing.

I think I did love her at that point, but I can't remember if I had told her that yet. I'm good at remembering moments and their places, but not exact dates and timestamps. Rebekah's the more detail oriented one in our relationship. I think she has a spreadsheet of every significant moment of our lives together, with dates, times and locations collated, the document notarized and signed by two witnesses. I wish I could tell you that that was a joke, but she is a Notary Public.

Crazy Train

After Rebekah moved into her tiny one-bedroom apartment in the summer of 2009, our life together really took off. I stayed over at her place throughout most of the second half of that year. We slept on her queen size bed, which I barely fit on by myself. I'm still not sure how we both managed to sleep on that thing.

This was around the time when my family was playing musical houses. My parents were living in the house that I had built for myself in Hickory Hollow, taking care of Caesar and Shep, and Carey and his family were living in Mom and Dad's house, trying to get on their feet. I was living sparsely in my model home, still for sale, on the golf course in Stonebridge, but I was only there during the days and on weekends.

While Rebekah was working Uptown, I would go to Stonebridge during the days to work on appraisals and give Max and Pumpkin some love and attention. In the evenings I would meet Rebekah back at her apartment, and we'd have dinner together, go to the gym, hang out and watch TV. We both enjoyed the amazing 2003 reboot of the sci-fi show *Battlestar Galactica*.

On the few occasions when I tried to go back to Stonebridge for the night, Rebekah would guilt me into staying with her at her apartment. She didn't really have to try too hard though. I was really enjoying being with her and wanted to stay. I just wished we could have fit a king-size bed in her cramped bedroom.

On the weekends, Rebekah and I would meet up with friends at bars and restaurants in the Plaza-Midwood district of Charlotte or go shoot pool together at a joint called Bailey's, just down the road from Rebekah's apartment. Chuck would usually hang out with us on weekends. I was happy that Rebekah and Chuck got along so well. The three of us would go to concerts and shows together and sometimes go down to Myrtle Beach to stay at Chuck's parents' condo for a few days. On quieter weekends, Rebekah and I would 'staycation' at my house in Stonebridge and relax in each other's company.

Over the holidays in 2009, Rebekah and I took a trip to Washington D.C. to get out of town and do something new for a change. We visited all the typical tourist attractions, like the Lincoln and Washington Memorials. We saw the Tomb of the Unknown Solider and watched the changing of the guard there. We also walked through the Museum of National History and saw one of Abraham Lincoln's hats on display, which delighted both of us.

Our trip to D.C. was the first of many traveling adventures Rebekah and I would eventually take. We both love to travel and do it very well together. She likes to navigate and map out our daily sightseeing stops, while I follow her lead and simply enjoy the ride. It works because I don't like doing the day-to-day planning stuff, whereas Rebekah finds joy in it. All I have to do is say, "Let's take a trip to Great Britain," and, within a few days, Rebekah will present me with a list of travel dates, a daily itinerary and budget. Who wouldn't love that kind of arrangement?

It was at Amos' Southend, a small concert venue in Charlotte, where I first told Rebekah that I loved her. *I already admitted that I don't remember the exact date.*

Rebekah and I went to see an Ozzy Osbourne tribute band at Amos', and the lead singer who performed was incredible. He looked, sounded and acted just like Ozzy, the band was tight and sounded amazing. I got to see the real Ozzy a few times in my youth and the band we saw that night sounded as good, if not better, than the real deal.

Now I may be overly romanticizing this in my memory, but I honestly remember hearing the song "Mama, I'm Coming Home" being played at the exact moment when I realized that I loved Rebekah. I may be wrong about that though, and it could have just as easily been "Crazy Train".

We were standing in the back of the venue, near the bar, because we had both just ordered beers, when the song started. When I looked over at Rebekah, she was swaying back and forth to the rhythm being played and singing along, with a beer in her hand and that gorgeous smile spread across her face. She looked angelic to me at that moment, cast in a soft blue light emanating from the stage.

Then it just hit me.

This is a woman I could spend the rest of my life with and be happy.

From the Castle to the Dungeon

At the beginning of 2010, I finally had to accept the fact that I was going to lose everything that I had worked for in the last ten years. The housing market was not recovering as I had hoped, and my financial situation was grim. Like so many other homebuilders caught with their pants down, the music had stopped, and I didn't have a chair to sit in. I was tapped out and could no longer afford to pay the mortgages on my three homes, which meant they would eventually be foreclosed upon and sold at auction to the highest bidder. So, at the start of 2010, I had no other choice but to move into a small, two-bedroom basement apartment of my own.

Because I was giving up my homes to creditors, my parents had to move out of the house in Hickory Hollow and back into their own house with Carey and his family while I took Caesar and Shep back to live with me in my dungeon apartment. Even though my new place was just a couple of miles from Rebekah's apartment, I would continue to go over and stay with her in the evenings. But I would routinely have to go back and forth to let the dogs out and feed everybody. It was such a chaotic time in my life, filled with uncertainty.

But having Rebekah by my side through all of it was a blessing. She never treated me like a failure, even though I felt like one at the time.

Instead, she encouraged me to keep working, persevere and have faith in the future. Rebekah was a beacon of hope to me during that period. I'm not sure I could've made it without her.

When the lease on Rebekah's one bedroom apartment ran up, we decided to get an apartment together and stop all the running around. Rebekah had a lot of anxiety about telling her parents that she and I were going to move in together. But her fears turned out to be overly exaggerated because her father agreed that it was a sound decision and gave Rebekah his support. Jim's not dumb. I'm sure he understood that Rebekah and I had been practically living together for a year already. Why waste money on two apartments?

So, in the summer of 2010, Rebekah and I officially moved into an apartment together, along with Caesar, Shep, Max and Pumpkin. It was my third move in 18 months and Rebekah's third move in two years. The apartment that we moved into was a two-bedroom, top floor unit that had come available in my apartment complex. I had to get out of my basement apartment. I think all four of the kids that lived above me were in the fucking marching band and it was driving me nuts.

Living with Rebekah has always been easy. From the beginning, we just naturally found an equitable rhythm in splitting household chores and duties. I usually do the cooking and grocery shopping while Rebekah takes care of paying the bills. We each take initiative in doing the dishes and laundry, taking out the garbage and such.

At night, we go to bed at the same time, and in the mornings, we get up together to start the day. That may sound passé, but I've found that getting on the same circadian rhythm as your partner is very important to maintaining a strong relationship. There's something to be said for starting and ending your day at the same time with your partner. It creates a natural balance in the relationship and provides ample time to talk and stay connected in each other's lives.

Our first year of living together was stress free for the most part. We were a bit cramped in a two-bedroom apartment with two large dogs and two cats, but we were happy and relatively comfortable. I continued to work in my appraisal business during the day while Rebekah maintained her position at the accounting firm in Uptown Charlotte, commuting every day.

The only real problem we had while living in our first apartment was navigating the two flights of stairs coming and going. One weekend Rebekah and I went to have breakfast at a nearby diner that we frequented. We had planned on going to see a movie that afternoon, but Rebekah got very sick after breakfast. At the diner that morning, we both had omelets, but Rebekah's had spinach in it and mine did not. Considering spinach is well known to carry E. coli and needs to be properly washed before cooking, it was easy to assume that food poisoning was the cause of Rebekah's digestive issues.

By mid-afternoon that day, Rebekah was laid up on the couch, looking pale and pitiful. She had been throwing up nonstop since we had gotten home from the diner and was dizzy, so she asked me to take her to the emergency room to see a doctor. Because she was so weak, I practically had to carry her down the two flights of stairs to get her into my truck. At one point she passed out on me while we were navigating down the stairs, and I had to shake her to get her to wake up. It scared the shit out of me.

When they took Rebekah back for examination at the E.R., I wasn't allowed to go with her because we weren't married. Jim and Maria arrived at the hospital shortly after we did though, and I was eventually allowed to see her. It turns out Rebekah was severely dehydrated from all the vomiting, and the nurses had to use five liters of saline to get her body back to equilibrium and rehydrated.

After that experience, I was kind of over apartment living and wanted to get back into a house without two flights of stairs to climb when coming and going. Especially when I would have to walk the dogs three or four times a day to go potty. I really missed the convenience of simply opening up the back door and letting the dogs out. Plus, Caesar and Shep were almost 10 years old and taking all those stairs was not good for them. Big dogs can easily develop hip and joint problems as they get older.

So, at the start of 2011, I kept an eye out for homes we could possibly move into at the end of our lease in the apartment. The problem with that was that I couldn't qualify for a mortgage after having gone through bankruptcy in May of 2010. But because my appraisal business was still thriving, and Rebekah and I were living well below our means, I had managed to save up a good bit of money and had enough for a down payment on a home.

I suppose we could have always rented a home to get out of our apartment, but I knew that that would be a short-term fix, and we'd end up having to eventually move again. And I was tired of moving every 6 or 12 months. The only other option we had was for Rebekah to take out a mortgage using the money I had saved up as the down payment. Basically, Rebekah had the credit, and I had the cash. There was just one snag to that plan: It would also require an engagement ring.

That really wasn't a snag though, because I knew then that Rebekah was the woman I wanted to spend the rest of my life with. I loved her and knew in my heart that my life was better having her in it. I was ready to take the plunge and, in early 2011, Rebekah and I started looking at engagement rings.

An Awkward Engagement

While Rebekah and I started to look at engagement rings and talk about getting married in the Spring of 2011, I continued to try finding us a home to move into. Thankfully, Rebekah wasn't interested in a very expensive ring. She's never been Madonna, *A Material Girl.* But she did take her time to see what was out there, and we looked at several jewelers around town before she eventually found a ring she liked. But before Rebekah found that ring, I found us a suitable home within a couple of miles of our apartment in the Stone Creek Ranch subdivision.

The house that I found was perfect for us. It had an open floorplan with the primary bedroom on the ground floor, and it sat at the end of a private street, with easy access in and out of the neighborhood. It even backed up to a wooded area for some added privacy and was located within ten minutes of both our parents. The only drawback to the home was that it was located close to the Interstate. But it was an all-brick home, which insulated it well against noise, and you couldn't hear the traffic from the Interstate while inside. Plus, it was a short sale offering, which meant that the owner had to unload the house, and we could probably get a good deal on it.

Rebekah fell in love with our home on Tom Short Road the first time we looked at it together. I didn't have to sell her on it at all. Like me, she was tired of living in apartments and loved the open layout of the home. So, we made a low-ball offer to the sellers and waited for them to get the bank's approval.

Buying a home out of a short sale is a very tedious and exhausting process. The seller has so many legal authorizations and bank procedures to go through that it can sometimes take months to get a signed contract returned, which is what I was anticipating.

While we waited to hear from the seller, Rebekah and I continued to spend weekends looking at engagement rings. I had not officially proposed at this point of course, but we both knew it was coming. After all, I had already trusted Rebekah with $40,000 to use as a down payment on the house. If the bank didn't approve the sale, she could have easily just walked away with my money and left me high and dry. But I knew she wasn't that type of person, and I had faith in what our future looked like together, so I was never worried.

I also realized that, to some degree, Rebekah and I were putting the cart before the horse by trying to buy a home together without first being married or even officially engaged. I wanted to try and at least surprise her with my marriage proposal. She deserved that after two and a half years of courtship. But coming up with ideas on how to propose to Rebekah proved to be difficult for me and, before I could devise a plan to put into action, the seller unexpectedly accepted our offer on the house and set a quick closing date, which meant Rebekah had to submit her loan application for the home sooner than I anticipated.

The mortgage broker that helped Rebekah and I buy our home on Tom Short was none other than my buddy Gary, the same broker who had helped me re-finance my first house in Walnut Crest after getting in over my head and going over budget. Gary was a good guy and had been in the mortgage game for a long time. I knew that he could help us navigate through the murky waters we were in. Nonetheless, it still got awkward when we met with Gary to fill out the paperwork.

Gary: *"I'm assuming you two are engaged, right?"*

Corey: *"Yes."*

Gary glances down at Rebekah's hand and smiles: *"So where's her ring?"*

Rebekah's eyes go wide as she gives Corey the 'Deer Caught in the Headlights' look.

Corey, caught off guard: *"Well, I haven't actually gotten down on one knee yet, but I did give her $40,000 for the down payment on the house. Isn't that enough?"*

Gary: *"Technically you have to be engaged when she submits this mortgage application. Otherwise, you can't gift her the money for the down payment. I'll need both of you to sign a statement that you are engaged when I submit the loan package tomorrow."*

So, technically, there is a legal document floating around somewhere that says Rebekah and I were engaged before I officially proposed. I didn't want it to happen that way. It just sort of all fell together quickly and in the wrong order I suppose.

I knew that Rebekah was scared when we left Gary's office that day. She was taking on just as big a risk as I was in all of this. If I walked away from her now and didn't propose, she couldn't make the mortgage payments on her own and be able to eat at the same time. If I got cold feet on her, she'd be in a real shit situation.

But it didn't end that way. It ended with me totally surprising Rebekah and catching her off guard when I proposed a month later. And, to my delight, she DID NOT see it coming.

Sneaky Bastard

In 2011, my mother turned 60. Her birthday is on August 16th. I had thrown my dad a surprise party for his 60th birthday a few years earlier at the local German restaurant, 'The Waldhorn', and really wanted to do something similar for Mom that year. It has always been difficult for me to try and pull one over on Mama Bear. She knows me all too well.

But being the sneaky bastard that I am, I devised a plan to play Rebekah and my mother against one another by organizing a joint surprise engagement/birthday party at the same time. And, to my delight, I snowed both of them.

I told Rebekah that I was planning a surprise birthday party for Mom, and I told Mom that I was planning a surprise engagement party for Rebekah. With both of them keeping their respective secrets from one another, the ruse came off flawlessly.

Somehow, without Rebekah knowing, I managed to secretly invite her family, friends and co workers to meet us at Maggiano's Italian Restaurant on Saturday, August 14, 2011. I also quietly invited a lot of Mom's friends and family to the party. I can't take all the credit in managing this though. I had a lot of help coordinating from Cami and Dad as well as Rebekah's friends Jessica and Sarah.

On the day I proposed, Rebekah initially got dressed in a long cotton gown for what she thought was a surprise birthday party for my mom. What she didn't know was that I had arranged to take Rebekah and my parents to the Winghaven Botanical Gardens in the Myers Park district of Charlotte that morning to propose, while guests arrived at Maggiano's for the surprise party afterwards.

While Rebekah looked beautiful in her cotton gown that she had originally chosen to wear that day, I thought she might regret that choice of wardrobe if she really knew what was going on. It was going to be a big day for both of us with a lot of pictures being taken. When I casually asked Rebekah if she would mind changing into one of her classier summer dresses for my mom's party, I thought for sure she'd get suspicious and catch on. But, to my surprise, she remained oblivious and changed into a cute purple sundress that showed off those gorgeous legs of hers.

It was a really hot day in Charlotte when I proposed to Rebekah. But the Winghaven Botanical Gardens and Aviary were well shaded and absolutely beautiful. Mom, Dad and Cami were with us. They all knew what I was about to do. I also had Jim and Maria hiding in the Gardens, by a small fountain, where they could watch and celebrate afterwards. If my folks were going to be there, I knew Rebekah would want hers there too.

Funny story about how I asked Rebekah's father for her hand in marriage. I took Jim out to dinner, and we talked about the house and all the renovations I planned to do before we moved in. I had a lot going on in my head during this time and everything just spilled out of me over dinner with Jim. I talked about how Rebekah and I were going to furnish the house and how I was going to propose to her and how I was also secretly planning a surprise birthday party for my mom to catch Rebekah off guard. I just rambled.

Jim and I have always gotten along well, so I felt bad when I got home from dinner that night and realized that I never *actually* asked him if I could marry his daughter. I instead just kind of told him I was. The next day I called Jim and apologized for not actually asking, and he laughed. He wasn't offended or upset. When I then asked him if I could marry his daughter, Jim said he had never seen Rebekah so happy in her life and said yes.

So everybody was in on it at the Gardens except Rebekah that day. On our way to the Gardens that morning, Rebekah wanted to know why. I told her that we were stopping at Winghaven to stall for some time.

"You know, we'll walk through the Gardens with Mom to kill some time and allow all the guests to show up at her surprise party before we arrive."

Rebekah bought it hook, line and sinker but still complained that it was going to be too hot and that her face was going to melt off.

As we walked through the Gardens, I kept Rebekah in front of me. When we reached the small water fountain I took a deep breath, pulled out the ring, got down on one knee and said, "Here we go baby. Are you ready?"

Rebekah, whose back was to me, replied, "Jesus, it's hot out here. Ready for what?"

"I guess that's about as good as I'm going to get at this point, huh?" I said dryly.

When Rebekah turned around to find me on one knee, her face went white for a moment, and she gasped. I didn't say it out loud, but in my head, I said, *"Gotcha!"*

To keep things succinct, here's a poem I wrote to describe what happened next:

I asked and she said yes.

She cried.

We were both sweating.

It was hot that day.

and my feet hurt.

My loafers were too tight

and I had soaked through my shirt

But she said YES

To being my wife

And, from then on after,

Everything was alright

We left Winghaven shortly after so we could get to our surprise engagement party, which we still kept Rebekah believing was a surprise birthday party for my mom. When we arrived at Maggiano's and opened the doors to a roomful of 90 people who screamed "SURPRISE", everybody jumped. Even I did, and I was expecting it.

To the very end, both Mom and Rebekah were snowed. Rebekah looked around the room and pointed to Mom that all her friends were there, and Mom was pointing out that all Rebekah's friends were also there. They both got confused, and I literally had to explain it to them. It was a proud moment for me. I should be working in the CIA. I can pull off a decent set up.

We had a great time at the party. I was happy to see so many of our family and friends show up. We had two cakes, one for Mom's birthday and one for our engagement. It was a special and memorable day.

The next month, when Rebekah and I actually closed on the house, we were officially engaged so no crime was committed at closing. Before we moved in, I arranged for some updates to be made to the home, like remodeling the master bathroom and painting some color on the walls.

In October of 2011, Rebekah and I officially moved into our first home together on Tom Short Road. It was a long road getting there for us. We started out in Rebekah's one bedroom apartment, eventually progressed to a two-bedroom apartment and now, we were moving into a three-bedroom home of our own. At the end of that move, we were both exhausted and agreed that we weren't going to move again for at least 10 years. We made it for 8 years.

Rose of My Heart

On the day I married Rebekah, I had no anxiety. I was actually really happy because the day that Rebekah and I had been planning for over a year was finally upon us and I could enjoy it. I was well aware that I was marrying up and proud of it. But between glad handing family and friends, posing for wedding photos and doing the dog and pony show, I really can't recall much of that day. However, one particular memory will always remain with me.

When the doors to St. Mary's Chapel opened and the bridal march began to play, I got my first glimpse at Rebekah in her wedding gown and was absolutely floored by her beauty. She was radiant and glowing and looked more beautiful than I could have possibly imagined as she walked down the aisle with her father.

In that moment I remember thinking to myself that, just a few years earlier, I was a defeated man. My health was poor, I was in a relationship going nowhere and my construction company was on the brink of going under. Somehow, I had managed to crawl out of that situation, reclaim my health, get back on my feet and was now standing on top of the world, about to marry the most beautiful and perfect woman I had ever met.

I found my perfect fit in the very first person I met. It was as if the Universe guided me to Rebekah and offered me a blessing when I crawled out of that hole and found the courage to go on. I have no idea if there is a purpose, plan or design to life, but I've experienced enough good fortune against odds to make me believe that, every now and then, someone or something will step in and wink at you from on high.

Our ceremony was brief. I only interrupted the Minister once, but it came off funny to everyone in attendance, so there was no foul. Rebekah and I said our vows to one another and performed the ancient Celtic tradition of handfasting before lighting a unity candle and exchanging rings. On the inside of Rebekah's wedding band I had engraved the words, *"A Perfect Fit"*. The whole ceremony just felt "right" to the both of us. There was no preaching or sermons, just a celebration of our love in front of family and friends.

When we took our wedding photos outside, I thank the Gods that it wasn't too hot. I really didn't want to sweat through my tuxedo before the reception because I had bought it new and had it tailored to fit for the wedding. But, thankfully, while the day of our engagement was a scorcher, the day of our wedding was not.

We managed to get a few goofy photos in our wedding shoot. My favorite is a photo of Rebekah ripping open my button-down shirt to reveal the iconic Superman sigil underneath my tuxedo. Rebekah has this big grin on her face in the photo, like she's Lois Lane just finding out Clark Kent's true identity. That photo is blown up on canvas and hanging in the dining room of our home. I smile every time I look at it.

Rebekah and I both think that our wedding reception was a huge success and that everyone had a blast. We rented a novelty photo booth where our guests could take goofy photos for our wedding scrapbook as well as have prints made for themselves as keepsakes. That was a big hit with everybody, and I still look at those photos often. They play in a slideshow on a digital picture frame in my office.

Jim was very generous in providing Rebekah and I with a fabulous wedding reception, but I wouldn't let him pay for the booze. I made a deal with Jim that I would pay for the open bar at our reception but also told our coordinator at The Big Chill that I had a $5000 hard cut off. After we hit that, it would become a cash bar. Our friends Ralf and Caroline flew over from Germany for our wedding, and I knew Ralf could put away some wine. I once saw him drink a cruise ship bar out of their entire white wine selection.

I don't know how we didn't hit the limit on the open bar that night. From the amount of dancing and fun everyone appeared to be having, I thought for sure that everybody was drunk. Rebekah and I did not get hammered though. With the exception of a few glasses of champagne and a couple of beers, we left our reception stone sober.

Our first dance was to Johnny Cash's "Rose of My Heart". We both love that song. Rebekah had never heard it before. When I played it for her, we both immediately agreed on it for our first dance. It's simple, beautiful and just aches with soul. Johnny recorded that song late in his career, after his wife June had died. And Johnny sings that song in heartbreaking fashion in that recording. If you've never listened to it, do yourself a solid.

We were first introduced as Mr. and Mrs. Maher while Metallica's "Master of Puppets" played. Rebekah agreed to that without objection, being yet another reason why I knew she was the one for me. "It's like I made you on my computer!" I said to her gleefully when she agreed.

We had cupcakes for the guests, while Rebekah and I had a small pecan pie wedding cake to cut into. We were kind though and didn't smear cake all over each other after we cut into it. She threatened my life. We noshed on that cake for a couple of weeks after the wedding. It was so good.

At the end of the reception, Rebekah and I bid our adieu and raced through a torrent of bubbles that our guests were blowing on us as we made it to our limo. We didn't go home that night though. We stayed in a suite at the Ballantyne Resort to spend our first official night as man and wife in romantic style. Everything was going splendidly with that plan until Rebekah remembered that she forgot to feed the cats before she left for St. Mary's Chapel that morning. Max and Pumpkin hadn't eaten all day.

"You want me to go home and feed the cats on our wedding night?" I asked her incredulously.

When Rebekah refused to accept my claim that a 24 hour fast was good for animals, I sighed heavily and grabbed my keys. I kissed her gently, told her that I loved her and that I wanted a divorce before I left.

It wasn't that big of a deal though. Our house was literally a ten-minute drive from our hotel, and I was only gone for 25 minutes. And in those 25 minutes Rebekah had taken the opportunity to slip into something more scandalous and was very generous in her apology for making me go feed the cats. The day ended exceptionally well. We had marriage locked down on day one.

Going for Distance

L ife was good in 2012. Rebekah and I took a trip with my folks to Ireland in the summer as well as planned our wedding, got married and had our honeymoon. It was a busy year, but I was happy and full of optimism and ambition once again.

Even though the global financial crisis of 2008-2009 was starting to recover and the markets were cautiously climbing out of the mess, my appraisal work was still slow. I had lost almost everything in my bankruptcy and needed to try to make up for lost time and start rebuilding for my future. So, I started to watch the financial news and follow the markets closely to start doing some day trading in the stock market.

I did fairly well in most of my trading. I was smart enough not to trade with a lot of money and didn't risk the house or anything like that. I was just trying to figure things out and work on my skills to read the markets. It was hard work and stressful, but I stuck to it. I was determined to find my way back to financial success and was confident enough once again to start taking risks, both financially as well as physically.

In the Fall of 2012, I convinced my buddy Jason to run the Spartan Beast with me. The Beast is a 13-mile obstacle course race with extensive trail running, mud crawls and grueling challenges, designed not only to test you physically but to challenge your mental fortitude as well. Jason and I ran the Beast in November of 2012 and, when we finished, we agreed never to do that shit again.

On the one-hour ride home from the Spartan Beast, I was so dehydrated my legs cramped up on me multiple times. When we finally made it home, I pulled into our driveway and literally fell out of my truck, I was so cramped and exhausted. Jason, of course, just laughed and took a picture of me as I tried to get up off the ground.

Running that race sucked. I gassed out too early and was made woefully aware of how weak my endurance was. But Jason and I apparently have short memories, because after we downed several beers, got a good night's sleep and weren't peeing brown anymore, we planned on running another Beast in 2013. So, to help build up my endurance, I decided to start running outside for distance every week as a part of my training regimen. I wanted to be able to run 13 miles at the next Beast without gassing out and crawling across the finish line, exhausted.

Growing up playing baseball, basketball and football, I usually sprinted whenever I trained. I was never a distance runner. In Junior High track, I ran the 100m and 400m events. Learning how to run long distances was difficult for me at first because I didn't understand how to pace myself or how to find rhythm and focus in my breathing to control my exertion of energy. But, eventually, after a few months of consistent effort, I was able to find a rhythm and pace that allowed me to run farther than I ever thought I was capable of.

The most important thing I learned while working on my long-distance running was how to control my breath. Through focused breathing, I could control my pace, which allowed me to manage my level of output and kept me from gassing out too early.

I eventually found a relaxed, natural rhythm to my breathing that would ebb and flow throughout my run. I even started to experience a "runners high" and would enter a state of flow, where I would simply lose track of all time and just run without thinking. I would often finish a run and not even realize that I had been running for over 2 hours. Physiologically, a runner's high is when the body releases a surge of endorphins in your brain that creates a state of euphoria and decreases stress levels.

A lot of times I would be so focused on my breathing that I would not even see other people on the public greenway, where I would often run. I had to apologize to a few friends who said they waved to me on the greenway, but I didn't wave back. I had to explain to them that I wasn't ignoring them. I simply wasn't paying attention to the people around me because I was focused on my form, my pace and my breathing.

As a result of this, I think I unknowingly began to meditate.

When most people think of meditation they think about sitting down with their eyes closed to try to clear their minds and become relaxed. Buddhist monks use chanting and sound vibration to enter a state of meditation. In western religions like Christianity, Islam and Judaism, prayer and silent contemplation are emphasized. In Hindu, the traditional practice of Yoga was achieved through the reciting of mantras, which are meant to bring about a state of interconnectedness between the body and the mind. The goal is to awaken the spirit and thereby reach a heightened state of consciousness, self knowledge and understanding.

But the fundamental principles of meditation are all the same. It's about focused breathing, connecting to the body's senses and being present in the moment, which is exactly what I was doing on my long runs. For a couple of hours every week, I was effectively emptying my mind while I was running and, in the process, began to find myself becoming more relaxed and less anxious in my everyday life. I found the mental health benefits to my running to be extraordinary and totally unexpected. I was just trying to increase my endurance and stamina so that I could run another Spartan Beast without feeling like I got hit by a truck when I crossed the finish line.

Now I might lose some of you here with what I'm about to say next because it's going to sound weird and a little hard to understand. Hell, I still have a hard time understanding it myself. Whenever I talk about this with friends or family, I can tell they don't understand and, most of the time, they end up looking at me like I'm nuts. But it is something that happened to me and it fundamentally changed my life, so I've got to write about it no matter how much of a quack I end up sounding like.

In the Spring of 2013, after having meditated consistently while running for several months, I had a very powerful, lucid dream. I've experienced lucid dreams before, mostly in childhood, and am familiar with them to an extent. But the dream I had in the Spring of 2013 felt so real and so powerful that my perspective and approach to life completely changed overnight. I woke up feeling reborn, with an overwhelming feeling of deepened wisdom and a significant decline in my fears about life. In short, I had a spiritual awakening.

The Dream of Rebirth

"I'm dying," was the first thing I remember thinking. I was weak and frail and felt like I was over 1000 years old with the memories of several lifetimes bottled up inside of me. I was ready to let go and wanted to die.

I was lying in a hospital bed with tubes and wires connected to various parts of my body. The machine I was connected to had little white lights on it that blinked in a hypnotic rhythm but made no sound. In fact, there was no sound at all. Not just quiet, but a void of sound.

I could sense the presence of others around me and had the strong sensation that I was not in my own world, but somewhere in the distant future, maybe even on another planet or in another dimension.

I've experienced lucid dreams since childhood, but this dream was unlike anything I had previously experienced. The level of conscious awareness and cognitive ability I had was extraordinary. I felt a profound sense of meaning and importance in the dream, as if I was being shown something and needed to pay attention.

"This is a weird hospital. There are no hard lines anywhere. No corners or edges or doors. I can't tell where the floor ends and the walls begin. Everything blends together so smoothly. It's beautiful, but disorienting."

The room was sterile and pristine, with a strange, yet comfortable, feel to it. Everything was white. The walls, ceiling and floor looked glassy, like white marble. The vase on the white table, next to the machine keeping me alive, was white. The flowers in the vase were also white and smelled like gardenias. It felt like a stage of set scenery, with everything placed purposefully and having meaning.

A large, concave window materialized in front of me, flooding the room with a rich golden glow that bathed me in a warm light. In my frail state, it took significant effort to shift my eyes to gaze out the window, but when I did, I was in awe at the vast desert landscape presented to me. Smooth, rolling sand dunes shimmered like water under a deep blue, cloudless sky. I could see each grain of sand in absolute clarity if I focused on them.

"It's too perfect," I thought to myself. *"This isn't real."*

I heard a sniffle from across the room, which broke the void, and I slowly turned my gaze from the window to see a large group of people gathering around me. They were sad and crying.

"There's Mom and Dad.... No, wait, that's not Mom and Dad .... Yes, it is. ... No, No, No.... there's Mom and Dad over there, next to... Mom and Dad. How do I know all of these people? I have strong memories with every single one of them... They are all my family, from different lives I've lived."

While I had a strong connection to my own consciousness, I also had the collective memory of many lifetimes previously lived. It was confusing at first, but not frightening. It felt natural, like I had done this many times before.

One by one, my family members stepped forward to say goodbye. Several of them kissed my hand or my forehead, wiping away tears from their eyes as they did. They didn't speak. Nothing was ever spoken. Every one of them looked me in the eyes, and I could recollect the memories I share with them vividly.

When my family finished the parade of tears and stepped away from me, my memories of them faded into clouds and I was left in a profound state of emptiness, which was comforting. I could feel myself slipping into eternal sleep.

I inhaled deeply, somehow aware that it would be my last breath. My family, still gathered around my deathbed, sobbed as I exhaled slowly. My eyes grew heavy as I turned away from them to look out the window. With my last breath gone, I focused on the horizon of the desert landscape outside.

Just before my eyes closed for the last time, I saw a brief flash of white light, far out in the desert, like someone used a mirror to reflect light directly into my eyes.

An eruption of energy exploded in my mind as a kaleidoscope of colors and sacred knowledge flowed through me like a river. I could feel myself becoming whole again, returning to unity and one with everything in existence. There was no pain or suffering, no comfort or relief. Everything I was experiencing was happening in one fluid state of consciousness. Nothing was separate from me.

When I decided to exit that state of unity and higher consciousness to return to a state of separate existence, I did it freely and of my own accord. I desired to experience separation again so that I could later experience becoming whole. When my eyes re-opened, my family gasped and backed away in fear. I had returned to the same hospital room. What had felt like an eternity of bliss and wholeness to me was a mere moment of grief for my family.

I was filled with renewed life. My once frail body began to regenerate and seemed to reverse in aging. As my body reformed and my new life took form, I began to pull the various electrodes, wires and tubes off of me because I no longer needed their support. Everyone around me was stunned and confused when I sat up and climbed out of bed, full of youth and vitality.

My family members trembled in fear at the sight of my rebirth. They couldn't understand what was happening. They had watched me die and now come back to life. To them it was unnatural. Somehow though, I retained the knowledge that there is no beginning or end to consciousness and that, fundamentally, there is nothing to be afraid of.

In front of me a large set of steps materialized, leading down into an immense mausoleum of catacombs and crypts. From out of the darkness below, several of my past reincarnations emerged. They came from many different time periods, some of which I recognized but many that I could not. I had the strong feeling that the ones I could not remember were from other dimensional realities. But they were all me, from lives that I had once lived. I had chosen them to accompany me in my rebirth.

As the various incarnations of my former lives marched slowly out of the catacombs, they lined up in front of me. Behind me, another set of steps materialized, this time leading up to an immense door that pulsed and radiated with the unique energy of "life".

I turned and began to climb up the steps towards the immense door. My former lives followed me up the stairs, leaving my family down below confused. With each step I took, every one of my previous incarnations fused into my being. I could feel all of them, with the knowledge and experience that they'd attained in previous existences, merge within me.

When I reached the summit of the steps and stood before the majestic door, I entered into a relaxed state and took my first breath. I could feel my lungs fill with air and knew I was about to return to my own reality. The door cracked only slightly before a blinding flash of light once again exploded in my mind. And I stepped through.

I woke up in the middle of the night, in my bed at our Tom Short house, shaking all over and sweating more than a hooker in church. My mind raced as everything I had just experienced flooded in at once.

"What the fuck was that?!" was my general state of mind for about 30 minutes. I just laid catatonic, in my sweat drenched bed sheets, and tried to get my head on straight. I kept trying to rationalize to myself that it was all just a lucid dream, but I just couldn't accept that. This dream was so tangible and felt so real, I couldn't dismiss it.

I could feel a change within me. My mental and emotional states were altered and my core values and priorities shifted. I felt like I was in a perpetual state of inner calm that I inherently trusted and had faith in.

It was, for lack of a better explanation, my spiritual awakening.

Fundamental Change

After my dream, I lost complete interest in day trading and following the financial markets. I realized that I was just chasing money and had been attacking my life like it was something to conquer and dominate, pushing and forcing my way towards a future that I believed to be ideal and that would bring me happiness.

I laughed at myself with the sudden understanding that, in fact, all I was doing was standing in my own way and was blinding myself to the many opportunities that life was subtly offering.

After experiencing that dream I felt like my entire consciousness shifted into a state of relaxation and calm, and I held on to a strong faith that if I could just quiet my mind, listen to that little voice deep within me and pay attention to what was happening in the moment, all of the answers to life would present themselves. I imagine it's how Neo felt at the end of the movie *The Matrix*, when he finally understood what Morpheus had been trying to explain to him. I became unafraid of life and stopped thinking about when it was going to end.

My interest in philosophy and spirituality soared after that dream. I dove, headfirst, into trying to understand what happened to me. Like I said earlier, whenever I would try to discuss it with my family and friends, even Rebekah, I would be met with blank stares. My enthusiasm for what I had been shown in my dream was confusing to most and I couldn't effectively explain it, so I stopped talking about it with people. But privately, I jumped into a rabbit hole and tried to read and understand as much information as I could to hopefully gain better clarity about what I had experienced.

In my research, I learned a great deal about eastern philosophy. I read and listened to many lectures by the 20th century philosopher and professor of religious studies, Alan Watts. And from my research, I came to believe that what I experienced in my dream was what Zen Buddhists refer to as Satori, which is a moment of awakening, signifying a deep, intuitive understanding of one's true nature and the nature of reality.

Don't get me wrong. I don't think I'm some sort of prophet or Buddha. I didn't start going to temples and chanting mantras or anything like that. It was just satisfying to me to learn that other people have been experiencing what I had experienced for as long as there has been recorded history. And to those that have not experienced it, trying to describe it can sound strange, superficial and sanctimonious. I get that.

If I haven't lost you completely by now and you are curious in trying to better understand what I experienced, I humbly suggest you listen to the lecture "Zen Bones" by Alan Watts. You can find it on YouTube. It's the best explanation I could find of what my spiritual awakening felt like.

I told you in the prologue of this book that I don't have the recipe for a fulfilling life, and I hold to that statement. I don't feel like I have any answers to give you from my brief moment of enlightenment. All I can say with certainty is that there is far more to reality than what our everyday senses can reveal. I do believe we all have the capability to connect with something deeper within ourselves and attain a better, more peaceful, acceptance of it all. I wish I could tell you how to do that, but it happened to me seemingly by accident.

The dream I had in the Spring of 2013 gave me the understanding and confidence to let go of my preconceived notions about what a fulfilling life is. I no longer approach life as something to beat into submission and conquer, but instead, I try to flow with it, like a sailboat adrift in the ocean. I can steer my rudder, hoist my sails and point my boat in the general direction I want to go, but I have no control over which way the wind is blowing.

In accepting that fact, I felt as if an enormous weight was lifted off of me, and I found a sense of freedom that I never thought possible.

Drama and My Misunderstanding

I've been a professional actor for over a decade now. And, if I'm completely honest, I'm not sure how I feel about it anymore. After what happened on my last acting job in October of 2024, I was forced to take a break from it. But I'll get into that later.

In high school, I took drama classes in my senior year and was in one stage production, Shakespeare's *Much Ado About Nothing*. Mr. Kusterer, my high school drama teacher, encouraged me to take drama classes after seeing me give a speech to the entire school when I ran for student government. I'm grateful to Mr. K for encouraging me to get on a stage and give acting a try but, admittedly, I wasn't ready to take acting seriously in high school. I was just too self-conscious and unsure of myself.

However, the greatest achievement I received in high school came from Mr. Curtis, my high school history teacher, who gave me an "Excellence Award" for my performance in "Much Ado About Nothing". Receiving an accolade from Mr. Curtis gave me a real boost of confidence because I respected him. Back then, I needed as much confidence as I could get because, like most people at that age, I was still trying to discover who I was and what my strengths and limitations were.

I liked having fun and playing over-the-top characters in my high school acting classes, but I found dramatic acting and working on character profiles to be boring and silly. I also found the warmup exercises that actors do at the start of class to be ridiculous. I had no intention of becoming an actor after I graduated high school. I did want to be a heavy metal rock star though. So, I guess, in a way, I did have ambition for the stage, just in another medium.

During my last semester of high school, a friend of mine named Allison Latta convinced me to attend a few acting classes at the University of North Carolina at Charlotte (UNCC) with her. Allison was a brilliant actor and very funny. She loved everything about theater and the dramatic arts and was planning on making a career out of it. I can't remember how Allison talked me into taking the classes with her at UNCC. I think I had a mild crush on her, but we never dated or "hooked up", although we did go to an R.E.M. concert together, which I thought was spectacularly boring.

While I did enjoy Allison's company, I did not enjoy the acting classes at UNCC. Most of the students in the class were phenomenal actors, and I felt completely out of my league being there. I was uncomfortable with dramatic scenes and playing characters that required me to show emotional vulnerability. It takes great courage to be a performing artist. Whether you are an actor, musician, singer, comedian or ballet dancer, you need an astounding resilience to rejection and criticism. All art is inherently subjective. I thought the R.E.M. concert was boring as hell, but Allison loved it and sang along to every song.

In college, I didn't study acting at all. I focused on business, finance and guitar. My brother Carey, however, obtained his Bachelor's degree in Theater from UNCC after transferring out of Appalachian State after his freshman year. Regrettably, I advised Carey not to get a degree in Theater because I thought it would limit his options in the workplace after college. I should have kept my mouth shut though and not said anything to Carey, because it created an even larger wedge between us. Things were never the same between us after he transferred out of Appalachian State.

In 1999, *Remember the Titans* was filmed in Atlanta, GA, which is about 200 miles south of Charlotte. The film starred Denzel Washington, and the casting department of the production was looking for local actors to be in the film. When they held an open audition to fill roles for the supporting cast, Carey wanted to audition but needed a scene partner to go with him, so I volunteered. I wanted to help him out and thought it would be a way for us to mend our strained relationship from college. Round trip, it's an 8-hour drive to Atlanta from Charlotte, and I was thinking the time in the car would give us a chance to talk again.

When Carey and I went to the open audition for *Remember the Titans*, we stood in line for a couple of hours with a hundred other actors looking for their big break. I remember everyone in the waiting room being nervous as hell, except me. I had no skin in the game and wasn't looking for a role in the movie. I was there to support my little brother.

Unfortunately, my plan backfired because after Carey and I performed our scene in front of the casting agents, I was the one that got a call back for a second audition, while Carey did not. I could tell Carey was pissed, and I truly felt terrible. However, I was intrigued that I had gotten a call back audition, so a week later I drove back to Atlanta by myself.

At my second audition for *Remember the Titans*, I had skin in the game and was nervous as hell. I didn't do well because I took it too seriously and, like a lot of actors, sabotaged my performance by getting in my own way. On that long drive back to Charlotte, after bombing in that audition, I deflected the rejection I was feeling by once again telling myself that acting was silly and a waste of time. I still didn't understand it.

In 2002, after my band Channel Black had disbanded and I had given up my rock star ambitions, Carey decided that he and a buddy of his were going to move to Los Angeles and take their shot at the big time. They arranged to drive across the country together and move into an apartment with a mutual friend, who was already living in Hollywood. At the last minute though, Carey's buddy backed out on him.

Mom and Dad didn't want Carey to make the cross-country trip alone, so they asked me, at the last minute, to go with him. Driving across the country with Carey was not as bad as I thought it was going to be. We had fun together on that trip. We both got to see the American West for the first time and were thrilled to see armadillos, tumbleweeds and cactus in the wild. We even detoured into the Rocky Mountains for a day, to get out of the heat.

When Carey and I finally arrived in Los Angeles after a long, four-day journey, I was not impressed with the city or its people. I thought it was dirty and full of hustlers. I stayed for a couple of days to help Carey settle in and then flew home to Charlotte to get back to my appraisal business and start making my own bad decisions.

It was tough saying goodbye to Carey in Los Angeles. I was genuinely heartbroken leaving him there.

Carey lived in L.A. for about a year and worked on a few studio films as a production assistant, but he never landed any acting roles. He eventually became disenfranchised with the glitz and glamour façade that is Hollywood and drove back home to start grad school at Appalachian State in 2003. He studied psychology and counseling, like Cami.

I'm proud of Carey for having the courage to go all in and take his shot at Hollywood. I don't think I could have done it. I often wonder why I never found the courage to take the same leap of faith with my ambitions in music. I suppose I'm just too pragmatic to be an "all or nothing" type of guy.

It would take me 20 years after high school to eventually find the courage to try acting again. I gained plenty of life experience in those years and was able to find myself in the process. I built my first house, started a construction company and then lost everything when the housing market crashed in 2008. My general health and well-being also suffered during that time because I got fat, stressed and depressed from all the pressure I was under. I also failed in love by ending the relationship with my high school sweetheart of 16 years.

But while working through all of that, I managed to reclaim my physical and mental health and move on to find true love with my wife, Rebekah. I developed a deeper understanding and acceptance of who I was. I experienced so much in those 20 years that it broke me down to my core and forced me to humbly accept failure and take a more relaxed approach to all areas of my life.

The Lounge

I was officially bitten by the acting bug in 2013. In the spring of that year, I had a very powerful dream which, overnight, seemed to reawaken a creative spirit within me. After that dream, I needed an outlet in which to focus that energy. I was bored reading in my free time and wanted something more engaging to sink my teeth into. It was time to feed the creative monster that had been dormant inside of me for many years.

On August 25, 2013, my buddy, Jason, and I ran our second Spartan race together at a ski resort in Virginia. The race was literally on the day of my first wedding anniversary with Rebekah, and she was rightfully a little miffed about spending our one-year anniversary at a mud run with Jason Kendlehardt.

I didn't feel too bad for Rebekah though because we had a two-week trip to Italy and Germany planned for the following month to attend the wedding of a friend. Plus, the ski resort where the Spartan race was being held had a day spa. While Jason and I were trudging through the mud, in one of the hardest physical challenges I've ever endured, Rebekah was getting pampered with a deep tissue massage and champagne. Of the two of us, Rebekah is obviously the smarter one.

After Jason and I finished the Spartan race, we took a picture together to commemorate our achievement, and I posted it on social media. A friend of mine jokingly commented that I looked like an action hero in the photo and should audition to be in the next *Expendables* movie, with Sylvester Stallone and Jason Statham. It was from that random comment that the seed to pursue acting again was planted in my brain.

In October of 2013, I was scrolling through social media and saw an advertisement for a professional acting studio in Charlotte that offered a wide variety of classes for all ages and experience levels, from beginners to professional working actors.

I had seen the ad for "The Actors Lounge" several times before but never had any serious interest in pursuing it. But after my powerful dream in the spring and then receiving a random comment that I should be in an action movie, my curiosity got the better of me, and I arranged to sit in on a beginner's class at "The Actor's Lounge" and observe.

To be honest, I wasn't sure if acting was something I would enjoy or want to pursue at that point. I remembered not enjoying the acting classes I took at UNCC with Allison Latta, while still in high school. I wondered if I would still find acting to be 'silly'. But I was curious enough to want to try it again. A newly awakened part of me kept screaming: *"PLAY AND EXPERIENCE LIFE!!"*

The instructor in my beginner's class at "The Actors Lounge" was a fantastic acting coach by the name of Pat Dortch. Pat is a little older than me and a veteran screen actor. When I walked into my first class at 'The Lounge', Pat took one look at me and said, "You should've played Jack Reacher, not Tom Cruise."

Jack Reacher is the title character in the best-selling book series by the author Lee Child. I wasn't aware of that in 2013 though. It wouldn't be until January of 2020 that I would randomly discover my first Reacher novel and become an immediate fan of the man who says nothing.

In 2012, the first Jack Reacher movie was released, starring Tom Cruise as the stoic ex-military wanderer who fights injustice wherever the wind takes him. Many fans of the books thought Tom Cruise was a bad choice to play Reacher because Mr. Cruise is only 5'7" tall, whereas Reacher in the books is 6'5", a much larger man. Personally, I thought Tom Cruise did a great job in the movies, but I can also understand the backlash from fans. Reacher's imposing physique is a trademark feature of the character.

After sitting in on a class taught by Pat Dortch at "The Actors Lounge", I enjoyed it and decided to enroll in the program. The classes were designed not only to train students in the fundamentals and methods of professional acting but also to provide insight into the business of filmmaking and television production.

Pat Dortch was a big reason why I enjoyed my return to acting. His teaching methods were relaxed, and his critique of students' performances was positive and constructive. Pat wasn't stuffy or snooty, like the acting coaches from my youth. He taught his classes in a manner which was fun as well as informative, like mentoring his students on the effective approaches to auditioning and providing firsthand experience on what to expect when working on a professional film set.

Acting at the age of 38 was a completely different experience for me than it was in high school. I was no longer uncomfortable working in dramatic scenes because I was more confident in myself. I wasn't embarrassed to show emotional vulnerability or demeaning values in front of people. I could let go of myself without worrying about what others were thinking. I found acting to be liberating in a strange way, like being given permission to stop being myself for a while.

After just two months of taking classes at "The Actors Lounge", Pat referred me to the talent agency that represented him and, by Christmas of 2013, I signed on and booked my first gig. It was a drug commercial that was filmed in a gym. All I had to do was workout in the background and be eye candy while another actor delivered lines into the camera. It was the first time I had ever been on a professional film set of any kind, so it was exciting.

Enrolling in "The Actors Lounge" was one of the best decisions of my life because it was the start of a wonderful creative outlet for me. Pat Dortch was one of the greatest teachers and influencers of my life. Taking his class at "The Actor's Lounge" allowed me to find joy in acting. In the years that followed, I would end up working on several big budget productions, alongside "A list" actors and directors. From that work, I was inspired to start writing, producing, and directing my own independent films, which ultimately led me to finding my voice and style of writing, acting and directing.

I had a lot of fun studying at "The Actors Lounge". I met some great people and developed some wonderful friendships there.

But unfortunately, I got kicked out after a year.

Wait, What?

At the start of 2014, I felt reborn in having a new creative outlet to explore. I decided that I wanted to be a professional actor and began looking for opportunities to work on professional film sets as often as I could. Most of the acting jobs that I did early on were working in "background". Background actors are the people who walk around in the peripheral of the scenes, without lines. They're more commonly referred to as "extras".

Working in background is the lowest level of acting on a film set, and it generally doesn't pay very well. But I really didn't care about the money. I was more interested in learning how professional film sets operated and wanted to get a feel for how the cast and crew performed their magic. I figured that obtaining as much experience as I could on studio productions would later help me to be more relaxed and comfortable when it came time for the cameras to be focused on me.

I worked in background on several different productions in 2014, including the films *Hunger Games* and *Ashby* as well as the television shows *Banshee* and *Homeland*. I had a few small speaking parts in various productions like the film *One and Two*, where I played a doctor, as well as the television show *American Genius*, where I portrayed the real-life rocket scientist, Werner Von Braun. I also played a Viking king on *The Originals*, a spin-off show from *The Vampire Diaries*.

In the summer of 2014, I signed up to go on a weekend acting retreat through "The Actor's Lounge". It was a Friday through Sunday workshop which focused on various acting methods for character development. The retreat was being held in the mountains at a small cabin resort, and it sounded like fun.

The weekend workshop was being run by the founder and owner of "The Actor's Lounge", who was also the instructor of my advanced acting class, to which I 'graduated' after successfully completing Pat Dortch's beginner's class. Unfortunately, I did not enjoy the advanced class as much as I did Pat's class. I found it to be stuffy and pretentious, like the acting classes from my youth. But I signed up for the weekend actors retreat anyway because I was curious.

After signing up for the retreat, I continued to submit for work in background and landed a featured role on the film *Masterminds*, the hilarious comedy starring Zach Galifianakis, Owen Wilson and Jason Sudeikis. The film was being shot in Asheville, NC and was directed by Jared Hess, who had also directed the films *Napoleon Dynamite* and *Nacho Libre*.

When I got the offer to play a featured background role on *Masterminds*, the shoot dates did not conflict with the weekend of the acting retreat. But as often happens on film productions, things got shifted around in the shooting schedule and my scenes were pushed to shoot on the opening Friday of the acting retreat.

When I called the owner of "The Actors Lounge" to tell him that I would be arriving a day late to the weekend retreat because I was obligated to work on *Masterminds*, his reaction took me completely by surprise.

Corey: "I'm sorry that I can't make it on the opening day of the retreat. I told the casting director on "Masterminds" that I could be flexible with my schedule when I accepted the job and I don't want to burn that bridge with her by canceling. She's cast me in quite a few different productions already."

Owner 'Meh': "I'm sorry to hear that, but you made a commitment to me and to yourself when you signed up for this retreat. Building a cohesive bond with the other students over the weekend is essential to everyone having a productive experience. If you can't be there at the start of the weekend's events on Friday, then I'm afraid you won't be able to participate at all."

Corey: "I understand. But can I not come directly to the retreat as soon as I wrap on "Masterminds"? I'm not trying to blow off my commitment to acting. In fact, the reason I'll be late is that I'll be working as an actor on a major studio production."

Owner 'Meh': "As I've said before in class, working in background is not real 'acting'. When you decide to take your craft seriously, you'll understand that. I'll refund your money for the retreat... In fact, I see that you're paid up through your classes already, so I think it's best if you just part ways from the Lounge at this point and take some time to think about what you want to do."

So...yeah, I got kicked out of "The Actors Lounge" because I chose to work as an actor on a major studio production instead of going to an acting retreat. I don't really understand why it happened. I didn't waste my time trying to grovel with the owner to get back in. I simply never went back to the Lounge after that.

I feel like I made the right decision though because I learned a lot from my experience working on *Masterminds*. I played an FBI agent at a press conference and stood directly behind the very funny Leslie Jones of *Saturday Night Live* fame. We shot several takes of that scene and Leslie had the entire cast and crew laughing in stitches. In my opinion, watching Leslie work was far more of an education on professional acting than I could have ever gotten at the acting retreat.

It was very frustrating for me when I was asked to leave "The Actors Lounge" over something so trivial. I was reminded that there are a lot of fragile egos in this world. You have to tread lightly sometimes so as not to offend people. But, at some point, you also need to let go of self doubt and the need for approval. I realized that I didn't need anyone's permission to be an actor.

Getting kicked out of "The Actor's Lounge" was actually the best thing that could have happened to me because it forced me out of the nest, so to speak. It gave me the confidence and determination to fly on my own.

You Have to Want It

In June of 2015, I auditioned for the television show *House of Cards*. A couple of weeks after I submitted my audition, I flew up to Baltimore, Maryland for a callback audition and met with the Casting Director. At the time, *House of Cards* (HOC) was the flagship production of the first streaming platform, Netflix. The premise of the show revolved around the seedy political arena of Washington and followed the exploits of a corrupted Senator, Frank Underwood, and his equally despicable wife, Claire. In its first two seasons, the show won several awards, including an Emmy and a Golden Globe.

Luckily, I nailed my call back audition and booked the gig. Getting to work on season three of *House of Cards* was a big win for me. It was like being called up to the big leagues. It also meant that I had to join the Screen Actors Guild (SAG) and officially become a professional union actor.

The day that I found out that I had booked the gig on HOC, I was absolutely thrilled. I immediately called Rebekah, and we made plans to go out to dinner that night and celebrate. Unfortunately, we never made it to the restaurant.

That afternoon, I sat outside on the patio with my dogs, Caesar and Shep. I wore my shoulder out throwing Caesar's ball continuously. He never got tired of chasing that damn thing. Caesar had the energy of 10 horses when it came time to play fetch. He could go all day. But after throwing the ball at least 50 times that afternoon, Caesar eventually trotted back to me and collapsed at my feet, panting heavily. I assumed he had just worn himself out from all the running. But as the evening progressed, Caesar's condition got worse and by nightfall he couldn't stand up on his own. He was very weak and obviously struggling to breathe.

Rebekah and I skipped dinner to take Caesar to a 24-hour veterinarian hospital to find out what the problem was. It was there that we received the heartbreaking news that Caesar's heart was enlarged and functioning at less than 20%. The poor guy wasn't getting enough oxygen into his blood and was slowly dying. Rebekah and I were both devastated by the unexpected news.

At the Vet's recommendation, we made the difficult decision to give Caesar mercy. I know it was the right thing to do, but it absolutely destroyed me. It was the first time that I had to make that kind of decision for a pet. I cried nonstop for a week after losing Caesar. It brought back many repressed emotions of death and mortality. The *Shadow Man* stole my big win that day by stepping into view and reminding me that time is limited.

I'm grateful that Caesar didn't suffer too much. It happened fast, and Rebekah and I were there with him when he crossed over. On the afternoon he died, he was chasing his ball and having the time of his life. By the end of that day though, he was dying and there was nothing we could do about it. It felt very similar to how Grandpa died, unexpected and quick.

Had I known that day that it would be last time I would ever throw the ball for Caesar, I would have been more present in the moment with him. But my mind was too busy racing with excitement and anticipation about working on *House of Cards*. I remember feeling guilty about that for awhile.

To be honest, most of the experiences I've had as a professional actor have come with unexpected frustrations and disappointments. Film and television production is a very unpredictable business. When I worked on *House of Cards* in July of 2015, I learned that last minute changes are to be expected and prepared for.

My contract on the show was initially scheduled to shoot two weeks before Rebekah and I were booked to fly to Italy for the Mediterranean cruise we took with our families that year. We had booked that trip months before I had even gotten the audition for *House of Cards*. At the last minute, the production for "HOC" pushed my scenes to shoot on the day before our flight to Venice.

When I showed up to set on "HOC", I sat in my trailer for 8 hours before being told that they couldn't fit my scenes in and they needed to push them to the following day. So, at the last minute, I had to rearrange my flight to Italy and fly into Venice a day later, separate from my family. Rebekah was pissed about that of course, but thankfully I shot my scenes the following day and I arrived in Venice just in time to make it onto the cruise ship. We had a wonderful time on that vacation, but I was nervous as hell getting there. I honestly didn't think I would make it in time.

In 2016, when I booked a five-day contract to work on *The Fate of the Furious*, one of the many installments in the *Fast and the Furious* franchise, I had a similar experience. My original shoot dates were pushed to the same week that my entire family had already rented a house on the beach for a summer vacation. I got to spend two days in the Outer Banks with my family before having to leave to drive down to Atlanta and film the project.

When I arrived in Atlanta to work on *The Fate of the Furious*, I ended up sitting in my trailer for five straight days, waiting to be called to set. At the end of the fifth day, the production told me that they couldn't get to my scenes and were writing them out of the film. I was paid for my time of course but was pissed that I wasted my vacation for nothing. I would have much rather spent those five days with my family at the beach.

I was so fucking upset by my experience on *The Fate of the Furious* that I almost called my agent, Rusty, to tell him that I was done with acting. The only good thing about that gig was that the money I made from the film helped Rebekah and I remodel our kitchen.

Most of the productions that I work on are shot in Atlanta, or "Hotlanta" as they call it now. Atlanta has become the new "Hollywood of the South", with many major studios setting up shop in Georgia to take advantage of the various tax incentives the state has implemented to attract film and television productions.

Atlanta is about 200 miles south of Charlotte, and the most direct route between the two cities is Interstate 85. I have made that drive more times than I care to remember, and it absolutely sucks donkey balls. The drive can take anywhere between 3 and 7 hours, depending on what time you leave and how brave you are.

I listen to audio books to pass the time when I drive to Atlanta because it's usually a white knuckling game of nerves having to dodge construction workers while playing a deadly game of Tetris with a symphony of 18 wheelers, all barreling down the Interstate at 90 miles an hour.

I'm not much of a believer in there being a heaven or hell, but if there is a hell, for me it would be driving back and forth from Charlotte to Atlanta for eternity. It's a dumpster fire gauntlet of trashy southern culture. I have seriously thought about quitting acting on at least half of the gigs that I've worked on in Atlanta and not just because of the drive. A lot of times, I usually don't feel like the gig was worth the effort. Half of the time, I'm preoccupied with the thought, *"Why the hell am I doing this?"* In all honesty, I still don't have an answer to that question.

Not all my experiences as an actor have been that way. I've also had some fantastic moments working as an actor. When I worked on *House of Cards* for the first time in 2015, my scene was a confrontational showdown between my character, a tough Secret Service Agent, and the seditious "Mrs. Claire Underwood", played by the very talented Robin Wright.

What was special about that gig was that Robin was also directing the episode we were filming. Together, she and I rehearsed the scene and worked through it before shooting it. For the rest of my life, I can say that I got to work, one on one, in a scene with Robin Wright, on an Emmy award winning show. Achieving that breakthrough, in less than two years after first stepping into a professional acting class, is an accomplishment that I'm proud of.

***

In 2016, Rebekah and I had to say goodbye to Pumpkin, the lovable little runt who showed up on my doorstep at Halloween in 2003. She was a sweet girl, with the most adorable high-pitched meow and tiny little tail. Even though she never got bigger than a salad bowl, her heart was always full.

Unlike Max, Pumpkin loved nothing more than to curl up in my lap and knead dough on my chest. Then she would nap on me for an hour or until had I to get up to go pee. I think she needed that physical connection because she was abandoned by her mother as a kitten. I'm very grateful that Pumpkin wandered into my life when she did because I think I needed her as much, if not more, than she needed me. Her adoration and gentle purring helped me through some of my toughest years. In 2016, Pumpkin's kidneys began to fail, and Rebekah and I had to again make a tough decision to ease her pain.

Losing Caesar and Pumpkin was tough on me. I found myself dealing with a lot of heartache and grief by the end of 2016. I knew that I did not have much time left with Max and Shep at the rate things were moving. I found myself thinking a lot about death and the *Shadow Man* again.

In 2017, I was invited back to *House of Cards* to reprise my role on the show. This time though the production had given my character a name. You can imagine my dumbfounded surprise when I received the contract and found out that my character's name was "Secret Service Agent Drake".

For some unknown cosmic reason, the name Drake has carried a special significance throughout my life. Drake was the name I had given my Dungeons and Dragons character in childhood. When I started my home construction company in 2005, I chose the name Drakestone

Construction, to bring a piece of my childhood into my adult life. Being offered a contract on *House of Cards* to play a character named Drake felt like more than a random coincidence. It felt like fate.

I mean, seriously, what are the fucking odds that I would be offered to play a character named Drake in just two years as a professional actor? The name followed me around for over 25 years. And this time it was handed to me at random. I felt like the name kept calling me back. I know I'm over thinking it. Maybe it was just a coincidence. But at the time, it felt like the Universe was winking at me. I was finally going to get an opportunity to catch my big break. I had been preparing to play "Drake" my entire life.

In another remarkable twist of fate, Pat Dortch, my first acting coach, also booked a role on *House of Cards* that season. We weren't working in the same scenes on the show, but we were shooting on the same day in Baltimore, so Pat and I had dinner the night before our shoot and talked for quite a bit, which I enjoyed.

My second gig on *House of Cards* was another terrific experience. My scene was shot in the production's soundstage, on a beautiful set design of the White House. I, again, got to shoot a scene with Robin Wright, this time in the Oval Office. It was an amazing experience. When I wrapped on *HOC* that second time, I felt confident and positive about the future of my acting career.

Unfortunately, two weeks after I wrapped on my second contract with *House of Cards*, the show was run aground by reports of inappropriate behavior involving the show's leading actor, Kevin Spacey. As a result of Mr. Spacey's impropriety, he was fired by the production and the entire season was scrapped, along with the scene that I had filmed. Shortly after

Mr. Spacey left the show, the production announced that a series ending season was being written, with no part in it for me.

So, my frustrations in the acting world continued and, again, I asked myself, "*Why the hell do I do this? What the fuck am I looking for by being an actor?*"

Asking for Forgiveness

I know you're supposed to love all your children equally, but my cat Max will always hold a special place in my heart. He was my first pet as an adult and came into my life unexpectedly. I had zero interest in wanting a cat before that little bastard suckered his way into my life. I didn't choose Max, he chose me. And he stayed with me for 18 years before he died.

When Max found me in 2000, I was just getting started in the world. After I built my first house in 2002, I adopted my dogs, Caesar and Shep. Max was not pleased with having dogs in the house, but he quickly established dominance over them in order to tolerate their presence. Despite them being at least ten times his size, Max ruled over Caesar and Shep with divine sovereignty. He always maintained his seat at the top of the hierarchy. He got along well enough with the boys, but he never played with them or showed them any love.

Max wasn't a very affectionate cat. When Pumpkin showed up on my doorstep in 2003, I could feel Max's agitation. For a while, he pretended to loathe Pumpkin. But eventually he grew to love her. Within a year, the two of them began napping together and bathing each other. They would often play, racing through the house in a violent game of cat and mouse. Max always won of course because Pumpkin was only half his size. He never hurt her. He was just grumpy at times.

OK, most of the time.

If Pumpkin was the runt of the litter, left behind by her mother for being weak, I think Max left home voluntarily because he was tired of everyone's bullshit.

Max showed his love through play. At night, when I was getting ready for bed, he liked to ambush me by attacking my feet. I would then chase him around the house, playing hide and seek, until he grew bored and let me catch him. When I would scoop Max up to claim victory in the game, he would gnaw on my hand aggressively, sometimes drawing blood, to remind me that he let me win. He was fiercely independent and much too proud to concede gracefully.

I could tell he was grateful though. On the rare occasion that Max showed affection, it was very sincere. He would sometimes climb into my lap and stand on my chest so that he could place his forehead against mine. He would stay there for a couple of minutes, purring softly, and the two of us would share a deep connection together. Then he would hop off my lap, give the dogs a spiteful look and walk out of the room. Maximus Achilles Khan was the coolest cat to have ever lived.

I have very few regrets in my life, but losing Max in 2018 is one of them. Shortly after Shep died in December of 2017, Max's health went downhill. He started losing his teeth and becoming mangy. He was always an indoor cat, which is why I thought he was becoming senile when he began to wait by the patio door to try and dart outside whenever someone opened it. He had never done that before. It took me a while to realize that Max wanted to go into the woods behind our house so that he could die on his own terms. But I was too much of a coward to let him go.

I knew that losing Max would be the hardest on me. I wanted to be there with him in the end, like I was for Caesar, Shep and Pumpkin. It was important to me because it gave me closure, allowing me to be with them in their last moments. I needed to show them love and to comfort them on their journey to the other side. And while Max's health was declining, I didn't think he was ready for that. He didn't look like he was in any pain. He was still moving around OK and eating. He hadn't gone deaf or blind. He was his otherwise ornery self, a crotchety old man who seemed to get up every morning just to spite the world.

Rebekah and I started spoiling Max with food and treats towards the end of his life. Rebekah would often give Max some of her runny egg yolk in the mornings after making soft boiled eggs. Max loved that and begged for it. Eventually Max began meowing incessantly at Rebekah, first thing in the morning, until she started cooking eggs.

I told myself that when Max started showing signs of pain or stopped eating, I would take him to the Vet and give him mercy. But I never got to do that.

In May of 2018, Rebekah and I took a vacation down to our favorite resort in Mexico, Secrets Maroma. We had asked Rebekah's parents to feed and look in on Max while we were gone and they were kind enough to do so. However, in the middle of our vacation, while we were on the beach, Rebekah's father, Jim, called to tell us that Max had died in the house overnight.

The news hit me like a shovel across the face. I cried for the remaining four days of our vacation thinking about Max. To this day I still feel so much guilt over the way he died. I hope he knows we didn't abandon him. I hope he wasn't in any pain and went peacefully in his sleep. But I'll never know.

All I kept thinking on that beach was, *"He was all alone"*.

The guilt I still feel about Max's death is still heavy. It tears me up inside whenever I think about it. I don't regret going on vacation. I don't regret not taking Max to the Vet sooner. I regret not letting him out the door when he wanted to do it himself. I should've let him go and do what he felt was natural, but I was too selfish and cowardly to let him.

I hope he can forgive me for that.

Momentum and Bust

Being a professional actor is all about building momentum within the industry. After my second stint on *House of Cards* in 2017, I lost that momentum when the production scrapped the entire season due to allegations of impropriety against the lead actor of the show, Kevin Spacey. In 2018, I submitted several dozen auditions to try to keep work flowing but, unfortunately, I didn't book anything. The life of an actor is truly feast or famine.

In 2019 though, I found a seat at the table again and booked work on three different studio productions. The first gig I booked that year was for the show *Manhunt: Deadly Games*, where I played an FBI Swat Commander. The show's story revolved around the hunt for Eric Rudolph, the man responsible for the 1996 bombing of Centennial Park during the Olympic Games in Atlanta.

Ironically, I was watching live commentary from the Olympics in Atlanta when that bomb exploded. It was 1:20 a.m. on July 27, 1996. The commentator I was watching was reporting just a few hundred feet from where the bomb went off. I heard the explosion live, over television, and watched as the scene in Atlanta broke down into chaos. Not a very shiny moment in our nation's history.

Manhunt was a great gig because I did good work and was proud of my performance. My scene partner on the show had a real mouthful of dialogue and we had to shoot the scene over several takes because she kept stumbling through most of her lines. When it came time to shoot my coverage of the scene, the director and crew were frustrated and ready to move on. Thankfully, I stepped up and nailed my lines on the first take.

After my performance there was a long pause before the director yelled *"Cut!"*. He then stood up from his monitor, with a big grin on his face, and said, "Excellent work Corey, moving on." Several of the crew members came up to me after that to say, "Nice job." It was a fantastic feeling. I was walking on cloud nine for a few weeks after that gig. That was undoubtedly one of the best experiences I've had working as a professional actor.

A month later, I was invited to return to *Manhunt* and reprise my role. But my second gig on that show was a bust because I sat in my trailer all day before being told by a production assistant that I was wrapped because they filmed the scene without me. They literally forgot to call me to set when they started shooting. I still got paid, of course, but it was one of those gigs where, afterward, I couldn't stop thinking, *"Why am I doing this again?"* <sigh>

The second gig I booked in the summer of 2019 was on the Sony film *Jumanji: The Next Level*, starring Dwayne Johnson, Kevin Hart and Jack Black. That was a big budget film with a $125 million budget and "A-list" actors walking around everywhere. There were so many people on set, it felt like being at a circus. The production had huge, elaborate set designs, crazy costumes and over the top characters. For my scene, I was dressed as a Viking warrior and had to stand next to a horse that was taller than me while I growled my lines. It was a lot of fun, and I loved it.

Unfortunately, though, when the movie was released, I was disappointed because my line had been cut. I am on camera for a brief second, but they cut my damn line. *"Why the fuck am I doing this again?"*

Adding to my frustration on that gig, I got a traffic ticket driving down to Atlanta for speeding in a construction zone. I had no idea it was a construction zone because it was in the middle of the night, with no construction work being done whatsoever. In fact, the construction cones were literally 30 feet off the side of road and not visible. Interstate 85 is the bane of my existence.

The third show I worked on in 2019 was the first season of the Netflix original series *Outerbanks*, which, thankfully, filmed in Charleston, SC. I didn't have to drive on Interstate 85.

Outerbanks became a huge hit among younger viewers. I played a Coast Guard captain organizing a search and rescue mission for a pair of runaway teens during a hurricane. The shoot was a big production, involving the entire cast of the show and about 100 background actors. There were huge, industrial size fans blowing all night to simulate hurricane force winds and several ambulance and police vehicles casting red and blue light all over the set. It was a fun gig, but I wasn't prepared for the long hours. I'm pretty sure I drank craft services out of coffee trying to stay awake that night.

The best thing about working on *Outerbanks* was seeing the excitement on my niece's face when she learned that I had worked on the show. Ella boasted to all her friends that her Uncle Corey was on *Outerbanks*. She was absolutely giddy that I got to meet the young stars of the show and wanted to know if the young male stars were really as good looking in person as they are on TV. I told her they were even dreamier in person. Just to make her jealous.

Working on *Outerbanks* finally gave me an answer for why I am pursuing acting. I became a star in Ella's eyes after that gig. Getting to bond with my niece over that show made all the acting struggles that I have gone through worth it.

By the end of 2019, I was confident that I had regained momentum in the industry. I was excited about the opportunities ahead, going into the New Year.

But then, a few months into 2020, a little global pandemic started, the entire industry ground to a halt, and everybody lost momentum. *<sigh>*

Traveling is Important

I 've been fortunate to do a good bit of traveling in my life. I've seen most of the eastern United States, from Maine down to Key West. I've been to Hawaii and Las Vegas a couple of times, seen the Grand Canyon and gone to a few shows on Broadway, in NYC. I have not really explored the American west or been to Alaska, but I intend to in the next decade.

In 2002, my brother and I drove across the United States, from Charlotte, North Carolina to Los Angeles, California. We made that 2500-mile trip in about 3.5 days, driving primarily on Interstate 40 in Carey's cramped two-door Chrysler coupe. It wasn't much of a sightseeing trip because about half of our time was spent driving through northern Texas, which was about as interesting as varying shades of brown can be. However, I do remember being delighted at seeing my first cactus tree in the wild and watching tumbleweeds blow across the desert, just like in the movies.

Growing up, the only traveling I dreamed of doing was touring the world as a heavy metal rock star. I wanted to ride into cities on a breeze, thrash and scream for thousands of adoring fans, receive thunderous applause and then blow out of town, riding high on the adrenaline of fame and outrageous fortune.

In the summer of 1995 though, when I was 20 years old, I developed a serious itch to travel after spending several weeks in Germany. I studied German (language) in college and minored in International Business. My German professor at the time, Uli Froehlich, encouraged me to apply for a student exchange program that Appalachian State had with a partnering university in the city of Würzberg. Thankfully, Mom and Dad agreed to pay for the trip. They thought it was a unique opportunity for me and as usual, they were right. Studying abroad that summer opened my eyes to the greater world and broadened my mind considerably.

I think everyone should have the experience of being a foreigner at some point in their life. Traveling and engaging with different cultures has a tremendous impact on a person. It forces you to step outside of your comfort zone and navigate through the chaos that comes with language and cultural barriers. It was Mark Twain who famously wrote: "Travel is fatal to prejudice, bigotry and narrow-mindedness."

During my summer semester in Germany, I only took two classes. But to be honest, I didn't do much studying. I spent most of that summer talking to people, absorbing the culture and history of the country and, of course, drinking lots of delicious beer. The beer in Germany is fantastic because the country still adheres to the *Reinheitsgebot*, or "Purity Law" of brewing. The law is over 700 years old, first enacted in 1516, *before* the discovery of yeast fermentation.

At the end of my summer semester in Germany, I traveled with a group of exchange students to a small town in the Austrian Alps called Hintertux. I hiked up a glacier and explored the natural beauty of the lush valley that the town was nestled in. At that point in my life, Hintertux was the most beautiful place I'd ever seen.

The most profound experience I had in Germany that summer was when I toured the grounds of Dachau, located just outside of Munich. Dachau was the first Nazi concentration camp established in Germany in 1933, just weeks after Hitler became chancellor. It's estimated that between 30,000 to 45,000 prisoners died there.

I was very uncomfortable walking through Dachau because I had never felt such a pervading sense of hopelessness and despair before. I don't really know how to put into words what it feels like to stand a few feet away from a blackened crematorium at a former Nazi concentration camp. I was curious and horrified at the same time and felt an intense feeling of shame for humanity.

The German government has wisely kept Dachau open for visitation, to provide a solemn warning to the world about the dangers of fascism. As I was leaving Dachau, I came across a large iron gate that had the words *"Arbeit Macht Frei"* welded into its frame. In English, it means "Work Sets You Free". The Nazis were so confident in their fanatical ideology that they welded their propaganda into the very bars of their prisons.

I stared at that gate for a long time, allowing the immense weight of the moment to sink into me. Out of respect, it was forbidden to take pictures inside of Dachau, but I felt compelled to take a picture of that exit gate before leaving. I framed the photo when I returned home and have kept it within my view for almost 30 years now. It's currently sitting on a credenza in my office, alongside happier photos of friends, family and pets. I include the memory of Dachau in those photos to remind myself to be grateful and maintain my humanity above all else in life.

From my experiences in Germany over the summer of 1995, I vowed to make traveling a part of my life going forward. When I was finally making enough money to travel on my own, I took advantage of every opportunity that I could. In March of 2006, I took my parents, Carey and Cami, along with Wendy, Brandon and Chuck to Germany. We rented a van, and I drove us around Bavaria. We had a fantastic time exploring the area and immersing ourselves in the culture. We drove through the Black Forest and toured the famous Neuschwanstein Castle, built by the "Mad King", Ludwig II. We explored the birthplace of Wolfgang Amadeus Mozart in Salzburg, Austria and even spent a couple of days in Zurich, Switzerland.

When we were in Salzburg, we took a walking tour of the town and stumbled across a very recognizable area, which we identified as being the location where a scene from the movie *The Sound of Music* was filmed. Dad went ape shit with excitement because that's one of his favorite movies.

Our family trip in 2006 was the first time my parents had ever traveled across the pond, and they had a blast. It was the happiest I've ever seen my parents, I think. Like me, Dad fell in love with German beer and Mom, who rarely drinks alcohol, got drunk off of the introductory glass of champagne at a candlelight wine tasting we attended in the cellar of the Palace Residence in Würzburg. Mom giggled like a little girl throughout the tasting. But we were respectful and got along well with our host and the other guests, who were all local Germans.

The host of the wine tasting did not speak English very well, so Cami and I had to do our best to translate for our group. Cami also studied German in college and spent a summer semester in Germany as well. At the end of the wine tasting, our host genuinely thanked us and offered us a toast. Everyone in attendance raised their glasses and wished us safe travels back to the United States. They were all hammered from the heavy pours made that afternoon, of course, but it felt good, nonetheless.

In July of 2012, right before Rebekah and I got married, we traveled with my parents and Chuck to Ireland, along with my Aunt Linda. That was my first trip to Ireland, and it was a magical time. Our family heritage, Maher, is of Irish descent. The Meagher clan originated in Tipperary County, Ireland and became a very powerful and respected family during the 12th Century Norman Invasion. We defended our lands from those Vikings and fought well.

Our family motto is *In Periculis Audax*, which means "Bold in Danger". I think that's pretty badass. If I were ever to get a tattoo, it would be our Latin motto. But I doubt I'll ever get one because I still regret getting that stupid fucking earring in high school.

We are related to the famous Irish revolutionary Thomas Francis Meagher, who participated in the Young Irelander Rebellion of 1848, against the English. He was captured, exiled from Ireland and sentenced to life in prison on Tasmania, the island off Australia.

Meagher, however, escaped Tasmania in 1852 and made his way to the United States, where he eventually became a Brigadier General for the Union army during the American Civil War. After the war, President Andrew Johnson appointed Thomas Meagher as the Territorial Secretary of Montana.

When my family visited the town of Waterford, Ireland in 2012, our hotel happened to be the very house in which Thomas Meagher was born. It was pure coincidence that we booked that hotel. Rebekah and I had no idea that it had roots to my family lineage. Dad and Aunt Linda both got teary eyed when they saw the large bronze plaque affixed to the hotel's entrance, which proudly proclaimed it as the birthplace of Meagher. That 2012 trip to Ireland was full of special moments like that and, in many ways, truly felt like being back 'home'.

In September of 2013, Rebekah, Chuck and I traveled to Italy, along with Rebekah's brother, David. The four of us went to attend the wedding of a childhood friend of Rebekah's named Caroline, who married a German named Ralf. The wedding was held in a beautiful castle located in the Dolomite Mountains. We started our two-week adventure in Rome and stopped in Florence before making our way up to the wedding venue in the town of Bressanone (Brixen), in northern Italy.

The only problem we had on that trip was when I got our rental car stuck down in a pedestrian only courtyard in Florence. It was embarrassing, and we ended up looking like quintessential American idiots. But, in my defense, we had no idea where we were going because the damn GPS in our rental car died just a few days into the trip.

Despite that minor inconvenience, walking through the Roman Coliseum and seeing countless other ancient ruins was remarkable. We toured the Vatican Museum and marveled at the incredible collection of rare art it held within. I was shocked at the enormous size and extravagance of Saint Peter's Basilica and feel privileged to have witnessed the genius of Michelangelo up close, from his breathtaking sculpture of the Pieta in Saint Peter's, to his iconic painting on the ceiling of the Sistine Chapel as well as his masterpiece, the statue of David in Florence.

We ended our 2013 trip in Munich, where Caroline and Ralf live, and were fortunate enough to attend the Wiesen, or Oktoberfest. Being a native German, Ralf was able to reserve us a table in the exclusive Augustiner-Bräu tent. We all dressed in traditional lederhosen and dirndls and danced the night away on top of the tables. We sang traditional German songs as well as American pop songs, alongside hundreds of other drunk and rowdy people. Apparently, John Denver and Neil Diamond are very popular in Germany.

We stayed at Oktoberfest until they closed the tents down. I don't remember how much beer I drank that night. You don't order more beer at Oktoberfest in Germany. It's simply brought to you whenever your stein runs empty. Chuck and I got separated from the group somehow and had to stumble back to Ralf and Caroline's apartment on our own. I'm not sure how we were able to do that because it's the only time in my life that I've ever gotten black out drunk on beer alone. It was a fantastic night.

The morning after though was not so great. I woke up severely dehydrated and promptly threw up in the bathroom. After hugging the toilet for awhile and swearing off beer for the rest of my life, I wandered into the kitchen to get a glass of water and found Ralf cooking breakfast for everyone. Ralf took one look at me, gave me a wry smile and then offered me a breakfast beer. I had to hold back my urge to wretch again and politely declined Ralf's offer before immediately walking out of the apartment to get some fresh air. I ended up wandering around Munich alone for a couple of hours that morning, eating fresh pastries and hydrating with water to regain my equilibrium.

Rebekah and I still see Ralf and Caroline often. They come to the United States frequently to visit Caroline's family and always make an effort to see us when they're in town. They are great friends as well as excellent travel partners.

Traveling is an important part of my life now. Rebekah and I don't drive fancy cars or own a boat. We don't wear designer clothes or have a collection of expensive jewelry. We live below our means and choose to spend our money on traveling, prioritizing life experiences over material possessions. It has made my life very fulfilling, and I would encourage you to consider doing the same.

An Orgy of Caffeine

I n the Spring of 2019, while still living in our home on Tom Short Road, Rebekah and I were the victims of a home robbery. Some idiot decided to kick in our side door in the middle of the night and snatch Rebekah's purse and my wallet off our kitchen island. It was a simple smash and grab. We never saw the thief. In fact, both Rebekah and I woke up to the bang of the door being kicked in, but both of us assumed it was a dump truck or backfire from a car on the Interstate, which was less than a quarter of a mile away from our house. So we heard the door kicked in, but both of us went right back to sleep without investigating. We didn't realize we had been robbed until the next morning.

We called the police, and a CMPD (Charlotte Mecklenburg Police Dept) officer came by to take our statement, collect our contact information and write up the official report of the break in. But the officer who showed up annoyed me almost immediately. I thought his demeanor towards us was callous and disinterested. Like we were just another upper-middle class Ballantyne couple who had their pocket change stolen. No big deal.

"Officer Meh" made it abundantly clear that morning that we shouldn't get our hopes up about the police catching the perpetrator because crime was rampant and there was a large backload of unsolved break-ins in the area with limited resources. Essentially, he told us that he was there to write up a report for us to file with our insurance company. To me, he treated our break-in like it was a traffic accident and not the serious and violent invasion of our home that it was.

Don't get me wrong, I get that the police have many crimes to deal with on a daily basis and that many of those crimes are far more heinous than ours. But 'Officer Meh' could have at least lied to us and told us that they'd do their best to catch the thief.

In hindsight, I realize that my demeanor that morning was also a little suspect. When the officer arrived, I was still keyed up and angry, wearing no shirt and answering his questions curtly. I know I came across rather beastly that morning because, while taking my statement and standing right in front of me, the officer casually texted Rebekah and secretly asked her if she was okay or if she felt like she was in danger – essentially asking her if I was holding her hostage or an abusive husband.

Thankfully, Rebekah laughed and diffused the idea immediately and explained to the officer that we were both just upset about the late hour break in of our home. I wasn't upset at "Officer Meh" for sending Rebekah that text. I thought it was smart and am glad he did it. It was a possible scenario, especially given my temperament that morning.

The break-in shook Rebekah up pretty badly, and it took her a while to feel safe and comfortable again when going to bed at night. She had never been a victim of a robbery. I'd had my share of them in my youth and while building houses. But, admittedly, never one which felt so violating, like having the door of your home kicked in in the middle of the night. Rebekah updated our home security system and had all the locks changed because she had keys to the house in her stolen purse.

Despite "Officer Meh's" disingenuous attitude to us that morning, the police did identify the thief shortly after we reported it because the dumb ass used my debit card, which was being monitored, to buy an energy drink and a pack of smokes at a nearby gas station. Using video surveillance footage from behind the gas station checkout counter, it was easy for law enforcement to identify our thief. The asshole also went to a Starbucks and helped himself to an orgy of caffeine, draining a well funded gift card from Rebekah's stolen wallet. I think that pissed Rebekah off even more than the actual break in. Never underestimate the power of a caffeine addiction.

About a month after the robbery, we were notified that the police had arrested our thief. He was in his 40s and was a habitual criminal with a string of robberies and even aggravated assault on his record. This surprised me as I was certain that our thief would turn out to be a teenager or 20-something with a drug habit. A 40-year-old habitual criminal gave me pause to reflect because I was in my early 40s at the time. I felt grateful that my life never degraded to the point where I was reduced to smash and grab robbery to buy a cup of coffee.

After the robbery I thought it was time we started looking at adopting another dog, for added security. Had Caesar or Shep still been alive during the break in, we certainly would have been alerted to the situation immediately and not have fallen back asleep unaware. But, in truth, I think the real reason why I thought it was time to get another dog was because I was lonely and the house felt dreadfully empty to me most days.

I work primarily from home, and during this time, Rebekah was still working Uptown – which was a hellish two-hour daily commute from our house. She would leave at 7:30am for work and then go to a yoga or circuit class after to avoid the rush hour traffic coming home. She typically didn't get home until after 8pm most weekdays. She had been doing this since we met in January of 2009.

So, I was alone in the house most of the day and I missed the camaraderie and companionship of my fur babies. I missed having a fuzzy butt randomly rubbing against my leg, wanting food or a scratch behind the ears. I missed hearing the gentle (and sometimes deafening) snoring of my boys sleeping on their beds in my office while I worked. I deeply missed running my hands through Max's long, soft fur when I picked him up. He would stretch out wide in my arms and open himself up to me with complete trust and vulnerability sometimes. I even missed Pumpkin's epic lap naps where, after sitting down on the couch, she would immediately hop into your lap and fall asleep, effectively cementing you into position for hours until you finally couldn't hold it anymore and had to get up to go pee.

Having a dog or cat in your home can really lift your spirit when you are blue. They are typically very sensitive and attuned to changes in your emotional energy and can provide a quiet, soothing connection for you during difficult times. But the cost of having a pet is steep because the emotional pain you feel when losing a pet is close to unbearable. I had lost Caesar, Shep, Max and Pumpkin by 2019, and it never got easier to say goodbye as they went. It's arguably worse than losing a relative or direct family member because your pet is typically in your life everyday and your care for them is a part of your daily routine.

When we lost Caesar, I cried like a little girl for days. When my grandmother, Daisy, passed away, I shed only a few tears at her funeral. For a long time, I felt ashamed of that. It's not that I loved my grandmother less than my dog. It's that my dog was in my everyday life when he died. And I hadn't seen my grandmother in years when she passed away. It took me quite a while to accept that about myself.

To love another is to eventually suffer. Throughout recorded history, countless poets, authors and songwriters have said this, so I won't try to add my own literary take on it. However, I personally think Hemingway said it best when he wrote, "If two people love each other, there can be no happy end to it."

This is especially true with pets, because most of the time we outlive them. If I were to make a top ten list of the most gut-wrenching days of my life so far, all five of the days that I had to say goodbye to one of my pets would be included.

David and Duke

Before I could broach the subject of getting another dog with Rebekah, she asked me if I would be okay with her younger brother, David, living with us for a few months while he saved up some money and got his feet underneath him. David was about 30 at the time, had a degree in computer science and a job. But he had been jumping around from apartments and rental houses, living with friends since college, never really settling down or finding a foundation. He was partying a little too much I think and eventually had a run in with the law. He was pulled over late one night and mouthed off to the cop, which landed him behind bars for a few hours. My father-in-law, Jim, had to bail him out, and David had to pay a fine and apologize to the officer for the charges to eventually be dropped.

I was hesitant at the idea of David living with us at first, but Rebekah and her parents thought it would be good for David, in the hope that it would help balance him out. At this point, I didn't really know David that well. He had traveled with us to Italy and Germany in 2013 and came to my Bachelor party weekend in West Virginia, but David and I had never really had a serious conversation before, and his true character was still unknown to me. It was obvious to me though that David was holding on to a lot of anger and was having a hard time letting go of it.

In truth, David reminded me a lot of myself. We had common ground in the fact that we both had a love for heavy metal music and were creative types. He plays guitar and likes going to concerts and shows. He had gone with us to a few shows – Iron Maiden, TOOL, In Flames and Metallica. But beyond cultural similarities, I didn't know what David and I would have in common. He's 14 years younger than me. We literally come from different generations.

But I remembered that, while I was growing up, we had a revolving door of cousins and relatives who lived with us. My parents always kept an open-door policy for anyone who was looking for a fresh start and needed somewhere to call home for awhile. So, I agreed to let David move in with Rebekah and me and, in retrospect, I'm very happy he did.

A couple of months after David moved in with us, I approached Rebekah about getting a new dog by asking her if she had any desire to move. I think she thought I was getting ready to drop a bomb on her – like I was unhappy in the marriage or something – because she paused for a long moment and gave me a cautious look before asking, *"No, why?"*

I said:

"I think it's time we start looking for another dog. Maybe two. But no more cats. I've had my fill of cleaning out litter boxes. I did that for about 18 years. And if we get another dog, we're going to need to fence in the yard. When we moved into this house, Caesar and Shep were already 10 years old and well behaved. They knew not to wander out of sight. But we can't risk that with a new dog. We'll need to install a fence. But I don't want to spend the money to fence in the yard if you have any desire to move out of this house anytime soon."

After breathing a sigh of relief and realizing that I wasn't asking for a divorce, Rebekah got excited about the notion of a new dog and, true to her nature, immediately started looking online at dogs available for adoption. Rebekah was excited because she had never had her own dog. She grew up in a house without pets. Her mother did not want the responsibility of animals in the house. And when we met, I already had Caesar, Shep, Max and Pumpkin. They were technically my "children", brought into our marriage. So, deciding to get another dog or two meant she would get to be involved in choosing our next fur baby and that delighted her.

So, in late spring of 2019, we fenced in the rear yard of our home for $5000 with the intention of getting another dog. And about 5 months later we decided to move. *<sigh>*

***

I t was in June of 2019, while still in the house on Tom Short Road, that my wife informed me she was in love with someone else, and his name was Duke.

Rachel Woodhouse, a friend of mine from the "Actors Lounge", was actively involved in volunteering at CMPD's Animal Control shelter (i.e. – the pound) to help find homes for animals up for adoption. Rachel was your quintessential animal lover. Early in my acting career, before I bought my own cinema camera, Rachel would help me film my auditions. I would go over to her house, and she'd record my auditions, edit them and submit them for me.

Going to Rachel's house was like visiting a petting zoo. She lived in a small ranch style home not too far from ours and had a few dogs, cats, birds and even a large pot belly pig that she kept *indoors*. In her backyard she had ducks and a small koi pond with huge fish. She even raised a colony of bees in her back yard. I'm not sure how well her neighbors appreciated the immense number of animals she kept, but I thought it was neat. Rachel, like my father, had a great love for all animals.

When Rebekah reached out to Rachel and told her that we were going to start looking for a dog to adopt, Rachel immediately began to send Rebekah profiles of dogs up for adoption at the CMPD animal shelter. And, not long after deciding to get another dog, Rebekah fell in love with the handsome face of an American bulldog named Duke.

Duke was estimated to be 5-6 years old and, according to Rachel, was found in an empty apartment with no food and living in filth. He had been abandoned by his former owner(s). I try very hard not to judge people and their actions, but for someone to abandon their dog like that simply infuriates me. I have to remind myself that I did not know Duke's previous owners' situation. They could have very well been in dire straits. Thankfully, I have never been in a financial situation where I had to choose between feeding myself or my dog.

Before we took Duke in, though, we learned that he had been previously fostered to a family for adoption but was returned because, according to the previous fostering family, Duke did not get along well with other dogs. Naturally, this made me suspicious that he would be too aggressive. And, too, it likely meant that adopting Duke would mean that we could only adopt one dog. But Rebekah was in love with Duke from his profile alone, and I wanted her to be happy, so I agreed to foster Duke on a temporary basis. Plus, I admit that I, too, fell in love with Duke's lovable smile and handsome face on his profile page.

I think it's funny that Duke entered our lives in very much the same way that Rebekah entered my life 10 years earlier. Just as my original interest in Rebekah came from her beautiful smile on her online dating profile, Duke joined our family based on his lovable grin alone too. I guess there's something to be said about the benefits of smiling in pictures. Especially in the digital age we live in now. You never know who may see your smile and alter the course of your life forever. Although I suppose that same notion could be applied in reverse and a serial killer could target you based on your smile, so forget I said anything.

In June of 2019, Duke entered our home and our hearts. He weighed about 80 pounds and had a white coat with caramel-colored spots, very much like an American Painted Horse. When he came to live with us, Duke was undergoing treatment for heartworms and was on medication and prednisone (a steroid). Prednisone is known for making dogs pee a lot and, on those first few nights we had him, Duke peed all over the kitchen floors, which was frustrating. I was concerned that he was not properly house trained. However, after a couple of weeks, when Duke's heartworm treatment was complete, we had no other problems with him peeing in the house.

From the beginning, Duke was always a very chill and relaxed dog. He didn't bark excessively, except when the doorbell rang or he saw someone on the front porch. But he was always friendly with guests and children. I never saw him be aggressive with a human being in the time we had him. Despite what Duke's previous foster family reported, we found that Duke was rarely aggressive to other dogs. He was just an alpha dog and would scrap with other alpha dogs who tried to be dominant over him. That only happened a few times though.

Ardrey

In August of 2019, while both Duke and David were adjusting to living with us, I was doing an appraisal on a home in the "Ardrey" subdivision, which was only a few miles away from our home on Tom Short Road. The subdivision, with its Charleston style, colorful homes and well-manicured, tree-lined streets, was always a favorite of mine in Charlotte. Whenever I received an appraisal assignment in Ardrey, I was always blown away by the neighborhood's beauty, as is almost everyone who visits it for the first time. In 2005, the subdivision won 'Community of the Year' by the North Carolina Homebuilder's Association for its impeccable design. I typically don't put much stock in those clever marketing types of awards, but in the case of Ardrey, it was well deserved.

The neighborhood is pretty much a life size diorama of a Norman Rockwell painting – a beautiful throwback to Americana craftsman style homes. There's a dog park anchored on the west side of the neighborhood and a large central park, which splits the neighborhood down the middle, with giant granite boulders and tall oak trees shading quiet park benches. All the homes in the neighborhood feature large, covered front porches, reminiscent of a time when neighbors actually gathered and talked to each other.

During the 4th of July, almost everyone in the Ardrey neighborhood hangs an American flag off their front porch. On Halloween and through the holidays, the neighborhood goes all out in decorating, and the subdivision becomes as colorful as downtown Disney. Featured every year in the local "The Best Neighborhoods to See Holiday Lights" article, it's not uncommon to see lines of cars, large tour vans and even horse drawn carriages riding slowly through the subdivision to experience the magic of the lights and seasonal atmosphere.

I've done many appraisals in the Ardrey neighborhood throughout my career and have watched it grow even more unique in character and popularity as time passed. While other neighborhoods with monstrous, modern McMansions developed all around the area, Ardrey remained a glittering jewel of boutique charm in south Charlotte. People who moved into the Ardrey neighborhood took on a high degree of pride in ownership, which was reflected in the strong demand and increasing values of its homes.

So, when I was working on an appraisal assignment in Ardrey in the summer of 2019 and came across a home for sale that had been on the market for over 6 months, it piqued my curiosity. Homes in this neighborhood usually sold within a few days. I wanted to know why this home wasn't selling, and eventually, when my curiosity got the better of me, I took Rebekah to go look at it.

Upon our initial viewing of what would become our second home together, Rebekah was not impressed. Walking through the home for the first time, I immediately understood why the home had been on the market for so long. It was built in 2006 and had no recent updates or renovations. The kitchen looked terribly dated and had a hideous backsplash. The master bathroom was horribly drab and was in desperate need of remodeling, the hardwood floors needed to be refinished, the lighting fixtures were cheap, and the back patio was in deplorable shape and needed to go. But the layout and design of the home was perfect for us. It had an open floorplan, ten-foot ceilings on both the first and second floors and eight-foot doors throughout, just like the homes I used to design. In short, the structural and mechanical components of the home were in good shape, it was just in desperate need of a home "makeover" – which is something I am quite capable of managing.

Also adding to the home's longer than normal duration on the market was the fact that it was owned by the Zillow Corporation, an iBuyer company, that had purchased the home from the previous owners six months earlier. iBuyer companies like Zillow, OpenDoor and Offerpad buy homes from people at a discount, or below market value, and then, when the owners move out, they give the home a cosmetic facelift (painting, carpet replacement, etc.) before listing it for sale with their own in-house real estate agents.

Being an expert in the Charlotte real estate market, I recognized almost immediately that Zillow had paid too much for the house in Ardrey when they bought it from the previous owners. And I smelled an opportunity. I really loved the house, despite its dated appearance, and wanted to live in Ardrey.

So, in September of 2019, after promising Rebekah that we would make significant updates to the home before we moved in, we made a fair offer on the house in Ardrey and Zillow accepted it, despite our offer being $30,000 less than what Zillow had paid for it six months earlier. I admit, that made me happy and brought me joy.

I spent October getting quotes and lining up contractors for the remodeling efforts we needed in our home in Ardrey, and by early November, we closed and immediately began those renovations before we started moving in around Thanksgiving.

We took our time packing up and moving out of our house on Tom Short Rd. I think Rebekah had a hard time letting go of it at first. We had lived there for 8 years and had many memories in it. We got married while living in that house. We lost Caesar, Shep, Max and Pumpkin while living in that house. We had many parties and family gatherings there. It was the first house Rebekah ever owned, and she was attached to it. Even Duke had anxiety during the move. After all, when Duke's previous owners packed up and moved, they abandoned him. I could tell he was afraid that we were going to do the same. Not a chance, buddy.

I, on the other hand, had no problems moving out of our Tom Short house. I always considered that house to be temporary housing – a place to lick my wounds and recover from my failed construction business and bankruptcy in 2010. I considered that home to be an investment and a jumping off point for the future.

By Christmas of 2019, our move into Ardrey was complete and our house on Tom Short Road was empty. So, in early January of 2020, I began the process of getting our Tom Short home ready to sell. Being located in a very desirable school district and within easy access of the interstate, I told Rebekah that I thought the home would sell quickly. But deep down, I was nervous. My track record and experience in selling homes was not exactly stellar. The last time I tried to sell a house, I found myself in a downward spiral, which ultimately resulted in me losing almost everything I had worked for in over a decade.

"How could it not sell?" I asked myself with a self-assured tone. *"The financial crisis is well behind us and the housing market is strong once again. We're priced right and in a great location. Barring some radical, unforeseen change in the entire housing or financial markets, we should get an offer rather quickly."*

So, in February of 2020, I pushed my nerves aside and placed our home on the market with every confidence that it would be sold by spring. Then, on March 27, 2020 – with no offers yet on our home – a radical, unforeseen change happened, which ground almost all markets across the entire world to a dramatic halt.

"Fuck my life!"

84 Cans of Soup

I NTERIOR KITCHEN

Corey returns home from an appraisal inspection and enters the kitchen with a perplexed look on his face. He drops his briefcase on the kitchen island and glances at Rebekah, who sits at the breakfast table with her laptop in front of her, working.

COREY: *"Why do we have 120 rolls of toilet paper in the garage?"*

Rebekah answers Corey without looking up from her computer

REBEKAH: *"My mom was at Costco this morning and she was able to grab us some before they sold out."*

COREY: *"Costco ran out of toilet paper?"*

Rebekah says nothing and shrugs her shoulders, continuing to work her fingers across the keyboard in front of her. The door into the garage suddenly opens behind Corey and David enters the kitchen, having just returned home from the grocery. David is carrying two large cardboard pallets of canned goods and sets them down on the counter without saying anything. He then turns and exits back into the garage

Corey picks up one of the cans David brought in.

COREY: *"Campbell's Chunky Soup?"*

Corey returns the soup can to the pallet and begins to quietly count how many cans of soup David bought. The door behind Corey opens again and David enters with yet another two pallets of the soup. Corey's eyes go wide as David stacks pallets 3 and 4 on top of 1 and 2.

COREY: *"Jesus Christ man! How many cans of soup did you buy?!"*

DAVID: *"84"*

Corey shakes his head in disbelief.

COREY: *"You bought 84 cans of chunky soup?"*

DAVID: *"It was all they had."*

Corey glances at Rebekah who, once again, simply shrugs her shoulders and says nothing, continuing to type feverishly. Corey cracks a joke to bring levity to the room.

COREY: *"I think we're going to need more toilet paper."*

David gives Corey a serious look.

DAVID: *"Sorry man. I looked but they were sold out."*

The amused look on Corey's face slowly fades as he glances back and forth between the soup, Rebekah and David. After a beat, Corey sighs heavily, picks up his briefcase and begins trudging up the stairs.

COREY: *"I'll be in my office."*

***

In March of 2020, the COVID-19 Global Pandemic began. And, judging by the immediate hoarding of toilet paper by the public, people were scared shitless. Or, perhaps more accurately, scared that they would never be able to take a shit comfortably again for the rest of their lives. It was a strange and confusing time. An "unprecedented time", as almost every news anchor in the world liked to report ad nauseam.

Admittedly, I was unnerved when it all started. It was hard not to feel uneasy when the entire world was placed in lockdown. Every government on the planet implemented some form of isolation protocol on its citizens. It had to be the most coordinated effort of global control ever attempted in human civilization.

"Nonessential" businesses had to either shut down or have their employees work remotely from home. You couldn't go out to eat or go to the movies. Kids couldn't go to school. You couldn't get a haircut. You couldn't go to the gym. You couldn't go on vacation. You couldn't visit with friends or family. Most manufacturing facilities shut down, and the price of most goods skyrocketed as global supply chains around the world ground to a halt. It felt as if human civilization was entering the End Times. A dystopian world of failed states, Marshall Law and all out anarchy seemed to loom on the horizon.

I've often wondered how many people, who were generally healthy and productive before the pandemic, became alcoholics during the isolationism. One of the things I found most interesting about the early days of the lockdown was that liquor stores were allowed to remain open because they were considered "essential" businesses.

The reasoning behind that was to not risk creating another epidemic of people going through alcohol withdrawal. According to a study done in 2023, 10% of people over the age of 12 were estimated to have Alcohol Use Disorder. *Yes, I said 12.* So, prohibiting the sale of alcohol risked creating an additional epidemic of alcohol withdrawal, which would have flooded hospitals with even more patients and been counterproductive.

When the pandemic first started, I remember trying to remain optimistic in telling Rebekah, "It'll only last for a few weeks. They just need to limit the spread of the virus to get it under control and help alleviate the immense burden on hospitals right now."

My buddy Chuck and his wife Emily were literally in the hospital when the lockdown began. Emily had just given birth to their first child, Thomas. They were understandably terrified and thankful to get out of the hospital when they did. Emily had gone through several rounds of in-vitro fertilization to conceive Thomas. So, when Chuck and Emily left the hospital with Thomas, went straight home and didn't leave their house for nearly three years, I understood completely. They weren't taking any risks.

But despite how scary the global lockdown was initially, it worked. There were no massive protests, riots or looting. There was no degradation of order or breakdown in moral conduct. People all around the world were ordered to stay in their homes and avoid contact with others and they did without resistance, for the most part.

Of course, there were a few jackasses who refused to wear a mask while out in public. And when the COVID vaccine was developed and approved by the USFDA in December of 2020, there were your typical garden variety conspiracy theory nut-jobs who claimed that the vaccine was a tracking device or a mind control substance. There will always be a small percentage of the population that will act irrationally. But, with all that said, I think the handling of the 2020 global pandemic was an impressive feat for humanity. Like a litmus test of civility in which we passed.

Abstract Expressionism in Poop

My appraisal work was considered an essential business during the pandemic as it is directly related to the financial services industry. People still needed to manage their money and take out loans, especially with so many people not working and needing money to ride out the storm until they found work again. So, with the exception of not being able to go to the gym, the lockdown did little to change my daily routine.

To continue some regimen of physical activity while my gym was closed, I bought some resistance bands and a pull-up bar and worked out in the garage. I also ran sprints around the dog park across the street from our house and did farmer's walks up and down the sidewalk with a 70lb stone block leftover from the patio remodel we completed before moving in.

Because the pandemic began only a couple of months after we moved into Ardrey, Rebekah and I did not have a chance to formally introduce ourselves to many of our new neighbors. So, the first impression that most of our neighbors had of me was watching me walk up and down the sidewalk, carrying a large concrete block, dropping it and then sprinting around the dog park like some kind of crazy lunatic. I could feel their eyes on me while I worked out, peeking out through the slim blinds of their windows, wondering just what kind of meathead has moved into the neighborhood. I secretly enjoyed that.

It was really just dumb luck that we moved into our home in Ardrey when we did. While our previous home on Tom Short Rd had plenty of room, we would not have been as comfortable there as we were in our new home in Ardrey. A big reason for that was meeting our new neighbors, Kristin and Eric.

It started with casual chit chat at the fence, progressing to having a drink or two by their firepit in the evenings, to eventually having dinner together. Kristin and Eric are similar to Rebekah and me in age and, like us, have no children. Like most residents of Ardrey, they're also 'dog people', which is something I've learned to be quite important when determining the quality of one's character.

In December of 2020, as social distancing protocols began to relax, Kristin and Eric decided to throw a holiday block party. They had moved into Ardrey only a year before us and were considered to be new kids on the block as well. The party was a phenomenal success, despite the fact that the power went out for about an hour in the middle of the party. It was a fun night. Rebekah and I got to know many of our new neighbors better and I was able to shed my moniker as 'cinder block guy'.

During the early days of the pandemic, Rebekah had a difficult time coping. Thankfully she was still employed and working from home, which helped alleviate some of her anxiety. For as long as I've known Rebekah, she has always found comfort in creating order out of chaos. By working out calculations in Excel spreadsheets, formatting legal documents and Powerpoint presentations, Rebekah was able to relieve some of the stress she was feeling in the isolationism. While the outside world was engulfed in chaos and uncertainty, my wife found solace in the arms of Microsoft Office.

In the evenings and on weekends though, when there was nothing to do or nowhere to go, Rebekah occupied her time with many new and interesting short-lived hobbies. She went through a puzzle phase, where she worked diligently on a variety of 1000 piece puzzle sets. She would finish one and then immediately buy another one online. She even started to glue some of her puzzles together, which I thought was strange.

When she got bored with puzzles, she tried her hand at painting. She bought an easel, some blank canvases and paint, and started her own little renaissance in the living room for a while. I thought she was quite good at it, but that endeavor didn't last too long either.

As 2020 progressed and the initial chaos of the pandemic slowly subsided, Rebekah began to relax. After her forays into puzzles and painting had faded, Rebekah began to listen to audio books around the house to keep her mind from wandering too much. I remember walking into the kitchen one afternoon, as she was preparing her lunch, and hearing a foreboding voice emanating from her phone. The story she was listening to had a dark tone to it, and I vaguely recognized the language and character names.

"What are you listening to?" I asked

Rebekah, fully involved in the story, paused the recording and answered, "Stephen King's *The Stand*. It's so good. I've never read it before."

I gave her a concerned look. "Do you think it's wise to be listening to *The Stand* right now? It's a little too close to the mark, don't ya think?"

Rebekah laughed and waved me out of the kitchen, saying "I know. I know. Now go away. This is a really good part." It was at this point that I realized Rebekah was going to be okay.

In the afternoons and evenings, Rebekah and I would take Duke for long walks around the subdivision, meeting other people in our neighborhood and getting to know them from a distance. Duke loved those long walks with us, and over the course of the pandemic, he provided Rebekah, David and I with much love and comfort. For the most part, he was a good boy. Although on one occasion, when he misbehaved, Duke hilariously paid the price when he ate something he shouldn't have.

David eventually ran out of Campbell's chunky soup and, one day for lunch, he had made himself a couple of sandwiches and left them in the kitchen unattended. Duke naturally assumed that one of those sandwiches was for him and when David returned to the kitchen to find one of them missing, it was easy to identify who the thief was because Duke's snout had swollen to the size of a grapefruit. Unbeknownst to us at the time, Duke was allergic to mustard. It wasn't serious though, and the swelling eventually went down after a few hours, but Duke never helped himself to anything off the counter again. He did, however, eat anything and everything he could find when outside.

Once, when a bird got trapped inside our screen porch, Rebekah tried desperately to safely shepherd it back outside. But Duke, ever the hungry boy, seized the opportunity for a snack and, in one swift jump, snatched the bird out of the air and gulped it down. I can still remember Rebekah's blood curdling scream that day.

On another particularly unpleasant morning, Rebekah and I woke up to find what I can only describe as a Jackson Pollack painting of Duke's poop all over the living room floor. We learned later that baby rabbits, which are everywhere in our neighborhood, can cause dogs to have severe indigestion and diarrhea. Thankfully, Duke must have learned his lesson that day too because we only had to clean up that disgusting mess once.

Just Be You

In July of 2021, Rebekah and I took another trip down to Mexico to drink spicy margaritas and unplug from the world for a while. By that point, I desperately needed a break from my appraisal work. Since the fall of 2020, I had been working 50-60 hours a week in my appraisal business due to interest rates dropping to record lows. It seemed like everyone in the country was refinancing their mortgage and the pile of work on my desk seemed to never end. Rebekah and I felt comfortable traveling to Mexico because we had both received our COVID vaccine shots just a few months prior.

While I was happy that I had so much appraisal work coming in, I was feeling that old familiar itch for a creative outlet again. In 2020, during the lockdown, I was able to scratch that itch by reading the entire Jack Reacher book series and campaigning for the role of Reacher in Amazon's production by creating a couple of short films playing Reacher. But, by September of 2020, Amazon had cast the role, and my campaign, as well as my creative outlet, dried up.

In 2019, before the pandemic started, I had a breakthrough year in my acting work. I booked roles on a few major productions including *Jumanji - The Next Level*, *Outer Banks* and *Manhunt: Deadly Games*. I had built quite a bit of momentum in 2019 and really thought I had finally broken through in the industry. But then COVID started and derailed my train to Hollywood glory as productions everywhere shut down.

Over the pandemic, the entire landscape of film and television changed because people stopped going to movie theaters. They also stopped watching network television. Streaming platforms, like Netflix and Amazon, became the new kings of the screen, as people stuck in their homes began to binge shows and movies commercial free.

By the middle of 2021, when filming was once again permissible, production studios seemed to be lost and without direction. The entire film and television industry was flipped upside down by the pandemic. Projects that had been green-lighted prior to the pandemic were placed on hold or scrapped entirely. Producers everywhere pulled back considerably and, as a result, the number of auditions I received from Rusty became few and far between.

With very few auditions coming in and no other creative outlets available, I decided I would write and produce another short film to feed my imagination. It was while sitting on a beautiful, white sand beach at our resort in Mexico, Secrets Maroma, after having consumed anywhere between six to ten liquor drinks already, that I started writing the script for my next short film, *The Curious Case at 1301*.

With resort stationery and pen in hand, I started outlining "1301" as an intense, dark thriller, where the lead character, to be played by me, comes home to find his wife missing and then begins to receive cryptic text messages from her, leading him on a mysterious game of cat and mouse. In my original outline of the film, the climax would reveal that the villain who kidnapped my wife was none other than my neighbor across the street. This would then set up an intense showdown between me and my neighbor battling it out while my wife's life hung in the balance.

But after a couple of hours of outlining this story on the beach – and switching from margaritas to rum punch – I thought to myself, "*This is lame*", and decided to take a nap instead.

When we returned home from Mexico I continued trying to brainstorm ideas for my next short film – this time with my brain not soaked in tequila, rum or champagne. I knew the project had to be something that could be easily shot in our home and with as few people involved as possible because the pandemic was still ongoing and social distancing was still a top priority. I also knew that I wanted my next film to be a step up in production quality – something I could submit to film festivals so that I could watch it on a big screen with a live audience, like I did with my first short film, *Trophies in the Attic*.

But as hard as I tried, I just couldn't come up with any new ideas. I felt creatively constipated, which is one of the most frustrating feelings for me. I still had my original outline of "1301", made on the beach, but the story still didn't sit well with me. It felt too passé – like just another thriller/action story with the hero saving the girl. There are a hundred films like that made every year. I wanted my next film to be something original and unique.

I shared my creative frustrations with Britt and Jason around that time and remember Britt saying, "You don't need to be some kind of badass hero man, just be you. You're so damn funny in real life I promise you people will like anything you do if you just be yourself." Britt's advice stuck with me, and I thought about it for quite some time.

Then, one afternoon, while I was having a stogie on the front porch, mindlessly scrolling through social media, I came across an old Gary Larson cartoon which I hadn't seen in a long time. Growing up I loved *The Far Side*. I thought Gary Larson was a genius in the realm of absurd comedy, much like Douglas Adams, who wrote my favorite book, *The Hitchiker's Guide to the Galaxy*.

The Far Side cartoon I saw that day was a classic of Larson's, depicting a mailman who gets eaten by a mailbox. I remember laughing at the ridiculous premise for a few seconds, then looking down at our own mailbox on the street and, in a flash of brilliance, a light bulb went off in my head and my creative juices kicked in.

Instead of "1301" being a run of the mill, "who done it'" thriller, why can't it be an absurd dark comedy where my wife isn't kidnapped by our neighbor across the street but is, instead, trapped inside of our mailbox? She could reach out to me for help by sending me cryptic messages through the mailbox, snail mail style. The climax would be me hilariously battling it out with my mailbox, trying to pull my wife free. The ridiculousness of the story delighted me because, as Britt suggested, it had "me" written all over it.

Excited to have new direction, I feverishly began writing the screenplay for "1301" and completed it in just a few days. With the screenplay in hand, I then decided to reach out to Collins White and his company at OtherVision Studios to see if he would be interested in shooting, editing and mastering "1301" for me. I first met Collins at the Tryon International Film Festival in 2018 where my first film, *Trophies in the Attic*, was screened. Collins was at the festival that year representing his own film, *13 Ghosts* – a short film about a hitman haunted by the ghosts of the people he murdered.

After watching Collins' film, I was struck with how unique his story was and how well the production value of his film appeared. I thought Collins and I would work well together, so I sent him my script. After reading it, Collins said he was intrigued by the premise of a man-eating mailbox story and agreed to help me produce it.

In late August of 2021, during a blisteringly hot heat wave, we shot *The Curious Case of 1301* at my home in Ardrey. And, let me tell you something, if you thought I got strange looks from my neighbors when I did farmers' walks with a cinderblock up and down the sidewalk during the lockdown, you should have seen the looks I got when I was out on the street screaming and fighting with my mailbox while Collins filmed me. I'm pretty sure everyone in my neighborhood thinks I'm completely nuts at this point.

We shot the film over three days and, by the end of 2021, after Collins and I both worked through the editing process and composer Neil Griffin – who worked with me on "Trophies" – provided a fun, complimentary score, *The Curious Case of 1301* was in the can. I was overjoyed with how well it turned out and couldn't wait to show it to a live audience.

We submitted "1301" to several local and national film festivals and it got accepted into quite a few. In Collins' hometown of Greenville, SC, the film was screened at the Reedy Reels Film Festival, along with 60 other films. To our humble surprise, the film took home the "People's Choice" award, which is, in my opinion, the most coveted honor you can achieve at a film festival. It means that the audience, not the film festival committee, liked our film the best.

The Reedy Reels Film Festival, in the Spring of 2022, was the first time I was able to see my original work on a big screen. My first short film was screened in a small art gallery on a flat screen television. Hearing the audience chuckle and roar nonstop throughout the film was simply euphoric to me. I felt as if I had finally found my audience. And all I had to do was just be me. *Thanks Britt.*

If any of you are wondering if there is any significance with the number "1301", I'll let you in on a secret: it was completely arbitrary. 1301 was our room number at the resort during that trip to Secrets Maroma in 2021. It was the first thing I wrote down when I started brainstorming ideas for the film because I was afraid Rebekah and I would be too drunk to remember it at the end of the day.

Writing and producing "1301" was both a personal and professional breakthrough for me. I felt like I had finally found my "voice" in producing that film – both as an actor and as a writer. I simply needed to stick to being me and bring my natural wit and sarcasm into my work as much as possible. So, it should come as no surprise that, immediately after Collins and I finished "1301", I started work on my next project, *The Birthday Butterfly.*

Who Doesn't Love Birthday Cake?

In February of 2022, shortly after Collins and I finished editing "1301", I began to start thinking about a story for my next film. I had just turned 47 and my birthday buddy niece, Nora, turned 8. We didn't hold a joint birthday party that year because the pandemic was technically still ongoing and, let's face it, no 8-year-old wants to share a birthday party with their 47-year-old uncle. It got a little weird after the age of 6.

But I miss those joint parties that Nora and I had together. They always provided a youthful energy to my birthday, softening the general malaise I've come to now feel every year on February 10. I remember those parties being very chaotic, with kids running around everywhere and parents trying desperately to maintain order. So, when I began to brainstorm ideas for my next film project, I thought a children's birthday party would be an ideal setting for an adult themed comedy.

Writing the screenplay for *The Birthday Butterfly* was actually much easier than my previous films because I finally knew, from the work I did on "1301", which direction I wanted to go in with my films. Comedy is what I enjoy most and what I feel like I am most natural at doing. So, when I began developing the central story and script for "Butterfly", I simply asked myself, *"What would be the most hilarious thing to happen at an 8-year old's birthday party?"*

After pondering this question for a while, I ended up focusing on writing my screenplay around a botched birthday cake. All good stories need to have a central conflict that the audience can relate to. And who doesn't love birthday cake?

In developing my story for *The Birthday Butterfly*, I needed to find a cake FAIL so awful that it would produce genuine panic from parents at a children's birthday party. Like one of those homemade birthday cakes meant to look like Remy from *Ratatouille* but instead looks more like a mentally deranged lab rat from NIHM. So, I took to the internet looking for a failed cake design to center my story around. *Kudos if you understand the reference to "The Secret of Nihm". It was one of my favorite movies as a kid.*

But after looking at hundreds of pictures of failed cakes online, I couldn't find anything wretched enough to incite real panic. So, I broadened my search parameters and dug deeper into the internet until, eventually, I struck gold when I happened upon a picture of a cake made for a "divorce party", which had a giant penis made from fondant on it and the words, "Happy Divorce, Cathy! Get That Dick!" written across it.

According to an article I found online in *The Law Review*, the divorce rate in the United States increased by 34% during the first year of the pandemic. That didn't surprise me though. Some marriages need a lot of space to breathe. If you take away that space, the marriage can become a pressure cooker, waiting to blow. I don't really understand why anyone would want to celebrate their divorce, but apparently some people do. And some of those people do it with a dick cake.

Can you imagine the panic a parent would have opening the box to that cake, with children and guests waiting in the next room, after a delivery mix up at the bakery??! I still laugh thinking about it.

Shooting *The Birthday Butterfly* in May of 2022 was a much larger undertaking than shooting "1301" a year earlier. When Collins and I shot "1301", we did it in three days and, on our busiest day, there were only 7 people on set, including a cast of 4 and crew of 3. When we shot "Butterfly" we did it over two long, three-day weekends and, on our busiest day of shooting, we had over 30 people in our house for over twelve hours.

"Butterfly" was an exhausting shoot, and most of the actors I cast in it were friends I had met at "The Actor's Lounge". Most of them had worked with me on my previous films. Even Rebekah had a role in "Butterfly", which I thought she played brilliantly. The shoot was both fun and frustrating at the same time because, with everyone getting along so well, trying to stay on a shoot schedule was a constant struggle. But Collins and I managed the set well and by the end of the shoot, I was thrilled with the footage we got.

In June of 2022, shortly after we wrapped the "Butterfly" shoot, Rebekah and I headed down to Secrets Maroma again for a well-deserved break while Collins began to rough cut the first edit of the film. By Halloween that year, the film was in the can, and we began submitting it to film festivals.

In early 2023, *The Birthday Butterfly* won "Best Short Film" at the Reedy Reels Film Festival, giving Collins and I back-to-back wins in his hometown. We won the "People's Choice" award for "1301" at Reedy Reels in 2022.

In February of 2024, "Butterfly" was screened at the Beaufort International Film Festival in Beaufort, SC. I know that doesn't sound like a big deal, but the Beaufort IFF is ranked as one of the top 20 film festivals in the world by Movie Maker magazine. "Butterfly" was selected out of 500 film submissions from over 40 different countries. Fifty-five films were selected for the Beaufort IFF, and it made me proud to be one of them.

Rebekah and I, along with my folks, spent a wonderful weekend in the coastal town of Beaufort, watching some pretty fantastic films. Legendary actor and humanitarian Gary Sinise (Lt. Dan from *Forest Gump*) was the guest of honor that year at Beaufort and Mom absolutely loved listening to his keynote speech at the closing ceremonies.

To top it all off, *The Birthday Butterfly* was nominated by the Beaufort film committee for both Best Comedy and Best Ensemble Cast, alongside many other amazing films, some of which had budgets 100 times larger than mine. The winner of Best Comedy that year was *The Martini Shot*, which starred an Academy Award winning actor (Matthew Modine).

The Birthday Butterfly was a triumphant success in my opinion. Writing, producing and directing that film was an absolute blast and will forever be a highlight of my life.

Up The Irons

By the spring of 2023, the United States economy was in trouble. Inflation was running high, and most Americans were feeling a significant pinch in their monthly budgets. Groceries and common household goods had increased in price by as much as 50% since the start of the pandemic. I could explain the economics behind it all and how the Federal Reserve, in my opinion, really screwed up by over stimulating the economy at the start of the pandemic.

But usually when I talk about economics with someone, I can literally watch their eyes glaze over in boredom and settle into a confused, middle-distance stare. So, for the sake of brevity and your attention, I'll just say that in the Spring of 2023, the Federal Reserve began to aggressively raise interest rates to try to stop the runaway train of inflation from derailing the economy.

As a result of the Fed's increase in interest rates, my appraisal business slowed down considerably, and I went from working 50-60 hours a week in 2020-2022 to working only 20-30 hours a week by early 2023. So, I began to find myself with a lot more free time.

In late 2022, shortly after Collins and I had *The Birthday Butterfly* in the can, I did write a new screenplay with every intention of starting production on it in 2023. The new screenplay I wrote, titled "The

Baked Sale", is a feature length follow up to "Butterfly", with the same characters and comedic tone. But because "The Baked Sale" is a feature length production (a full 80–90-minute movie), it would require a much larger financial investment than my previous short films. So, I had to place the project on hold. I wasn't making nearly as much money as I was before, and I wasn't about to overextend myself again. I learned that lesson with Drakestone Construction. I'm hoping I get the chance to produce "The Baked Sale" in the next few years as I really think it could be a hit.

With more free time on my hands and not enough money to start my next film project, I found myself in a state of limbo in the spring of 2023. After finishing Lee Child's Jack Reacher series in early 2021, I discovered author David Baldacci's world of crime and espionage stories, with characters like Will Robie, Amos Decker and John Puller. I quickly ate my way through many of Baldacci's novels in 2021-2022 and by early 2023, I was getting tired of reading all the time. Reading is a great way to pass the time, but after a while, I get fatigued and bored. What I needed was a new creative outlet.

So, in May of 2023 I decided to do something I hadn't done in over 20 years – I pulled out my guitars and started playing again. I had put my axes down in frustration in late 1999 after my band, Channel Black, disbanded. Thankfully I never got the inclination to sell my guitars or gear. I kept them all, untouched, for almost 25 years, dragging them with me through five different homes and a couple of apartments over that time. Deep down I think I always knew I'd come back to music. And, for whatever reason, in May of 2023, the timing felt right.

However, trying to play guitar again was very frustrating. I had forgotten 90% of what I had previously learned, which admittedly wasn't much. I had taught myself how to play guitar in the early 90s and never had any formal lessons. So, when I started to try playing again, I found myself unable to play even the simplest Metallica songs that I had learned and enjoyed playing endlessly in my youth. I couldn't even remember how to play my own songs, the ones we had written in Channel Black.

But with age comes wisdom and patience. Despite the frustrations I felt at not being able to play even the simplest of chords, I couldn't deny the joy that I felt in having an axe strapped over my shoulder once again. So, I dedicated myself to starting over with music and began using the endless resources now available online to educate myself on learning to play the guitar.

By the end of 2023, I was practicing guitar for about an hour a day and spending another hour or two a day learning music theory online. I learned more in those six months than I did in the 7-8 years when I first learned to play guitar. However, because I was practicing in my office, with my rig set up in the corner, I had to be mindful not to be too loud because Rebekah was still working from home during the days.

In December of 2023, I decided to create a soundproof practice room out of the walk-in attic in our home so that I could play as loud as I wanted, whenever I wanted, without bothering Rebekah or the neighbors. Creating a space dedicated to nothing but my love for music reasserted me even more, and for most of 2024, I spent 1-2 hours a day playing guitar. I eventually became more versatile and skilled at the guitar than I ever was in my youth.

It's truly amazing how much easier it is to learn almost anything nowadays. With online platforms like YouTube and millions of tutorial apps now available, learning how to play guitar or speak a different language or write computer code or install a toilet is all within the palm of your hand. The Age of Information is certainly a wonderful time to be alive.

It seems to me that the only limitations of someone living in the modern world now are those that are self-imposed. All you need to have is the desire, determination and dedication to want to learn. Hopefully future generations of humanity don't take that for granted.

Brotherly Love – Part 2

Rebekah and I were very lucky to move into the Ardrey neighborhood in fall of 2019. We wouldn't be able to afford a home in our own subdivision now, in 2025. The COVID pandemic created a lot of havoc in the national real estate market. When the lockdown started, builders had to stop building, which created a shortage of new homes. When the Federal Reserve cut mortgage rates down to historic lows, below 3%, it created a surge in demand for homes. A shortage of homes being met with a surge in demand for homes created an environment of hyperinflation in the entire national real estate market.

Within four years of buying our home in Ardrey, the market value of our house has nearly doubled, as did the value of our home on Tom Short. I suppose it was a blessing that our Tom Short house didn't sell in early 2020 when I put it on the market. We ended up leasing it out to an attorney for three years and watched the value of it increase dramatically. When the lease on that home ended, we tried to sell the home again but were too late and missed the buying spree. By late 2023, when the lease ended on Tom Short, interest rates had shot back up and demand in the market dropped dramatically.

I'm fucking cursed at not being able to sell homes.

Carey and his family came into some hard times because of all this housing market turmoil in 2024 as well. Carey moved to Houston, TX at the very beginning of 2020, before the pandemic started, after accepting a promotion at his company OfferPad, an iBuyer like Zillow. Carey helped Offerpad go public and was actually on Wall Street for the ringing of the bell on the day Offerpad opened for trading. The company did well from 2020 through 2023, when interest rates were low and the market was in hyperinflation. Carey bought a beautiful home and was happy. I am proud of him.

But by 2024, Offerpad and most iBuyer companies were struggling in the high-interest rate environment. Carey had to fire nearly 90% of his team as the company cut costs to stay afloat. Eventually Carey had to leave his position at OfferPad in the Spring of 2024, put his beautiful house up for sale and move back to Charlotte to start over.

Carey was going through in 2024 what I had gone through in 2009. He got caught in the crosswinds of a turbulent housing market and got laid out. I understood what he was going through and my heart felt heavy for him. Life is not fair, and it sucks sometimes. It's a lesson I've been reminded of repeatedly in my life.

When Carey moved back to Charlotte, he moved in with Mom and Dad with his son Quinn while Brandy and his daughter, Lorelei, stayed at her mother's. Carey was in a state of anxiety and depression when he moved home, and it was obvious. He felt defeated and angry, like I did in 2009, and to compound his emotional instability, he was split up from his family. Carey finds his strength in his family and while he was separated from them for a brief period in Charlotte, he started to unravel.

I invited Carey and Quinn over for dinner one night and we talked at length about his situation. Luckily, he had already found a new job and was working. Being split up from his family though was killing him. His problem was that his house in Texas hadn't sold yet, and he couldn't qualify to rent a house for his family because of his huge mortgage in Houston.

The solution was obvious. As fate would have it, our home on Tom Short was still on the market. Rebekah and I had an empty home.

We offered Carey the home to bring his family together and get Lorelei and Quinn into school before the school year started. Two weeks after Carey moved in, he got lucky and his home in Texas sold quickly. I was truly happy that his circumstances turned around so quickly.

Unfortunately, things between Carey and I took a turn for the worse after that. I'm not going to air our dirty laundry here, but we both said some hurtful things to each other out of frustration. I admit that I should have been more understanding of his emotional state and still shitty situation. He took a big loss on his house in Texas in selling it so quickly.

The truth is, Carey and I haven't communicated very well in the last 20 years. I feel like I have a very open and loving relationship with Cami and my parents. But it feels like Carey keeps me at arm's length, and I don't understand why. We've gone through a few periods in the last 20 years where we've been on no speaking terms, and it has really eaten me up inside. I know Carey has raised a family of four children in the last 17 years and has had very little time to do anything else while working full-time.

Maybe I don't try hard enough. Carey and I got along well in our youth, and I'd like to have that kind of relationship with him again one day.

By the end of 2024, Carey and I would find middle ground again. He and his family are still living in our home on Tom Short right now but he's under contract to buy a home being built out in the country with some acreage to spread out on and will move out by the summer.

And after he moves out, I'll have to try selling that fucking house again.

God Help Me.

Humpty Dumpty and the Fall of 2024

M ost days I roll out of bed at 7:30am and need two cups of coffee, a hot shower and 30 minutes of quiet time before I am safe to approach. I've never been much of a morning person. But on the morning of October 22, 2024, I jumped out of bed at 6:30am, energized and ready to start the day.

I was starting my first day of work on the television show *Blue Ridge* and my call time was 7:40 a.m. The month before, I had worked one day on the NBC production *Found*, playing a maximum-security prison guard. Prior to working on *Found*, I had not had a paid acting job since the fall of 2019, when I worked on the Netflix production *Outerbanks*. The pandemic and subsequent SAG strikes in 2023 were a real kick in the nuts to me and a lot of other people in the film and television industry.

The silver lining for me though was that during my five-year hiatus from studio productions, I used that downtime to write and produce two award winning short films of my own, *The Curious Case at 1301* and *The Birthday Butterfly*. I learned a lot creating those films, particularly the process of screenwriting and character development. On the production side of filmmaking, I learned how to get out of my own way by delegating and trusting others and how to collaborate with other creative people more effectively. Filmmaking is a challenging art form. Trying to go it alone can drive you mad. During the years 2020 through 2024 I think I found my unique voice as an artist and discovered a direction to go in with my future projects.

All that said, getting to work on a large production set again as a paid actor felt pretty damn good after five years. When I worked on *Found* in September of 2024, I had to drive down to the show's sound stage in Atlanta to film. And you know how I feel about driving to Atlanta. But *Found* turned out to be a great gig. The drive down and back wasn't too bad, and the cast and crew on the show were super friendly. I also got to see my cousin Kelly while in Atlanta. We talked for a couple hours and were able to catch up on each other's lives a bit. Something we hadn't done in a long time.

Having a good experience on *Found* was what I needed after not working on a studio production for five years. I didn't drive home from that gig asking myself, *"Why the hell are you doing this again?"*

So, when I woke up at 6:30 a.m. on that Tuesday morning to go to work on *Blue Ridge*, I was confident and excited about the day. To begin with, the show filmed in Charlotte, which meant I didn't have to deal with a grueling 8-9 hour round trip drive to Atlanta. The location I was filming at on *Blue Ridge* was only a 20-minute drive from my home, which meant I would wrap at the end of the day and be able to spend a comfortable night at home sleeping in my own bed.

Another big reason I was excited was that I was going to be working with producer Gary Wheeler, "Blue Ridge's" creator and showrunner. Gary has produced a lot of studio projects in the Charlotte area, and when I auditioned for *Blue Ridge*, he and I hit it off immediately. Like me, Gary grew up in Charlotte and went to Appalachian State University. During my callback audition, Gary and I talked for quite some time about all things Charlotte and ASU, so much so that the Casting Director had to cut us off to stay on schedule.

So, when I got the offer from Gary for a three-day contract to work on *Blue Ridge*, I felt like another door was opening for me. I was finally going to be working on a studio production in my hometown with a producer with whom I could hopefully collaborate more in the future. All I had to do was show up on time, know my lines and not screw up.

I arrived at the *Blue Ridge* base camp about ten minutes early that morning. I met one of the production assistants, who showed me to my honey wagon, which had my costume already in it. Then I immediately went to hair and make up because I was due on set by 8:00 a.m. to rehearse the first scene of the day. The role I was hired to play in *Blue Ridge* was called "Ice Man 3". Essentially, I was playing a bad guy who chases the good guy, Sheriff Wise, through the woods after discovering him snooping around my Crystal Meth operation. It's not exactly Shakespeare but, hey, I'm getting paid to be a professional actor in a major television production, so who am I to complain?

Once I was out of hair and make up and into my costume, I started introducing myself to the other cast members and crew. Gary was on set that morning and he and I chatted for a few minutes before Stephen Maddocks, the 1st A.D. (assistant director), gathered everyone around to hold the morning production meeting and start the day. I could tell almost immediately it was a great crew in the first few minutes of that meeting. There was no palpable tension or anxiety floating around and everyone seemed to be getting along famously. Stephen introduced me to everyone at the close of the morning meeting and then we all headed off to set – which was about 50 yards away – to start shooting.

The set was a lightly wooded area with a gently rolling terrain and the scene we were shooting was pretty straight forward. My character (Ice Man 3) and another character (Ice Man 2) are two guards, patrolling the grounds around our hidden meth lab for intruders, when we happen upon an empty campsite with a tent and smoldering fire. We toss the campsite, searching for clues as to who it could belong to, when the Sheriff and star of the show, played by Jonathan Schaech, would spy on us looting his campsite from afar. Then the Sheriff would discover my character's truck nearby and scurry off unnoticed to slash one of my tires. My buddy and I would hear the tire pop, spot the Sheriff and chase after him through the woods. Sounds simple enough, right?

Oh, how I wish I could tell you that it was.

Slip Slidin' Away

For the first couple of hours that morning, we shot footage of me and my partner tossing the Sheriff's campsite and tent, looking for clues. Then they turn the cameras around and shoot footage of the Sheriff sneaking up to his campsite unnoticed, watching us toss it. Then the crew moves over to the truck, about 30 yards away on the outskirts of the tree line, to film the Sheriff pull out his knife and pop one of the tires on my character's truck.

At around 10:30am, the crew began to set up the shot of me and my partner hearing our tire pop, spotting the Sheriff and then chasing after him through the woods. As the camera crews set up for our chase scene, my meth dealer counterpart and I got into our positions at the campsite.

Now, for over 16 years, since 2008, I have made physical fitness and health a priority in my life. I've raced in mud runs, like the Spartan Race, and completed Marine obstacle course races, all of which include long distance trail running, rope climbing, scaling ten-foot walls, barbed wire crawls and more. I ran a marathon before my 40th birthday. I go to the gym everyday to stretch, strength train and do cardio. Core strength, balance and stability are things I work on daily. So, when I tell you that I am absolutely confounded at what happened next that morning on the set of *Blue Ridge*, please believe me.

"Cameras rolling! Sound speeding!" I heard from outside the tree line. Then, finally Stephen called, *"ACTION!"*

My partner and I pretend to hear the 'POP' of one of the tires on our truck and spin around to spot the Sheriff take off into the woods. Then we start chasing him through the woods.

At this point things get a little fuzzy in my memory because, as I was running through those woods, for some inexplicable reason my legs just went out from underneath me. I never saw it coming and I didn't trip over anything. It was as if I just ran straight off a cliff and fell, watching helplessly as the horizon raced up and over me, like the veil of reality was suddenly being ripped off my head to reveal a completely alternate reality. It happened so fast, it felt like a dream, or more accurately, a nightmare.

I hit the ground HARD, with thunderous force, landing straight on my shins and knees. Then my upper body immediately fell backwards, with my legs still underneath me. I remember hearing little 'pops' in my ears, like sinus pressure being released. The pain from the impact hit me almost immediately as I cried out in agony.

I took a couple of seconds to calm down and assess my situation before trying to get up. I tried getting up on my right leg first but, as I did, I felt a 'squishy' material move around in my knee. Then I felt my kneecap slide away completely. The horror and realization of what I had done started to set in as I then attempted to get up using my left leg. But, again, I felt my left kneecap slide away too, up into my quadricep. I couldn't get up.

That's when I started to scream. The pain was so excruciating, I screamed like bloody murder. My mind went into a hazy fog, and everything got a little blurry as I desperately continued to try getting up. At first, I think everyone thought I was acting and had fallen to my knees on purpose. But after I continued to scream when Stephen yelled *"Cut!"* everybody on set realized I was not OK.

Mark Wells, the Production's on set medic, was on me almost immediately after that, to get his assessment of the situation. By that point I had managed to roll myself over and was sitting up, leaning against a rock or a tree, with my legs still underneath me.

"I think I just dislocated both of my knees," I remember telling Mark through clenched teeth.

Mark gently helped me slide my legs out from underneath me. I remember trying to look down at my legs, but my eyes were blurry, and my mind was not firing on all cylinders. I then looked at Mark and immediately recognized the panicked look in his eyes when he saw my legs and yelled for someone to call 911. He remained calm though and quickly found a blanket to drape over my legs so that I wouldn't look at them. Apparently, the bulges in my pant legs, where my kneecaps were supposed to be, were sitting up high, in my quadriceps. The cast and crew began to gather around to see what happened and one of the cameramen sat down next to me, talking to me calmly as the initial pain began to subside.

"What the hell did I trip over?!" I kept asking repeatedly. We had been out in this wooded area filming for over two hours before I fell. I remember walking around the area, before the cameras were even set up, looking for any significant holes or drops in the terrain to avoid. "What did I not see? What did I miss? How did this happen?", I kept asking.

Nobody seemed to be able to answer me. The cameras and crew were set up near the truck, a good distance from where I fell. Between the distance and vegetation blocking their view, no one on the crew saw what happened with any clarity. My scene partner and meth lab counterpart didn't see what happened either. Like me, he had been doing his job, watching the Sheriff run and then giving chase. He wasn't paying attention to me.

As the shock began to fade, my mind began to become clear again and I became suddenly aware that all eyes were on me. I was so fucking embarrassed. Humor has always been my defense mechanism, so when Mark knelt beside me to ask me for my wife's phone number so that he could call her and have her meet me at the hospital, I remember looking up at him with a boyish grin and answering, "Do we really have to call her? She'll get really upset at me if we do." This prompted a few hearty laughs from Mark and the crew.

When the laugh track faded though, the full realization of what I had just done began to set in.

"How badly did I just fuck myself?" I thought. *"How long will it be until I'll be able to walk again? Will I ever be able to walk normally again? Will I make a full recovery from this? What am I going to do about work? I have an appraisal inspection set up for Friday."*

I tried to quiet my mind and find a center, but between the pain and shock it was difficult.

After what felt like a relatively short period of time, two EMT trucks responded to the 911 call and arrived on set to help transport me to the hospital. After Mark, a former EMT himself, apprised the paramedics of my situation, they decided to give me morphine before trying to roll me onto a rigid backboard and carry me out of the woods.

The last lucid thing I remember that day was one of the EMTs trying to find a vein in my arm to administer the morphine. The EMT, who was still in training, kept missing the vein in my arm. After his third unsuccessful attempt, I remember smiling at him coyly and asking, "How bout we let one of the other guys try now, OK?" The EMT trainee blushed as his veteran peers laughed out loud. Apparently, I was just one big joke that morning.

After I was successfully loaded up with morphine and placed in a foggy state of existence, the EMTs carried me out of the woods and laid me on a proper gurney for transport. As they were loading me into the back of one of the ambulances, Stephen came up beside me to wish me well. I remember looking at Stephen, humbled and embarrassed (and high), and repeatedly apologizing for screwing up his day and making him behind in his shooting schedule. I also told him to give my apologies to Gary, who was probably on the phone, alerting the studio of my accident and preparing the insurance documents for my arrival at the hospital.

Riding the Dragon

They took me to a hospital in Monroe, NC, about 20 minutes from the set and 40 minutes from our house. I remember riding in the back of the ambulance with the EMT trainee on the way there, chit chatting with him a good bit. I recall him being a very nice guy, but because I was so high on morphine, I really don't remember what we talked about. I hope I didn't say anything too stupid.

Shortly after I was admitted into the E.R., Rebekah arrived at the hospital in a state of anxiety and panic. She had been working in her office uptown that day when she got Mark's call and immediately dropped everything she was doing to rush down to Monroe to be with me. When I saw her walk into my room in the E.R., I remember smiling at her and saying, "You didn't have to come all the way down here baby. I'm fine."

Can you buy morphine over the counter? Cause that shit is great.

When Rebekah stepped out of the room to talk to the doctors and the *Blue Ridge* production assistant who followed us to the hospital, I remember being alone and pulling the blanket off my legs to get a sneak peek at the damage I had done to myself. The first thought I had as I gazed down at my bare legs was, "*Where the hell are my pants?*" I assume they must've cut them off me when I arrived.

The second thought I had was *"I don't have a scratch on me"*. I thought for sure I was going to find a blotchy mess of crimson and purple on my legs, but there was no blood or bruising at all. Except for my kneecaps not being where they were supposed to be, everything looked normal. I suppose if I wasn't on a heavy narcotic at the time, I would've freaked out. But, instead, all I did was chuckle. Then I took my phone out of the costume jacket I was still wearing and snapped a couple of pictures of my displaced knees. Later that day, when Rusty and some of my friends found out about the accident and began texting me, asking me how I was doing, I told them that I was fine and then sent them those pictures of my knees. I probably shouldn't have done that. But, again, morphine is a helluva drug.

Not long after Rebekah arrived at the hospital, my family started to show up. As I sat in my little corner of the E.R. alone, with a curtain drawn around me, I could hear my mom's voice right outside, talking to a nurse. When the nurse came into my room to check on me, the first person I saw as the nurse drew back the curtain was Carey. He and I locked eyes for a moment and gave each other our patented shit-eating grin that said, *"You're such a dumbass."* Then, after a brief check of my vitals, the nurse left and closed the curtain behind her, leaving me alone once again.

Seeing Carey standing outside of my room for that brief few seconds brought out a flood of emotion in me, and I started to get teary-eyed. Carey and I had been at odds with one another for the past few months and weren't really talking at the time. Our current beef was just typical brotherly angst, petty and selfish, with harsh words said out of frustration by both of us. But as I sat there in that E.R., unable to move my legs, all that bullshit seemed to just disappear. I was so grateful that he came to see me.

I guess it was around mid afternoon that day when they took me to have an MRI done on my legs. I really had no concept of time anymore and had been admitted into the hospital overnight at this point. A few hours after the MRI was done, a surgical resident came to my room and told Rebekah and I that I had ruptured both of the patellar tendons in my legs.

The patellar tendons are what hold your kneecaps in place, attached to your quadriceps above the knee, and then to the shins below the knee. Apparently, I fell so hard and with so much force that I managed to rip both of my patellar tendons off of the bottom of my knees. That's why they were now floating up high in my legs. Those sinus pressure 'pops' that I had heard when I fell was the sound of both of my tendons being ripped clean off of the kneecap.

As bad as that sounds though, the surgical resident told us that it's not an uncommon injury. It's typically seen in athletes, as it takes quite a bit of force to rupture the tendon off the bone. The good news was that my tendons could easily be reattached to my knees with surgery and that I should make a full recovery. The surgery would involve drilling small holes into the bottom of my kneecaps and then sewing the tendons back in place to reattach to the bone. It would take about three months for the tendons to heal and then another 9-12 months of physical therapy to regain full use and stability in my legs. For athletes, a ruptured patellar tendon is considered a season ending injury, not a career ending one – similar to an ACL tear.

The bad news, however, was that I ruptured both of my patellar tendons at the same time, which is quite uncommon. Most people only rupture one tendon, leaving them with one good leg to move around on and recover with. The orthopedic surgeon who eventually performed my operation would later tell me that, in his twenty-year career, he had only one other patient rupture both patellar tendons at the same time – a basketball player who dove out of bounds for the ball and fell hard on his knees, similar to what I had done. The surgeon also said that my recovery would be far more difficult and frustrating because I would be healing both tendons at the same time, without a good leg to get around on. So, lucky fucking me.

At the end of that day, long after the excitement I had started my day with had vanished, I found myself lying in a cramped hospital bed, doped up on morphine and awaiting surgery to repair my two dislocated knees. That night, as Rebekah lay beside me in a reclining chair, sleeping restlessly, I replayed the events of the day over and over again in my head so that I wouldn't forget them. I had begged Rebekah to go home and get some rest, but she refused. I knew that I would need to lean on her heavily in the coming months for help with just about everything. And I hoped that it wouldn't do any long-lasting damage to our relationship.

The last thought I remember having before I dozed off to sleep that night was, *"If anybody ever tells me to 'Break a Leg' again, I might have to punch them in the mouth."*

I'm Better than That

T rying to sleep in a hospital really sucks. Zero stars, would not recommend.

Throughout the night, various nurses come in and out of your room to check on the multitude of beeping and blinking electronic devices you're connected to. And other nurses come in periodically to wake you up and ask you how your pain level is so they can give you more drugs based on your answer.

Don't get me wrong, I am eternally grateful for everything the hospital staff did for me, but if you're looking for a quality night of sleep after a hellishly bad day, try not to do it in a hospital.

But it wasn't just the constant bombardment of nursing staff that made me uncomfortable. I was also dealing with something I had never experienced before: residual trauma.

Throughout that first night, and for many subsequent nights to come, I would wake up in a cold sweat, with my body shaking uncontrollably, as my subconscious mind replayed the fall repeatedly in my head, trying to figure out what happened. The primary purpose of the mind, after all, is to keep you alive. Its sole function is to scan the environment, collect data, analyze and process experiences and categorize dangers as things to watch out for in the future.

When a child touches a hot stove and burns themselves, the brain processes that experience as being a threat and then creates a gag order in your mind to not do that again. But my brain couldn't understand **how** I fell and continually replayed the memory of it in order to analyze what I had done wrong and how to avoid doing it again in the future.

Every time it happened, my conscious mind would take over and I would repeatedly begin to ask myself: *"What did I trip over? What didn't I see? Was I just careless and not paying attention? Did I just run off a sheer cliff inadvertently, like an imbecile? Maybe it was a hidden sinkhole, covered up with leaves. How could I have possibly missed that and not seen it coming? I'm better than that."*

Over and over again, while both sleeping and awake, my unconscious mind would randomly replay the moment of my fall and send a jolt of fear and anxiety coursing through my veins. I've always considered myself to be of strong mind and discipline, able to willfully clear my head of limiting beliefs and negative feelings. I've had a lot of practice with that over the years. But the residual trauma I was now experiencing was something new. Something I didn't know how to control or stop.

Under the Knife

On Thursday, October 24, 2024, I underwent surgery to have my patellar tendons reattached. Thankfully, the procedure went smoothly and, when I woke up, I found my legs wrapped in thick foam isolation braces, secured with heavy Velcro straps, and with rigid metal rods running down the back of them to ensure I didn't bend my knees while they healed. I would have to wear these leg braces morning, noon and night for the next four to six weeks. And let me tell you, those damn things were terribly uncomfortable. They didn't breathe very well and made my legs and whole body sweat. And the metal rods running down the back of them would sometimes dig into my hamstrings at night, making it impossible to sleep at times.

On Friday, the day after my surgery, the surgical team cleared me to go home. But not before I was visited by a cardiologist, who came to tell me that during my surgery, the anesthesiologist found that my heart was in atrial fibrillation (a-fib), meaning my heart will sometimes beat irregularly or "skip beats". They then ran an EKG test on me to confirm the anesthesiologist's findings, which it did.

Being diagnosed with atrial fibrillation is not as bad as it sounds though. Most people diagnosed with a-fib show no symptoms at all and lead perfectly active lives. It's basically an electrical problem that can cause your heart to beat out of synch from time to time. The threat of a heart attack or stroke is very low, but if left unchecked and untreated, atrial fibrillation could enlarge the heart over time and become a major issue later on down the road.

Rebekah freaked out about my atrial fibrillation at first, but I wasn't too concerned. My mother has lived with a-fib her entire life, as her mother did before her. I guess I picked the winning lottery ticket on that genetic condition. But I'm an active guy and have never felt any heart palpitations or other symptoms linked to atrial fibrillation, so I wasn't too worried. I was far more concerned about my immediate problems, like how I was going to poop on my own with straight leg braces on.

Because I couldn't bend my knees for the next four to six weeks, it meant that I couldn't climb stairs. And our home in Ardrey has stairs at every entrance – lots of stairs. So, to get me home the hospital put me on a list to be transported by an EMT unit, who would have to carry me up the stairs to get me into our house.

We waited all day and night for an EMT transport to become available that Friday, long after they cleared me for discharge. But because my condition was considered stable, we were getting bumped to the bottom of the list for transport because all available EMTs kept getting called out for emergencies. By 9 p.m. that night, Rebekah was losing her mind wanting to go home, and I finally convinced her to go ahead of me and prepare the house for my arrival. Right after she left the hospital, I called Kristin, our next-door neighbor, to give her the heads up that Rebekah was on her way home. I asked Kristin to check in on Rebekah when she got home and give her some comfort, which she so kindly did.

Finally, after spending three nights in a hospital and undergoing surgery to have my knees repaired, an EMT unit became available at 11p.m. to take me home. I was elated to be going home but also terrified of how the next few months would unfold.

When we arrived at our home in Ardrey around midnight, I was alarmed to find a fire truck parked outside our front door with several firefighters standing around.

"Oh God, What now?" I thought to myself.

It turns out the two EMTs who drove me home didn't think they could handle carrying me up a full flight of stairs on their own and called the Charlotte Fire Department for backup. It eventually took two EMTs and five firefighters to carry me up the front steps of our house and into our bedroom on the first floor. After the EMTs and firefighters left, Rebekah climbed into bed with me and immediately fell asleep.

As I lay there that first night back in my own bed, I remember staring into the dark void of our bedroom unable to sleep. Before this accident, I had never ridden in an ambulance, never been admitted into a hospital and never undergone surgery, if you don't count having my wisdom teeth pulled about a decade earlier. This little fall of mine, just a few months before my 50th birthday, checked all those boxes off for me and then left me with a heart condition diagnosis as a parting gift. I did not feel like the man of steel anymore. I felt beaten and broken.

I tried to suppress my anger and fear as best as I could. I knew I needed to stay positive and prepare myself mentally for the challenges to come. But, in truth, I was an emotional mess. I had never felt so helpless and vulnerable in my life. The emotional and residual trauma of my accident was still ever present, and I wondered how well Rebekah and I would be able to manage my situation over the coming months. The surgeon said that I should make a full recovery in about six to nine months, but on that first night home, lying in the dark and unable to move my legs even an inch, six months felt like a lifetime.

Oh, How the Mighty have Fallen

"One, Two.... THREE."

Rebekah grunted as she picked up my legs and pulled them off the side of our bed while I used my arms to slide my butt and upper body over to the edge. She placed my heavy legs down gently on our bedroom floor as I gripped the walker in front of me for dear life and carefully hoisted myself up to stand. I can't imagine how hard that would have been for me 20 years ago, when I was forty pounds overweight and had no upper body muscle.

For the first few weeks, Rebekah had to do most of the heavy lifting in helping me get in and out of bed and on and off the couch. One of the things I was not told by the doctors and didn't anticipate was that my legs would be pretty much useless for the first 3-4 weeks of my recovery. After my surgery, my quadriceps seemed to shut down altogether, as if my brain stopped sending electrical signals to them completely. From a seated or laying down position, I couldn't lift my legs up even an inch. It felt like I was paralyzed from the waist down to some extent.

Once I was vertical though, I could still use my hips, glutes and hamstrings to walk (more like shuffle), but my balance was complete shit, and I felt like I would topple over at any second if I didn't have something to hold on to. It was a truly humbling feeling. I felt like Seamus, the pirate with two wooden legs on the TV show *Family Guy*.

In the beginning of my recovery, I couldn't swing my hips out wide enough to step up just two or three inches, which meant I couldn't step over the six-inch threshold of our shower. So, I had to bathe with a washcloth at the sink. Every few days, when I started to feel gross, Rebekah would get into the shower, and I'd lean my head in so she could wash my hair.

"Oh, how the mighty have fallen," I remember thinking to myself as Rebekah scrubbed shampoo through my greasy hair. I couldn't do my own scrubbing because I had to hold on to my walker and maintain balance while I was leaning in.

Sleeping at night became uncomfortable because the isolation braces I was wearing kept my feet pointed straight up all night. This caused my heels to rub raw on the bed sheet. As hard as I tried, I couldn't lift my legs up or turn my feet to reposition them on my own. On a few occasions, I had to wake Rebekah up in the middle of the night to help give me some much-needed relief by moving my feet around and applying a soothing salve to my heels. We eventually started to use a towel underneath my calves to elevate my feet a couple of inches, keeping my heels off the bed sheet and preventing me from going mad.

The heavy foam braces on my legs didn't breathe very well and trapped in body heat, making my legs and body sweat profusely. Because I couldn't roll over on to my side with the braces on, I was sleeping on my back all night, sweating, which made my back break out in a rash that was itchy and irritating. After one week of wearing those isolation leg braces 24/7, I finally couldn't take it anymore and took them off to let my legs breathe. During those first few weeks, letting my legs air out in the morning after breakfast became the best part of my day. It felt like heaven.

When I took the isolation braces off, it was easy to figure out why my legs were sweating so much. My knees were almost hot to the touch. They were radiating so much heat from the healing process that you could have probably slow cooked a pot roast inside my leg braces while I had them on.

Despite the discomfort of my heels being rubbed raw at night and the leg braces causing me to constantly sweat, the pain level in my knees was quite minimal. It was just a dull throbbing pain, which is something I'm quite accustomed to from my daily strength training. The doctors had prescribed me Oxycodone for pain management before I left the hospital, but I never touched the stuff once I got home. I didn't want to develop an opioid addiction on top of everything else I was going through. I know a few people who had to fight that horrible addiction, and it wasn't something I cared to go through personally.

During those first few weeks, my emotional state was fragile, to say the least. In addition to the continuing residual trauma that would creep in my head every now and then, I found myself breaking down in tears whenever one of our neighbors or friends would stop by to bring us meals or to take Duke for a walk. My good friend and fellow appraiser Chuck took over my appraisal business temporarily, keeping my clientele in place until I was able to start working again. Rebekah's brother David was kind enough to bring my standing desk and work computer downstairs so that I could check my email and forward any work-related matters to Chuck throughout my recovery.

Even Rebekah's office was kind enough to let her work from home during my recovery so that she could care for me properly. When Rebekah would go to a yoga class or run errands, Mom would come over and play cards with me. We'd gossip like two little girls for a couple of hours and cackle at old memories. I really enjoy spending time with Mom like that. I know she does too.

Throughout my hospital stay and recovery, Stephen Maddocks, the 1st A.D. on *Blue Ridge,* kept in constant contact with Rebekah and I to get updates on how I was doing. Stephen would send us video updates from the set to try cheering me up and let me know I wasn't forgotten. On Halloween Day, I was completely surprised when Jonathan Schaesch, the star of *Blue Ridge*, stopped by our house and surprised me with an acoustic guitar signed by the cast and crew of the show. Mark Wells, the show's medic, and Gary Wheeler, the *Blue Ridge* producer and show runner, also reached out to me regularly to check in and wish me a speedy recovery. Rusty, of course, also kept in touch and even took the time to talk to me at length about his experience with residual trauma when he had broken his hip while mountain biking a few years earlier.

All these simple gestures of kindness from friends, family and the *Blue Ridge* production helped Rebekah and I tremendously throughout my recovery, and I would occasionally be flooded with so much gratitude that I would break down and cry. Emotional vulnerability is not something I am used to, but it was truly inspiring to know that so many people cared about us. I will forever be grateful to everyone who lent us a hand or reached out with words of encouragement during that period of my life.

Baby Steps

During the first four weeks of recovery from my patella tendon surgery, I felt like I was under house arrest because I was literally incapable of leaving the first floor of our home. Boredom set in pretty fast, but having Duke around helped a lot. He was my isolation buddy during my recovery, providing me with some much-needed company and attention while Rebekah worked during the days. I hated that I couldn't get down on the floor with Duke to give him his nightly belly rubs. And I really missed taking him for a walk in the evenings. It was a multitude of little things like that that constantly reminded me of how much I took for granted in my life. One of the things I looked forward to the most during my recovery was being able to give Duke all the loving he needed and deserved.

To offset my boredom, I read quite a bit, chewing through several of Michael Connelly's novels I still had in my library. Hieronymus Bosch, the no nonsense L.A. detective at the center of many of Connelly's stories, is one of my favorite literary characters of all time.

I also played guitar to pass the time. David brought my Fender Strat downstairs so that I could play for an hour or so every day. But because I prefer to play guitar while standing, the daily practice regimen I had developed before my accident got thrown out the window. I simply couldn't stay on my feet for too long during those first few weeks.

I'm not sure I'm comfortable with using the term "silver lining" to describe anything about what happened to me in the fall of 2024 because there was nothing comfortable about it at all. But one thing I am grateful for is that it happened while I was working on a studio production carrying workers' compensation insurance. All the medical bills associated with my injury and recovery were being paid for and coordinated by *Blue Ridge's* insurance. And, I have to admit, they really took good care of me. Had my accident happened on one of my own films or in my private appraisal practice, Rebekah and I would have had to deal with insurance directly, which everyone knows can be an absolute nightmare.

One of the biggest challenges we had to overcome early in my recovery was figuring out how I was going to get out of the house to go to my four-week follow-up appointment with the surgeon. All the exits in our home required navigating stairs, which I was simply unable to manage in my isolation braces. If you recall, it took two EMTs and five firefighters to carry me into the house when I came home from the hospital.

To figure out a way to get me out of the house, the insurance company sent a contractor to our home to see if a temporary ramp could be installed. But that investigation proved to be futile as the contractor concluded there simply wasn't enough room for a ramp to be installed anywhere. The contractor instead suggested that a wheelchair lift be installed in our garage, which would have required the contractor to disassemble the stairs in our garage completely and then drill into the concrete floor. I seriously wanted to avoid that, so by the third week of my house arrest, Rebekah and I figured out a way for me to break free and get out of the house, without the need of a wheelchair lift or a ramp.

Using a pair of Rebekah's sturdy cork yoga blocks, she and I figured out how to cut the distance I needed to step up in half. Stair treads are typically 9 inches high and Rebekah's yoga blocks are, conveniently, about 4.5 inches high. By week three of my recovery, I had regained just enough mobility and strength to swing my hips out wide enough to clear the 4.5 inches of one of Rebekah's yoga blocks and could step up on to it.

So, together, Rebekah and I began to practice climbing up and down the stairs in our home. She would place one of her yoga blocks down, in front of the stairs, and I would carefully take a hip-swing step up onto it and then take another step up to the actual stair tread, essentially creating two smaller steps to climb up one full stair tread. I was quite proud of coming up with that solution to getting out of the house.

After we informed the insurance company that we didn't need a wheelchair lift and had instead devised an alternative method of navigating the stairs, they were skeptical and wanted a physical therapist to observe our escape plan to make sure it was safe. When Rebekah and I demonstrated our stair climbing technique to my physical therapist, she was floored by its simple ingenuity and effectiveness, even suggesting that we patent the idea.

Being able to get out of the house after four weeks of isolation was a big step forward in my recovery. It was empowering to me to know that I had successfully devised a simple and safe escape plan from my own home that no one from the insurance company or physical therapist's office could even conceive of. I felt like fuckin' MacGyver. Once I was on *terra firma* again, it was easy enough to slide into the back seat of Rebekah's car and go to my four week post operative consultation with the surgeon.

Finding small wins like that, as often as you can, is the key to any successful recovery, I think. In fact, I'd say it's one of the most important fundamental lessons that one can learn about life. In my youth I often got frustrated and gave up on a goal or passion because it was just "too hard". Well, news flash kid, everything's hard. Life certainly didn't get any easier as I got older. I simply got wiser and came to understand that consistency and dedication are the keys to success. Taking a large goal and breaking it down into smaller, achievable objectives is paramount to maintaining momentum. I needed to climb a step that was nine inches high but physically couldn't manage it. So, I decided to create two small steps out of it and managed to reach the summit and achieve my goal.

The accident I experienced on October 22, 2024, turned my life upside down and offered me a very different perspective on what it means to survive. In one moment, I went from being able to climb 100 flights of stairs in 20 minutes to needing significant help in getting out of bed in the morning. The first four weeks of my recovery were definitely the most challenging weeks of my life. It was a test of resolve and endurance. While I would never wish the experience on anyone, dislocating my knees was a life changing moment that ushered in me a new understanding of patience and showed me just how strong I can be with the support and love of my friends and family.

As New Year's Day and 2025 approached, I began to feel really good about the future. With my 50th birthday rapidly approaching, I was hoping to be able to start driving again soon. Reaching that goal would finally unlock my full independence and allow me to drive myself to physical therapy and doctor's appointments. It also meant that I could start going back to the gym regularly. I had no intention of pushing myself too hard though. I simply wanted to have a normal routine back in my life.

But with as much joy and optimism as Rebekah and I had during those final days of 2024, the Universe had yet another dick punch to throw our way, a sucker punch, that took us completely by surprise and left Rebekah and I weeping for days, well into the New Year.

You Are My Sunshine

Regardless of which one of us rolled out of bed first in the morning, letting Duke out to go potty was numero uno in the order of business. Duke rarely had an accident in the house and, when he did, he was usually sick or on medication. To keep it that way, every morning either Rebekah or I would open the back door, and Duke would trot out into the yard to do his business and then he would race back inside, all excited because he knew it was time for breakfast.

Duke always got excited when it was time to eat. He would prance around like a giddy little girl with his butt wiggling 100 miles an hour as I walked him to his bowl for breakfast, lunch or dinner. And, being an American bulldog, every time Rebekah or I pulled out his afternoon treat – a milk bone – he would drool all over the floors. Very similar to how I drooled over Cindy Crawford in her cut off jeans and tight tank top from her Pepsi advertisements in the 90s. I had a poster of Cindy on my wall for many years growing up.

If we were ever late giving Duke his lunch or dinner, he'd usually hunt us down and attempt to herd us in the direction of the laundry room, where his food and water were kept. This happened at least twice a year. It's not easy trying to explain Daylight Savings to a 90-pound bulldog.

On the morning of Friday, 12/27/2024 I slept in. Usually, Rebekah and I alternate on who gets up first to let Duke out and go get coffee for the two of us. And although I could get out of bed on my own by this point, I was still recovering from my knee surgery and finally sleeping well because I was no longer having to wear my leg braces at night. So that morning I milked it and slept in. I'm not exactly sure what time Rebekah got up because I didn't hear her get out of bed. What did wake me up that morning though was hearing Duke yelp loudly from the living room.

While Duke was always such a good boy, he had to sleep in the living room at night because, frankly, he snored and farted so much that I couldn't handle it in our bedroom. I think I do enough of that on my own to not need any help. *Ha!* Now, before you start to call us insensitive about not letting Duke sleep in our bedroom with us at night, let me first tell you just how spoiled he was in our living room.

Duke slept on three...yes, three large dog beds, stacked on top of each other in the living room. The floor was covered in various stuffed animals and dog toys which he absolutely loved to cuddle, chase and play tug of war with around the house. Every night, when we'd go to bed, we would wrap him up in one of the many blankets he had and tuck him in goodnight. Rebekah would often sing Duke a lullaby before we went to bed – usually "You are My Sunshine".

So, by the time we finally turned out the lights and said goodnight to Duke, he was the happiest dog in the world, with genuine love in his eyes and sporting a soft smile that truly showed his appreciation. When we woke up in the mornings to let Duke out, we were usually met with those same lovable eyes and handsome grin. Sadly though, on that Friday morning when I slept in, none of us were able to muster a genuine smile.

When I heard Duke yelp from the living room, my eyes slowly opened, and I slid out of bed carefully before peg legging it out of our bedroom to see what the commotion was about. When I entered the living room I found Rebekah on the floor comforting Duke, who was lying on his three beds and panting heavily.

"What happened?" I asked

"I don't know. He came back in all excited for breakfast and I guess he slipped on the floor," Rebekah replied. "I didn't see it happen; I was closing the door and had my back to him. He just yelped and then hobbled over to his bed and plopped down. I think he sprained his foot or maybe twisted his ankle or something."

"He slipped inside the house?"

"Yeah, right here, by the door."

Duke had taken a few spills and tumbles around the house before, but only a couple of times while inside. The hardwood floors were a little slippery for his paws and when he got excited and raced around, he'd occasionally slip and strain his back or legs. The few big tumbles he took happened when he was going down our front steps, when we'd take him out for a walk. But he always managed to push through the pain and walk it off, especially with the prospect of going into the dog park or getting a treat after his walk.

"Did he eat?" I asked Rebekah, but I was still groggy and not fully awake.

"No. Not yet," she replied, with concern in her voice.

I bent down as much as I could with my stiff knees and gave Duke some love, scratching him behind his ears and telling him good morning.

Then I carefully moved his back legs around, trying to better understand what was giving him problems. But Duke didn't yelp or seem to be uncomfortable with anything I did to his legs.

"Maybe he just slipped and scared himself again," I said in a hopeful tone. "You want some breakfast?!"

Duke's face erupted in a smile as he attempted to get up, but it was painfully obvious he was having a really hard time getting his back legs to work properly and, after trying valiantly for a few seconds, he simply plopped back down and continued to pant heavily. Rebekah and I shared a concerned look. We both knew that if Duke couldn't get up at the prospect of food, something was definitely wrong.

We ended up bringing Duke's breakfast into the living room for him that morning and he ate it ravenously. He certainly hadn't lost his appetite. But by mid afternoon Duke still hadn't moved from his bed. He tried a couple of times to stand up and walk, but whatever was hurting him was too much for him to bear and he would simply give up and settle back down on his bed.

Rebekah eventually took Duke into the vet later that day and was told by the vet that Duke had probably bruised his spine or ruptured a disc. The vet seemed optimistic though and said Duke would probably just need 48 hours of rest before he was healed enough to get around on his own. The vet gave Duke some steroid medication to help him with his recovery.

But over the next 48 hours Duke's condition did not improve. He just couldn't move his back legs, no matter how hard he tried. Whenever we tried to help him up to walk, he would simply drag his back legs behind him, like he was paralyzed from the waist down. When Rebekah and I eventually had to carry him outside and down a flight of stairs to go to the bathroom, he wouldn't go because he couldn't stand up.

On Sunday morning, 12/29/2024, Rebekah and I both woke up early and got out of bed together to check on Duke. It was a miserable, rainy morning with whipping winds and storms rolling into the area fast. Duke had managed to reposition himself in the middle of the night, but he still hadn't peed in about 36 hours, which told us that his kidneys probably weren't functioning properly.

Because it was such a nasty morning, Rebekah and I decided to take Duke out through the garage to try getting him to go potty. Maybe being in the front yard, within view of the dog park, would give him the motivation he needed to make an effort and stand up on his own. But, once again, after carrying him outside on our own, Duke couldn't hold himself up and simply plopped down in the wet grass, still panting heavily.

After pleading with Duke for half an hour to go potty, Rebekah and I finally had to give up because the rain began to fall heavier and both of our phones alerted us to a tornado watch in effect in our area. When we tried to carry Duke back inside though, he yelped and fought us when we started climbing up the garage stairs. He didn't want to go back in. So, we laid Duke down on the garage floor and sat with him while we quietly listened to the drumming of the rain that was coming down outside.

At that point, Rebekah and I both knew what we needed to do, but neither one of us could bear to say it out loud. We had been through this nightmare before and had to make this gut-wrenching decision a few times together already, with Caesar, Shep and Pumpkin.

After listening to the rain pelt and the wind howl for what felt like an hour, I finally found the courage to say it.

"It's time baby. He's in pain and getting worse. We need to show him mercy. I can't do to him what I did to Max."

"I know," said Rebekah, between soft sobs.

Before we put Duke in Rebekah's car to take him to the emergency vet, I went inside and pulled out a leftover ribeye I had cooked the night before. I cut it up for Duke, just the way he liked it, and stuck his 'steakies' in the microwave to warm up while I started to cry. I knew it would probably be the last time I would fix Duke his most favorite treat.

When I came back into the garage, I found Rebekah cradling Duke in her arms and singing "You Are My Sunshine". That moment was so beautiful and tragic at the same time that it ripped my heart to pieces.

After Duke devoured every bite of his ribeye breakfast, Rebekah and I put him in the back seat of her car. But when I tried to get into the passenger seat of Rebekah's car, I couldn't do it. My knees still wouldn't bend enough for me to get into the front seat. I may have been out of my braces, but I had yet to even start physical therapy at this point and was still very limited in what I could do.

I remember feeling absolutely crushed and defeated at that moment. The emotional trauma that I experienced after my fall and had been working through and coming to peace with over the last 9 weeks, came flooding back over me like a tsunami. *Why is this happening?* I kept asking myself. *What could I have possibly done to deserve so much pain?* It's selfish thinking, I know. But it's how I felt.

Once I was able to get my shit back together, Rebekah decided to call her brother David to see if he could come and help us. Of course, David came immediately, as did Carina. I was able to get into the back seat of his Tesla, and we followed Rebekah and Duke to the same emergency vet where we had taken Caesar nearly a decade earlier.

Thankfully, being a Sunday morning with terrible weather, the Vet's office was empty when we arrived. Duke was taken in right away for examination, but it didn't take long for the Veterinarian to come out and talk to us. Duke had apparently ruptured his spine when he tripped Friday morning coming back into the house. The Vet said it was likely Duke was suffering from a degenerative spine but the only option, to be sure, was to do an $8,000 exploratory surgery. And, even then, the Vet explained, Duke would probably not be able to recover or possibly even survive the surgery. He told us that euthanasia was the merciful and right thing to do.

Through the very end we were in the room with Duke. I know he was hurting and scared, but Rebekah and I and David and Carina were with him. I petted him, scratched behind his ears and kissed his forehead. Rebekah pulled out some of Duke's favorite treats she had brought with her and let him gobble them up out of her hands. Even the Vet gave him a Hershey's kiss. A sweet parting gift for such a sweet lovable soul.

I could see the pain leave him in the end. His body relaxed and his head grew heavy. But he smiled right before he went under. Not one of his big handsome smiles though. More like a soft, understanding smile. As he slowly closed his eyes for the last time, I thanked him once more for being such a good boy.

God, the Hit Man

The Fall of 2024 will be remembered as one of the most painful periods in my life. The physical, mental and emotional trauma that I experienced in those 10 weeks will forever be ingrained in my memory and permanently branded to my body by the scars on my knees.

Losing Duke so soon after my accident broke me down to the core. For a couple of weeks after his passing, I became lost in despair and agony. I was angry and felt a tremendous guilt permeating my soul. Duke's accident mirrored mine so much that I found myself diving down a rabbit hole searching for answers. We both fell and no one really saw it happen. We both lost the use of our legs. *Why am I the one who got to recover and live?*

For awhile I thought God was a gangster who, for some inexplicable reason, decided to put a hit out on me. First, he crippled me, then he crippled and killed my dog.

I consider myself to be a fairly rationale guy, putting my trust first in science, reason and logic. But for all the wonderful advancements that those fields have provided humanity, the big questions still elude us. *Why are we here? Why must the experience of life have to come with so much pain and suffering attached to it?* Once again, I circled back to the very same questions that have haunted me since I was 11 years old. The *Shadow Man* still stands in the corner of my room.

Religion attempts to answer those questions for us, but I still put little trust in those answers. Nobody really knows what's going on. No one has the definitive answer to life, the universe and everything. And anyone who claims that they do is most likely trying to sell you something.

A lot of people buy into it though, and I can't say that I blame them. Perhaps blind faith is a more suitable alternative to the madness that not knowing can manifest. When I was 38 years old, I had that powerful dream and experienced something that I considered to be bliss and understanding. But after the Fall of 2024, I guess I'm still on the fence about what I believe. *I wonder how my feelings about that will change over the second half of my life. Will I look back on this time, ten years from now, and see it in another light or from a much different perspective? Probably.*

When I look back on my failed construction business and bankruptcy now, I don't become bitter and wish that it had never happened. If it had not happened, I would most likely not be where I am today and have all that I am grateful for now. It reminds me of the Zen story about the Chinese farmer. You can look that story up on the internet easily if you're interested. I prefer to listen to the telling of that story by Alan Watts, the 20th century philosopher and Professor of Religious studies.

I know that things could be worse. Like Duke, I could've broken my back when I fell and become paralyzed for life. From a wider perspective, I suppose I've actually been quite fortunate in my life in avoiding injury, pain and suffering. While the last few months of 2024 were chock-full of disastrous surprises, I was also shown tremendous love and support from everyone around me. I am grateful that Duke was with me through the most challenging months of my life. Maybe God delayed his passing to help ease my suffering during that period. But I'm still torn up inside that I never got the chance to get on the floor with him again and give him belly rubs and snuggles like I did before my accident. I never got the chance to take him on that final walk.

I don't know what I would've done without Rebekah by my side through it all. She has proven to be my center and balance in life. For a while, she was the sole reason I kept getting out of bed in the morning and making an effort. Without her I would have surely spiraled out in a rage of self pity, anger and regret.

About a week after Duke passed, I started writing this book. I had been contemplating writing down my life experiences for some time, long before my accident happened. That little unconscious voice in the back of my mind has been telling me to write it all down for the last few years. But after the events of the past few weeks, that little unconscious voice became thunderous and demanding. Maybe everything that has happened to me over the last several weeks was a push to get me to finally start writing.

I'm not quite sure what will become of this book. At the very least I think it will bring me a better understanding and appreciation of all that I have experienced and everything I have to be thankful for. Perhaps if I end up sharing this book and my experiences with others, it will inspire them to do the same.

Despite all that I've gone through, I still have much to be grateful for. I don't really believe that God is a gangster.

But it sure does feel that way sometimes.

Embrace the Suck

"I hate these fucking things Sammy. They suck complete donkey balls."

"Good," Sammy growls, in that deep baritone voice of his. "That's what we want."

My depleted legs shake and spasm as I wipe the sweat from my eyes and begin to pump out another set of leg presses. When I hit the 15th repetition, Sammy gives me a sadistic smile, "Now hold it there for five seconds."

I fight desperately to maintain my legs at a slight bend, allowing the weight of the machine to bear down on me, fully engaging my quadriceps.

"Embrace the suck!" Sammy says, noting my struggle. "Three...two...one...and release."

I drop my legs in exhaustion and let the machine catch the weight as I gasp for air. Sammy gives me a nod of approval. "Good. Now walk it off."

As I roll off of the leg press, my knees sound like a popcorn machine, clicking and snapping from the scar tissue and cartilage still caked around my kneecaps and patella tendons. I groan heavily as I walk gingerly around the physical therapy room trying to catch my breath. The muscle fibers in my legs visibly twitch and dance uncontrollably.

I catch some of the other patients in the room stealing a glance at me. I'm pretty sure I scare most of them. Especially when training with Sammy. At six feet, six inches tall (two meters) and 265 pounds (120 kilos), Sammy is one of those rare individuals that can make me feel small when I stand next to him. He's got four inches in height and 40 pounds of muscle on me.

Most of the other patients in physical therapy are older than me and recovering from routine procedures, like knee and hip replacements. They're not having to rebuild nearly as much muscle or mobility as I am. When I train with Sammy at physical therapy it kind of feels like we're two muscle hungry meatheads working out in a nursing home.

Embrace the Suck. What a perfect summation of my life over the last 12 months.

For 10 weeks following my surgery I was off of my feet, allowing my patella tendons to heal and reattach to my knees. During that time, my quadriceps completely atrophied and the next challenge in my recovery became re-building the strength in my legs. I was shocked at how weak my legs were when I started physical therapy in January of 2025. I was so out of balance I could have farted and knocked myself over.

The things that suck complete donkey balls are the Blood Flow Restriction (BFR) cuffs strapped around my upper thighs. I've been wearing them for several months now during my physical therapy sessions. They're just like a typical blood pressure cuff, except the ones

I'm wearing are designed for strength training. At the start of my physical therapy they are pumped full of air to restrict up to 50% of the blood flow into my legs. This creates added strain by depriving my muscles of oxygen, allowing me to get a high intensity workout using lower weight. It's a physiological stress that tricks the body into thinking it's working harder than it actually is, effectively activating the same muscle-building pathways that occur with heavy lifting. While BFRs are highly effective, they suck complete ass. It's like trying to jog with a plastic bag over your head.

"Can I take these damn things off now?" I ask Sammy through gritted teeth.

Sammy watches my legs shake uncontrollably for a moment before grinning. "Yeah, I think you're done for the day."

I eagerly reach under my gym shorts to find the pressure release valves on the BFRs. As the blood begins to flow freely into my legs once again my muscles eagerly drink up the precious oxygen held within. The relief is blissful, borderline orgasmic. I've never tried autoerotic asphyxiation, but I imagine it's a similar feeling.

As I hobble over to retrieve my gym bag to leave, Sammy begins wiping down the sweat soaked BFRs with disinfectant. "Rest 'em for two days and then hit 'em again at the gym on your own Friday," he says. "I'll see you next Tuesday for more fun."

Did he say 'fun'?

For the last nine months I have been coming to physical therapy once or twice a week for this hellish penance. It's about as much fun as getting a root canal. On the days that I don't go to P.T., I go to the gym on my own to stretch and continue to work on rebuilding my physical form. I'm doing everything I can to claw my way back to some level of normalcy. It has been a monumental effort in patience and perseverance. I can guarantee you one thing: I'll never skip leg day again.

As arduous as my recovery has been though, I am very grateful to Sam, Kyle, Rich and all of the other physical therapists who have guided me this past year. Their knowledge and support has helped me tremendously and I have made significant progress. I still can't jog, jump or hop. My quads are simply not strong enough yet and my fast-twitch motor units (nerves) aren't fully re-developed. Progress is painfully slow and tedious, but I'm determined to make a full recovery.

Walking down a flight of stairs is still a delicate situation. I need a hand rail for balance and have to walk down sideways to engage more of my hamstrings and glutes. If I try to step directly down, like a normal person, my knees can lock up and potentially throw me off balance. Typically the rule of thumb for recovery from muscle atrophy is that for every day that a muscle is not used, it takes approximately ten days of resistance training to regain that strength. Based on that math, my full recovery should take about 18 to 20 months. So I still have a way to go.

The year 2025 has been a rebuilding year for me, and not just in my legs. The arrhythmia diagnosis (a-fib) I received in the hospital, immediately after surgery, turned out to be a bigger deal than I initially thought. My cardiologist suspects that the traumatic nature of the accident released a tremendous burst of adrenaline through my body which caused my heart to literally skip a beat, like a record player being bumped into at a raucous party.

To correct the arrhythmia, I had to go through another MRI of my heart to look for any blockages and then undergo a cardioversion procedure, which is where they literally shock the heart with 100 joules of electricity in an attempt to jump start it back into sinus (normal) rhythm. When I woke up from that procedure, I literally had electrical burns on my chest and back and felt like Frankenstein's monster. *"It's Alive.... IT'S ALIVE!!"*

Needless to say, it's been a helluva year, but I'm hopeful that the worst is now behind me. When I started writing in January of 2025 I had no expectations or intentions of this becoming a book. I honestly didn't know how much I would write or how deep I would go. I was simply searching for a way to get the poisonous thoughts (i.e. depression) out of my head at the time. The last three months of 2024 turned my life upside down and forced me to be still and reflect. As if the Universe, in her divine wisdom, cut me down at the knees and insisted that I sit down, shut up and think about what I've done.

Digging deep into my past and examining all that I've been through in my life has been extraordinarily cathartic. I wasn't expecting the sense of liberation that writing this book has given me. Reviewing all of the important moments of my life with as much objectivity as possible has given me a renewed sense of peace and understanding.

I feel like I've cleaned out the attic, so to speak, and let go of a lot of unresolved feelings and deep seeded regrets. There are still a few dusty boxes rattling around in the corners of course. I suppose there are some things that we can never let go of. But by re-examining my life from a humbled position, with the wisdom and knowledge that only 50 years of life experience can bring, I've accepted most of my failings and forgiven myself of many of my misguided decisions.

I know my story is not terribly tragic, exciting or unique. Compared to most people, my struggles are champagne problems. I recognize that I have much to be thankful for.

As the year 2026 looms on the horizon, I feel as if my life is at the start of a new beginning. The intermission of 2025 is winding down and the house lights are starting to blink, reminding me that the second act is about to get underway. And while I feel relaxed and ready to take the stage once again, I honestly have no idea what scene comes next or what my lines are. But I'm confident that I can improvise my way through the unscripted life that lies ahead.

I just need to watch my fucking step.

Acknowledgments

Typically, this is the part where I would thank my family and friends for their love and support. However, considering that gratitude is one of the foundations of this book, I fear it would be redundant to list everyone again. So, I shall simply say: You know who you are and that I love you. *Yes, even you Jason.*

I would like to thank my editor, Dr. Alwin Baum, for his help in the final development of this book. Despite the alarming number of grammatical mistakes in my original copy, Dr. Baum was very patient and supportive throughout our work together.

I would like to thank *YOU, the reader*, for taking the time to read my story. In a world of short attention spans, with more content available online and in print for any one person to digest in several lifetimes, I am honored that you gave your time to me. I hope you related to my story at some level or, at the very least, got a few laughs out of it. It is my sincere desire that this book will inspire you to reflect on your own life a bit more and perhaps share your story with others.

With so much content floating around in the world nowadays it's often difficult to discern between what is substance and what is noise. That's why honest reviews and recommendations are vitally important in the confusing age of information. That said, I would be tremendously grateful if you would leave a review of this book online. You can follow the link below to do that.

https://www.coreymaher.net/the-backstory

Until next time,

Cheers.